Communication: Principles for a Lifetime

Portable Edition

Volume 1: Principles of Communication

STEVEN A. BEEBE
Texas State University–San Marcos

SUSAN J. BEEBE
Texas State University–San Marcos

DIANA K. IVY
Texas A&M University–Corpus Christi

PEARSON

Boston   New York   San Francisco
Mexico City   Montreal   Toronto   London   Madrid   Munich   Paris
Hong Kong   Singapore   Tokyo   Cape Town   Sydney

Editor in Chief: *Karon Bowers*
Series Editorial Assistant: *Jessica Cabana*
Marketing Manager: *Suzan Czajkowski*
Production Supervisor: *Beth Houston*
Editorial Production Service: *Lifland et al., Bookmakers*
Composition Buyer: *Linda Cox*
Manufacturing Buyer: *JoAnne Sweeney*
Electronic Composition: *Publishers' Design and Production Services, Inc.*
Photo Researcher: *Helane Prottas*
Cover Administrator: *Joel Gendron*

For related titles and support materials, visit our online catalog at
www.ablongman.com.

Between the time website information is gathered and then published, it is not unusual for some sites to have closed. Also, the transcription of URLs can result in typographical errors. The publisher would appreciate notification where these errors occur so that they may be corrected in subsequent editions.

Library of Congress Cataloging-in-Publication Data

Beebe, Steven A., 1950–
   Communication: principles for a lifetime/Steven A. Beebe, Susan J. Beebe,
Diana K. Ivy—Portable ed.
      v. cm.
   Includes bibliographical references and index.
   ISBN-13: 978-0-205-58066-8
   1. Communication. I. Beebe, Susan J. II. Ivy, Diana K. III. Beebe, Susan J.
IV. Ivy, Diana K. V. Title.
   HM1206.B44 2009
   302.2—dc22   2007051355

ISBN-13: 978-0-205-58066-8   ISBN-10: 0-205-58066-1

Printed in the United States of America

10 9 8 7 6 5 4 3 2 1   RRD-IN   11 10 09 08

Credits appear on page 231, which constitutes an extension of the copyright page.

Contents

1.6 Adapting to Others: Bridging Culture and Gender Differences   177

Preface

This portable edition of *Communication: Principles for a Lifetime* is for students on the move—those who, on a daily basis, commute, travel, or work and therefore must study in nontraditional settings. The portable edition contains four separate volumes, enabling students to take with them wherever they go, for both reading and self-assessment purposes, only the volume they need.

Students may take only one course in communication during their entire college career. Yet they need to remember essential communication principles and skills for the rest of their lives. In this portable edition of *Communication: Principles for a Lifetime*, our goal is to provide a cogent presentation of what is fundamental to human communication by applying to the study of communication five principles that are inherent in the process of communicating with others.

Communication is essential for life. We want students to view this course not simply as another course in a string of curricular requirements or options, but as a vital, life-enriching course that will help them enhance their communication with others.

The Challenge of a Fundamentals of Communication Course

Most introductory communication courses cover a vast terrain of communication concepts, principles, and skills. Besides several theories of communication, students are presented with what may appear to them to be abbreviated courses in interpersonal communication, group communication, and public speaking. In addition to developing a conceptual understanding of communication, students are expected to master communication skills, including group discussion and problem-solving skills, listening and paraphrasing skills, conflict management skills, and informative and persuasive public speaking competencies. When a typical introductory communication fundamentals course is over, both students and instructors have covered an astounding amount of information and skills; they may not, however, have a coherent vision of what is fundamental about human communication. They may finish the course viewing communication as a fragmented area of study and having little understanding of what is truly fundamental about how we make sense out of the world and share that sense with others.

The Solution

To help students remember and integrate essential information, we've organized the study of human communication around five fundamental communication principles. By synthesizing essential research and wisdom about communication, these principles provide a framework for understanding the importance of communication. They are designed to help introductory communication students see the "big picture"—the role and importance of communication—both as they sit in the classroom and as they live their lives.

Although the communication principles we highlight are included in some way in most introductory communication texts, they are not often used as a scaffolding to lend coherence to the entire course. In most texts, principles are introduced in the first third of the book and then abandoned, as material about interpersonal, group, and public communication is presented. We carefully discuss each principle in the Introduction following this Preface. Then, throughout the four volumes, we gently remind students how these principles relate to interpersonal relationships, group and team discussions, and public presentations. In other words, we cover classic communication content but organize it around five principles.

What are the five fundamental principles?

Principle One: Be aware of your communication with yourself and others.
Principle Two: Effectively use and interpret verbal messages.
Principle Three: Effectively use and interpret nonverbal messages.
Principle Four: Listen and respond thoughtfully to others.
Principle Five: Appropriately adapt messages to others.

A subtext of these five principles is the importance of communicating ethically with others. Throughout the volumes, in a feature entitled *Ethics and Communication*, we invite students to consider the ethical implications of how they communicate with others. We believe that, to be effective, a communication message must achieve three goals: It must be understood, achieve its intended effect, and be ethical. Our five communication principles for a lifetime are designed to help students realize these three goals.

The relationship among the five communication principles is illustrated with a pentagonal model. When a principle is introduced or discussed, the corresponding segment of the model is highlighted.

In addition to knowing the five communication principles, we want students to see how these principles relate to the classic communication contexts of interpersonal communication, group and team communication, and presentational speaking. We link the five communication principles with specific content by using a margin icon to identify a discussion of a skill, a concept, or an idea related to one or more of the principles. The icon, illustrated in the margin here, is explained in detail in the Introduction and appears in each volume to indicate applications of the five principles.

Overview of the Book

The text is organized into four volumes. In Volume 1, Chapter 1.1 covers the fundamentals, and then each principle is discussed and illustrated in a separate chapter. These chapters help students see the value of each principle and its centrality in their lives. Chapter 1.2 discusses the principle of being self-aware. Chapter 1.3 focuses on using and interpreting verbal messages. The emphasis of Chapter 1.4 is on using and interpreting nonverbal messages. Chapter 1.5 discusses the interrelated processes of listening and responding, giving special attention to the importance of being other-oriented and empathic. The last principle, appropriately adapting to others, is presented in Chapter 1.6; we use this principle to illustrate the importance of adapting one's behavior to accommodate to culture and gender differences among people.

Volume 2 links concepts and strategies for understanding interpersonal communication with our five communication principles. Chapter 2.1 helps students better understand the nature and function of communication in relationships. Chapter 2.2 identifies strategies that can enhance the quality of interpersonal relationships with others. Appendix A includes practical strategies for being interviewed and for interviewing others, relating interviewing skills to the five communication principles. Appendix B helps students balance the use of technology with interpersonal communication.

Volume 3 discusses how the five communication principles can enhance communication in small groups and teams. Chapter 3.1 explains how groups and teams work. Chapter 3.2 offers practical strategies for collaboratively solving problems, leading groups and teams, and running and participating in meetings. Volume 3 concludes with Appendix C, relating technology to group communication.

The final volume, Volume 4, presents classic content to help students design and deliver speeches, with references to contemporary research and the latest technological tools. Our popular audience-centered approach to developing a presentation emphasizes the importance of adapting to listeners while also being an ethical communicator. Chapters 4.1 through 4.5 offer information and tips on coming up with ideas for presentations, organizing and outlining messages, delivering presentations (using various kinds of presentational aids), crafting effective informative presentations, and developing ethically sound persuasive messages. Appendix D describes the use of technology in giving presentations. Appendix E includes two examples of recent presentations to illustrate what effective, well-planned presentations look like.

Special Features

A textbook is essentially a "distance learning" tool. When we write the book, we are separated by both time and space from the learner. To help shorten the distance between author and reader and engage students in the learning process, we've incorporated a variety of learning resources and pedagogical features. As noted in the text, information alone is not communication. Communication occurs when the receiver responds to information. Our special features help turn information into a communication message that can affect students' lives.

Principles Model and Icon   Our pentagonal model and margin icons help students see connections among the various communication concepts and skills we present. Throughout the volumes, we provide an integrated framework to reinforce what's fundamental about human communication. We want students to remember the five fundamental principles long after the course is over and they have forgotten the facts they memorized for exams. The principles can also help them remember strategies and concepts for enhancing their interpersonal relationships, improving group and team meetings, and designing and delivering effective presentations.

Principles for a Lifetime: Enhancing Your Skills   In addition to providing a margin icon to highlight text material related to one or more communication principles, we conclude each chapter with *Principles for a Lifetime: Enhancing Your Skills*, a summary of the chapter content organized around the communication principles. In Volume 1, these summaries distill essential information about the individual principle presented in a given chapter. In Volumes 2–4, we summarize the chapter content using all five communication principles for a lifetime as a framework. Miniature versions of the principles icon highlight the five fundamental principles. The purpose of this chapter-end feature is to help students integrate the descriptive and prescriptive information presented in the chapter with the five principles that provide the foundation for it.

Ethics and Communication   To help students apply ethics to what they learn about human communication, each chapter includes a feature called *Ethics and Communication*. In this revised and expanded ethics feature, we present a case study and then pose ethical questions for students to consider, asking them to ponder how they would respond to a specific ethical dilemma. The thought-provoking questions are designed to spark insightful class discussion or to be used in combination with a journal assignment or other learning method to help students see connections between ethics and communication.

Technology and Communication   Because of the importance of technology in our lives today, each chapter includes a feature entitled *Technology and*

Communication. This feature is intended to help students become sensitive to the sometimes mind-boggling impact of new technology on communication with others. The importance and role of technology are also discussed in several chapters throughout the volumes, as well as in appendixes to Volumes 2, 3, and 4. The prevalence of technology in students' lives gives rise to powerful teachable moments, which can be used to help students learn and apply communication principles.

On the Web   We do more than just talk about technology. By including Web resources that link to the topic of each chapter, we encourage students to reach out to the vast array of learning resources on the Internet. These annotated Web links provide background, context, and activities to help students apply course content.

Diversity and Communication   Each chapter includes a *Diversity and Communication* feature to help students see the importance of diversity in their lives. Yet we don't relegate diversity only to a boxed feature. Because diversity is such an important issue in contemporary society, we discuss it not only in a comprehensive chapter on the fifth principle of communication (appropriately adapting messages to others), but throughout the text as well.

Developing Your Presentation Step by Step   The chapters in Volume 4, Presentational Speaking, contain a series of boxes that follow one student's progress through the steps in preparing and giving a presentation. Students receive tips that they can readily apply as they prepare their own presentations.

Comprehensive Pedagogical Learning Tools   To help students master the material, we've built in a wealth of study aids:

- Learning objectives
- Chapter outlines
- Concise Recap boxes that distill key content
- Boldfaced key terms with definitions
- Chapter-end narrative summaries of the chapters
- Chapter-end summaries of the five communication principles
- Chapter-end questions for discussion and review
- Skill-building activities and collaborative learning exercises
- Practice tests

MyCommunicationLab   In this Portable Edition, you will find icons throughout each chapter that refer students to interactive materials available on this book's MyCommunicationLab (www.mycommunicationlab.com; access code required).

- **Watch** icons link to relevant and interesting video clips that supplement a topic being covered in the textbook.

- **Explore** icons link to activities that allow users to gain more knowledge of major topics in the book, reinforcing key concepts taught in the text.

- **Homework** icons link to assignments for students that reinforce material covered in the text.

- **Quick Review** icons link to practice tests that provide reinforcement of key concepts in the context of the book. These Quick Review assessments are not graded and give students an opportunity for self-study.

- **Visual Literacy** icons link to images that help illustrate important concepts.

- **Profile** icons link to relevant self-assessments, which enable students to test and evaluate their communication skills in different contexts.

In addition, the following tools appear in MyCommunicationLab (but not in the printed text).

- A **pre-test icon** appears at each chapter-level page. This icon prompts students to complete a pre-test before reading the chapter in order to gauge their prior knowledge of chapter contents. Results from the pre-test will be stored in the students' individualized study plans.
- A **post-test icon** appears at each chapter-level page. This icon prompts students to complete a chapter post-test after reading and reviewing the chapter content that will indicate a level of understanding of the chapter's material. Results from the post-test will be stored in the students' individualized study plans (see below).
- The results from the chapter pre-test and post-test generate a customized **study plan** for each student, identifying specific areas of weakness and strength. The study plan is organized by chapter and major topic area. Each time a pre-test and/or post-test is taken, the study plan is instantly updated to indicate which topic areas need to be reviewed. The study plan, as well as the pre-test and post-test, are for the students' use only and will not be shared with the instructor. This personalized study and review strategy allows students to track their progress in a topic and to prepare for their tests. This tool allows students to efficiently master the text and course material, save time studying, and perform better on exams.
- **MyOutline** provides students with the opportunity to create customized and specific outlines for their speeches.

In-Text Practice Tests In each chapter of the printed text, we've provided a practice test to help students simulate the test-taking experience. Written by Richard J. Sabatino, Texas State University–San Marcos, these practice tests are derived from the Study Guide that accompanies the main version of this text. Each test gives students the opportunity to gauge their comprehension of the chapter concepts. Answers to the practice tests can be found at the end of each volume.

Our Partnership with Instructors

A textbook is only one tool for helping teachers teach and learners learn. We view our job as providing resources that teachers can use to augment, illustrate, and amplify communication principles and skills. We also offer an array of materials designed for students, to enrich their learning experience.

Instructor Supplements

As part of our partnership with instructors to facilitate learning, we offer an array of print, electronic, and video resources to help teachers do what they do best: teach. Combined with the vast array of learning resources built into the text, this dazzling package of additional resources will help instructors forge both intellectual and emotional connections with their students.

- *MyCommunicationLab.* A place where students learn to communicate with confidence, MyCommunicationLab (www.mycommunicationlab .com) is an interactive and instructive online solution designed to be used as a supplement to a traditional lecture course or as a complete online course. MyCommunicationLab combines multimedia, video, communication activities, research support, tests, and quizzes to make teaching and learning more relevant and enjoyable. Students benefit from a wealth of video clips that include student and professional speeches, small group scenarios, and interpersonal interactions—some with running commentary and critical questions—all geared to help students learn to communicate with confidence. Access code required.
- *Instructor's Resource Manual* by Travis Russ, Rutgers University. For each chapter, the Instructor's Resource Manual provides at-a-glance grids that link text objectives to the manual's content as well as to other supplements. Additionally, each chapter includes an outline, discussion and journal questions, classroom activities and assignments, and Internet suggestions. Available electronically through the Instructor's Resource Center (www.ablongman.com/irc). Access code required.
- *Test Bank* by Sue Stewart, Texas State University–San Marcos. The Test Bank contains over 1,500 questions in multiple-choice, true/false, matching, fill-in-the-blank, short answer, and essay formats. Available electronically through the Instructor's Resource Center.
- *Computerized Test Bank*. The Test Bank is also available through Pearson's computerized testing system, TestGen EQ. This fully networkable test-generating software is available for Windows and Macintosh. The user-

friendly interface allows instructors to view, edit, and add questions, transfer questions to tests, and print tests in a variety of fonts. Search and sort features allow instructors to locate questions quickly and to arrange them in a preferred order. Available electronically through the Instructor's Resource Center.

- *A Guide for New Teachers of the Basic Communication Course: Interactive Strategies for Teaching Communication*, Third Edition, by Susanna G. Porter, Kennesaw State University. This guide helps new instructors teach an introductory course effectively. It covers such topics as preparing for the term, planning and structuring your course, evaluating speeches, utilizing the textbook, integrating technology into the classroom, dealing with challenges, and much more.

- *Blockbuster Approach: Teaching Interpersonal Communication with Video*, Third Edition, by Thomas Jewell, Bergen Community College. This guide provides lists and descriptions of popular videos that can be used in the classroom to illustrate complex concepts of interpersonal relationships. Sample activities are also included.

- *Great Ideas for Teaching Speech (GIFTS)*, Third Edition, by Raymond Zeuschner, California Polytechnic State University. This book provides descriptions and guidelines for assignments successfully used by experienced public speaking instructors in their classrooms.

- *Video Workshop for Introduction to Communication*, Version 2.0, by Kathryn Dindia, University of Wisconsin. Video Workshop is a way to bring video into your introductory communication classroom to maximize learning. This total teaching and learning system includes quality video footage on an easy-to-use CD-ROM, plus a Student Learning Guide and an Instructor's Teaching Guide. The result? A program that brings textbook concepts to life with ease and that helps students understand, analyze, and apply the objectives of the course.

- *Allyn and Bacon Digital Media Archive for Communication*, Version 3.0. This CD-ROM contains electronic images of charts, graphs, maps, tables, and figures, along with media elements such as video, audio clips, and related Web links. These media assets are fully customizable and can be used with the pre-formatted PowerPoint™ outlines or imported into the instructor's own lectures. The images are available for both Windows and Mac platforms.

- *Allyn and Bacon PowerPoint Presentation for Introduction to Communication*. This PowerPoint presentation includes approximately 50 slides that cover a range of communication topics: public speaking, interpersonal communication, group communication, mass media, and interviewing. Available electronically through the Instructor's Resource Center.

- *PowerPoint Presentation for Communication: Principles for a Lifetime*, Portable Edition, by James R. Smith, State University of New York, New Paltz. This text-specific package consists of a collection of lecture outlines and graphic images keyed to each chapter in the text. Available electronically through the Instructor's Resource Center.

- *Lecture Questions for Clickers: Introduction to Communication,* by Keri Moe, El Paso Community College. An assortment of questions and activities covering culture, listening, interviewing, public speaking, interpersonal conflict, and more are presented in PowerPoint. These slides will help liven up your lectures and can be used along with the Personal Response System to get students more involved in the material. Available through the Instructor's Resource Center.
- *Communication Video Libraries.* Adopters can choose appropriate video material from Allyn and Bacon's video libraries for Public Speaking, Interpersonal Communication, and Small Group Communication. Please contact your Pearson representative for a list of available videos. Some restrictions apply.

Student Supplements

We also offer an array of materials designed for students to enrich their learning experience.

- *MyCommunicationLab.* A place where students learn to communicate with confidence, MyCommunicationLab (www.mycommunicationlab.com) is an interactive and instructive online solution designed to be used as a supplement to a traditional lecture course or as a complete online course. MyCommunicationLab combines multimedia, video, communication activities, research support, tests, and quizzes to make teaching and learning more relevant and enjoyable. Students benefit from a wealth of video clips that include student and professional speeches, small group scenarios, and interpersonal interactions—some with running commentary and critical questions—all geared to help students learn to communicate with confidence. Access code required.
- *ResearchNavigator.com Guide: Speech Communication.* This updated booklet by Steven L. Epstein of Suffolk County Community College includes tips, resources, and URLs to aid students conducting research on Pearson Education's research Web site, www.researchnavigator.com. The guide contains a student access code for the Research Navigator™ database, offering students unlimited access to a collection of more than 25,000 discipline-specific articles from top-tier academic publications and peer-reviewed journals, as well as the *New York Times* and popular news publications. The guide introduces students to the basics of the Internet and the World Wide Web and includes tips for searching for articles on the site and a list of journals useful for research in their discipline. Also included are hundreds of Web resources for the discipline, as well as information on how to correctly cite research.
- *Speech Preparation Workbook*, by Jennifer Dreyer and Gregory H. Patton, San Diego State University. This workbook takes students through the various stages of speech creation—from audience analysis to writing the speech—and provides supplementary assignments and tear-out forms.

- ***Preparing Visual Aids for Presentations***, Fourth Edition, by Dan Cavanaugh. This 32-page booklet provides a host of ideas for using today's multimedia tools to improve presentations and includes suggestions for planning a presentation, guidelines for designing visual aids and storyboarding, and a PowerPoint presentation walkthrough.
- ***Public Speaking in the Multicultural Environment***, Second Edition, by Devorah A. Lieberman, Portland State University. This booklet helps students learn to analyze cultural diversity within their audiences and adapt their presentations accordingly.
- ***Outlining Workbook***, by Reeze L. Hanson and Sharon Condon, Haskell Indian Nations University. This workbook includes activities, exercises, and answers to help students develop and master the critical skill of outlining.
- ***Study Card for Introduction to Communication.*** Colorful, affordable, and packed with useful information, Pearson's Study Cards make studying easier, more efficient, and more enjoyable. Course information is distilled down to the basics, helping you quickly master the fundamentals, review a subject for understanding, or prepare for an exam. Because it's laminated for durability, you can keep this Study Card for years to come and pull it out whenever you need a quick review.
- ***Introduction to Communication Study Site.*** Accessed at www.abintro-comm.com, this Web site includes Web links to sites with speeches in text, audio, and video formats, as well as links to other valuable Web sites. The site also contains flashcards and a fully expanded set of practice tests for all major topics.
- ***Speech Writer's Workshop CD-ROM***, Version 2.0. This interactive software will assist students with speech preparation and will enable them to write better speeches. The software includes four separate features: (1) a Speech Handbook with tips for researching and preparing speeches plus information about grammar, usage, and syntax; (2) a Speech Workshop that guides students through the speechwriting process and includes a series of questions at each stage; (3) a Topics Dictionary containing hundreds of speech ideas, divided into subcategories to help students with outlining and organization; and (4) a citation database that formats bibliographic entries in MLA or APA style.
- ***Video Workshop for Introduction to Communication***, Version 2.0, by Kathryn Dindia, University of Wisconsin. Video Workshop includes quality video footage on an easy-to-use CD-ROM plus a Student Learning Guide. The result is a program that brings textbook concepts to life with ease and that helps students understand, analyze, and apply the objectives of the course.

Acknowledgments

Although our three names appear on the cover as authors of the book you are holding in your hands, in reality hundreds of people have been instrumental in making this book possible. Communication scholars who have dedicated their lives to researching the importance of communication principles, theories, and skills provide the fuel for the book. We thank each author we reference in our endnotes for the research conclusions that have led to our contemporary understanding of communication principles. We thank our students who have trusted us to be their guides in a study of human communication. They continue to enrich our lives with their enthusiasm and curiosity. They have inspired us to be more creative by their honest, quizzical looks and have challenged us to go beyond textbook answers with their thought-provoking questions.

We are most appreciative of the outstanding editorial support we continue to receive from our colleagues and friends at Allyn and Bacon. We thank Joe Opiela for helping us keep this project moving forward when we wondered if the world needed another communication book. Vice President Paul Smith has been exceptionally supportive of our work since we've been members of the Allyn and Bacon publishing family. Karon Bowers, Editor in Chief, has continued to provide valued support and encouragement. Our thoughtful and talented development editor, Carol Alper, helped us polish our ideas and words. Karen Black, Diana Ivy's sister, who conducted permissions research, was a true blessing, providing skilled assistance with important details and administrative support. We acknowledge and appreciate the ideas and suggestions of Mark Redmond, a valued friend, gifted teacher, and skilled writer at Iowa State University. His co-authorship with us of *Interpersonal Communication: Relating to Others* significantly influenced our ideas about communication, especially interpersonal communication.

We are grateful to the many educators who read the manuscript and both encouraged and challenged us. We thank the following people for drawing on their teaching skill, expertise, and vast experience to make this a much better book:

Lawrence Albert, Morehead State University
Leonard Assante, Volunteer State Community College
Dom Bongiorni, Kingwood College
Michael Bruner, University of North Texas
Jo Anne Bryant, Troy University
Cherie Cannon, Miami–Dade College
Diana O. Cassagrande, West Chester University
Dan B. Curtis, Central Missouri State University
Terrence A. Doyle, Northern Virginia Community College
Dennis Dufer, St. Louis Community College
Julia F. Fennell, Community College of Allegheny County, South Campus

Annette Folwell, University of Idaho
Thomas Green, Cape Fear Community College
Gretchen Harries, Austin Community College
Mike Hemphill, University of Arkansas at Little Rock
Teri Higginbotham, University of Central Arkansas
Phil Hoke, The University of Texas at San Antonio
Lawrence Hugenberg, Youngstown State University
Stephen Hunt, Illinois State University
Carol L. Hunter, Brookdale Community College
Dorothy W. Ige, Indiana University Northwest
A. Elizabeth Lindsey, The New Mexico State University
Xin-An Lu, Shippensburg University of Pennsylvania
Robert E. Mild, Jr., Fairmont State College
Timothy P. Mottet, Texas State University–San Marcos
Alfred G. Mueller II, Pennsylvania State University, Mont Alto Campus
Sara L. Nalley, Columbia College
Kay Neal, University of Wisconsin–Oshkosh
Penny O'Connor, University of Northern Iowa
Kathleen Perri, Valencia Community College
Evelyn Plummer, Seton Hall University
Kristi Schaller, University of Hawaii
David Shuhy, Salisbury University
John Tapia, Missouri Western State College
Charlotte C. Toguchi, Kapi'olani Community College
Beth M. Waggenspack, Virginia Tech University
Gretchen Aggert Weber, Horry-Georgetown Technical College
Kathy Werking, Eastern Kentucky University
Andrew F. Wood, San Jose State University
Debra Sue Wyatt, South Texas Community College

We have each been influenced by colleagues, friends, and teachers who have offered support and inspiration for this project. Happily, colleagues, friends, and teachers are virtually indistinguishable for us. We are each blessed to know people who offer us strong support.

Steve and Sue thank their colleagues at Texas State University–San Marcos for their insights and ideas that helped shape key concepts in this book. Cathy Fleuriet and Tom Burkholder, who served as basic course directors at Texas State, influenced our work. Tim Mottet, currently a basic course director at Texas State, is a valued, inspirational friend and colleague who is always there to listen and freely share his ideas and experience. Richard Cheatham, Dean of the College of Fine Arts and Communication, continues to provide enthusiastic encouragement for this project. Kosta Tovstiadi, from the University of Oklahoma, provided skilled research assistance to help us draw on the most contemporary communication research. Michael Hennessy and Patricia Margerison are Texas State English faculty who have been especially supportive of Sue's work. Finally, Steve thanks his skilled and dedicated support team at Texas State. Administrative Assistant Sue Hall, who continues to be Steve's right hand, is a cherished friend and colleague. Manuscript typist Sondra Howe and technical support expert Bob Hanna are two other staff members who provide exceptional support and assistance for this project and many others.

Ivy is grateful to her students, colleagues, and friends at Texas A&M University–Corpus Christi for their patience and unwavering support for her involvement in this book project. In particular, Michelle Maresh, Jason Pruett, Kelly Quintanilla, Flicka Rahn, Nada Frazier, Chair Don Luna, Deans Paul Hain and Richard Gigliotti, and Provost Sandra Harper constantly reaffirmed the value of a well-written, carefully crafted book—one that speaks to students' lives. Their support of Ivy's research efforts, along with constant "fueling" from her wonderful students, has made this project a real joy. Ivy's deepest thanks also go to Steve and Sue Beebe for their generosity in bringing her into this project, and for their willing mentorship.

Finally we express our appreciation to our families. Ivy thanks her ever-supportive family, parents Herschel and Carol Ivy, sister Karen Black (who supplied the permissions research and constant encouragement), and nephew Brian Black (whose humorous e-mails provided great comic relief). They have been constant and generous with their praise for her writing accomplishments. Ivy is especially grateful to her father, Herschel Ivy, for lovingly offering many lessons about living the highly ethical life.

Sue and Steve especially thank their parents, Herb and Jane Dye and Russell and Muriel Beebe, who taught them much about communication and ethics that truly are principles for a lifetime. They also thank their sons, Mark and Matthew Beebe, for teaching life lessons about giving and receiving love that will remain with them forever.

Steven A. Beebe
Susan J. Beebe
San Marcos, Texas

Diana K. Ivy
Corpus Christi, Texas

Communication Principles for a Lifetime

Underlying human communication are five principles that provide the foundation for all effective communication, whether we are communicating with others one on one, in groups or teams, or by presenting a public speech to an audience. We will emphasize how these principles are woven into the fabric of each communication context. The five communication principles for a lifetime are

Principle One:	Be aware of your communication with yourself and others.
Principle Two:	Effectively use and interpret verbal messages.
Principle Three:	Effectively use and interpret nonverbal messages.
Principle Four:	Listen and respond thoughtfully to others.
Principle Five:	Appropriately adapt messages to others.

These five principles operate together rather than independently to form the basis of the fundamental processes that enhance communication effectiveness. The model on the next page illustrates how the principles interrelate. The first principle, being aware of your communication with yourself and others, is followed by the two principles that focus on communication messages: Principle Two on verbal messages and Principle Three on nonverbal messages. The fourth principle, on listening and responding, is followed by appropriately adapting messages to others (Principle Five). Together, these five principles help explain why communication can be either effective or ineffective. A violation of any one principle can result in inappropriate or poor communication.

Principle One: Be Aware of Your Communication with Yourself and Others

The first foundation principle is to be aware of your communication with yourself and others. Effective communicators are conscious, or "present," when communicating. Ineffective communicators mindlessly or thoughtlessly say and do things that they may later regret. Being aware of your communication includes

Communication Principles for a Lifetime

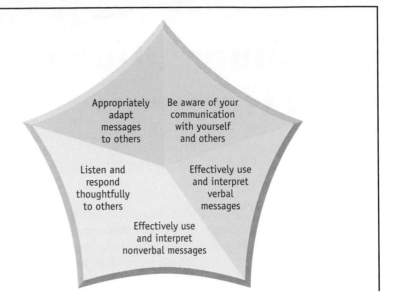

Appropriately adapt messages to others

Be aware of your communication with yourself and others

Listen and respond thoughtfully to others

Effectively use and interpret verbal messages

Effectively use and interpret nonverbal messages

being conscious not only of the present moment, but also of who you are, your self-concept, your self-worth, and your perceptions of yourself and others. Being aware of your typical communication style is also part of this foundation principle. For example, some people realize that their communication style when interacting with others is emotional. Others may be shy.

Self-awareness includes being conscious of your intrapersonal communication messages. **Intrapersonal communication is communication that occurs within yourself, including your thoughts, your emotions, and your perceptions of yourself and others.** Talking to yourself is an example of intrapersonal communication. Although our intrapersonal communication is often the focus of psychologists, our intrapersonal messages also form the basis of our communication with others.[1]

Competent communicators are aware of the choices they make when they communicate both intrapersonally and with others; incompetent communicators react to others' messages with thoughtless, quick, knee-jerk responses. Because they do not mindfully censor themselves, they may blurt out obscene, offensive, or profane words. Ineffective communicators operate in an unthinking "default" mode. Being aware of our communication is a foundation principle because all of the choices we make when communicating rest on our ability to make conscious choices when we respond to others.

Human communication is the process of making sense out of the world and sharing that sense with others. Being aware of who we are and how we perceive, or "make sense" of, what we observe is a fundamental principle that helps explain both effective and ineffective communication. In Chapter 1.2, we develop this principle and foreshadow how it relates to a variety of communication situations.

Principle Two: Effectively Use and Interpret Verbal Messages

The second principle we introduce here and elaborate on in Chapter 1.3 is using and interpreting verbal messages effectively. Verbal messages are created with language. A **language is a system of symbols (words or vocabulary) structured by rules (grammar) that make it possible for people to understand one another.**

A symbol is a word, sound, gesture, or other visual signal that represents a thought, concept, object, or experience. When you read the words on this page, you are looking at symbols that trigger meaning. The word is not the thing it represents; it simply symbolizes the thing or idea.

Your reading skill permits you to make sense out of symbols. The word *tree*, for example, may trigger a thought of the tree you may be reading under now, a tree in your own yard or a nearby park, or a giant sequoia you saw on your family vacation in Yosemite National Park. Effective communicators use appropriate symbols to create accurate meaning. Author Daniel Quinn once commented, "No story is devoid of meaning, if you know how to look for it. This is as true of nursery rhymes and daydreams as it is of epic poems."[2] Meaning is created when people have a common or shared understanding.

The effective communicator both encodes and decodes messages accurately; he or she selects appropriate symbols to form a message and interprets carefully the messages of others. The process of using and interpreting symbols is the essence of how we make sense out of the world and share that sense with others.

Words have power. The words we use to describe ourselves and our world have considerable influence on how we perceive what we experience. Any good advertising copywriter knows how to use words to create a need or desire for a product. Political consultants tell politicians how to craft sound bites that will create just the right audience response. And words can hurt us. Words have the ability to offend and create stress. For example, derogatory words about someone's gender or race can do considerable harm. We will present strategies and suggestions for selecting the best word or symbol to enhance your listeners' understanding.

Principle Three: Effectively Use and Interpret Nonverbal Messages

Messages are also nonverbal. Nonverbal communication is communication by means other than written or spoken language that creates meaning for someone. Nonverbal messages can communicate powerful ideas or express emotions with greater impact than mere words alone. An optimistic hitchhiker's extended thumb and an irate driver's extended finger are nonverbal symbols with clear and intentional meaning. But not all nonverbal symbols are clearly interpreted or even consciously expressed. You may not be aware of your frown when someone asks if he or she may sit next to you in a vacant seat in a restaurant. Or your son may excitedly be telling you about his field trip to the fire station while you stare into the pages of your newspaper. You have no intention of telling your son he is not important, but your lack of nonverbal responsiveness speaks volumes.

One of the most important reasons our unspoken messages are significant is that they are the primary way we communicate feelings and attitudes toward others. With someone whom you like or love very much, you may spend a very small percentage of your time verbalizing your affection and friendship. The other person can discern your interest and admiration based on your nonverbal expressions and the amount of time you spend together. Your eye contact, facial expression, and tone of voice communicate your pleasure in his or her company. You may also know someone who doesn't like you. This less-than-friendly person may never have to come right out and say, "I don't like you." But you know you're not on friendly terms based on nonverbal cues: A scowl, an uninterested tone of voice, and a lack of eye contact signal that you're not held in high esteem. Our nonverbal messages communicate how we feel toward others.

When there is a contradiction between what you say and what you do, your nonverbal message is more believable than your verbal message. When asked how your meal is, you may tell your server that the meal is "great," but your nonverbal message—facial expression and tone of voice—clearly communicates your unhappiness with the cuisine. Our nonverbal cues often tell people how to interpret what we are saying.

Effective communicators develop skill in interpreting nonverbal messages of others. They also monitor their own messages to avoid unintentionally sending contradictory verbal and nonverbal messages. It's sometimes hard to interpret nonverbal messages because they don't have a neat beginning and ending point—the flow of information is continuous. It may not be clear where one gesture stops and another begins. Cultural differences, and the fact that so many different nonverbal channels (such as eye contact, facial expression, gestures, posture) can be used at the same time, make it tricky to "read" someone's nonverbal message accurately. We amplify our discussion of the power of nonverbal messages in Chapter 1.4.

Principle Four: Listen and Respond Thoughtfully to Others

So far, our list of principles may appear to place much of the burden of achieving communication success on the person sending the message. But effective communication with others also places considerable responsibility on the listener. Because communication is a transactional process—both senders and receivers are mutually and usually simultaneously expressing and responding to symbols—listening to words with sensitivity and "listening between the lines" to nonverbal messages join our list of fundamental principles.

Listening can be hard because it looks easy. You spend more time listening than performing any other communication activity—probably more than any other thing you do except sleep.[3] Despite spending the greatest portion of our communication time listening, there is evidence that many, if not most, of us do not always listen effectively. What's tricky about listening? Both psychological, or internal, noise (our own thoughts, needs, and emotions) and external distractions (noise in the surroundings in which we listen) can create barriers to effective listening. The fact that it is perceived to be a passive rather than an active task makes listening and accurately interpreting information a challenge. Effective listening is *not* a passive task at all; the effective and sensitive listener works hard to stay on task and focus mindfully on a sender's message.

At the heart of this principle is developing sensitivity to others. By sensitivity we are not talking about the touchy-feely, emotional, what-I-hear-you-saying approach to interpersonal relationships. We are, however, suggesting that you develop an orientation or sensitivity to others when you listen and respond. **When you are other-oriented, you consider the needs, motives, desires, and goals of your communication partners while still maintaining your own integrity.** The choices you make in both forming the message and selecting when to share it should consider your partner's thoughts and feelings.

Most of us are egocentric—self-focused. We are born with an innate desire to meet our own needs. As we grow and mature, we develop a consciousness of more than our own needs. Scholars of evolution might argue that it is good that we are self-focused; looking out for number one is what perpetuates the human race.

Yet an *exclusive* focus on ourselves inhibits effective communication. Do you know anyone who is self-absorbed? Most of us find such a person tedious and uncomfortable to be around. People who are skilled communicators both listen and respond with sensitivity; they are other-oriented.

Principle Five: Appropriately Adapt Messages to Others

It is not enough to be sensitive and to accurately understand others; you must use the information you gather to modify the messages you construct. It is important to adapt your response appropriately to your listener. **When you adapt a message, you adjust both what is communicated and how the**

message is communicated and make choices about how best to formulate a message and respond to others to achieve your communication goals. Adapting to a listener does not mean that you tell a listener only what he or she wants to hear. That would be unethical. Adapting involves appropriately editing and shaping your responses so that others accurately understand your messages and so that you achieve your goal without coercing or using false information or other unethical means. To adapt a message is to make choices about all aspects of message content and delivery.

Regardless of whether you are giving a presentation, talking with a friend, or participating in a small-group meeting, as an effective communicator you consider who the listeners are when deciding what to say and how best to say it. One of the elements of a message that you adapt when communicating with others is the structure or organization of what you say. Informal, interpersonal conversations typically do not follow a rigid, outlined structure. Our conversation freely bounces from one topic to another. Formal presentations delivered in North America, however, are usually expected to have a more explicit structure—an introduction, a body, and a conclusion. The major ideas of a formal presentation are expected to be clearly identified. North American audiences also seem to prefer a presentation that could be easily outlined. Other cultures, such as those in the Middle East, expect a greater use of stories, examples, and illustrations, rather than a clearly structured, outlined presentation. Knowing your audience's expectations can help you adapt your message so that it will be listened to and understood.

You also adapt the general style or formality of your message to the receiver. If you are speaking to your lifelong best friend, your style is less formal than if you are speaking to the president of your university. The language you use and jokes you tell when around your best chums will undoubtedly be different than your language and humor when you are attending a meeting with your boss or with faculty members from your school. Our point is that effective communicators not only listen and respond with sensitivity; they use the information they gather to shape the message and delivery of their responses to others. In Chapter 1.6, we will discuss this principle in greater detail by discussing the diverse nature of potential listeners and how to adapt to them. Adapting to differences in culture and gender, for example, may mean the difference between a message that is well received and one that creates hostility.

Throughout the volumes of this book, we remind you of how these principles can be used to organize the theory, concepts, and skills we offer as fundamental to human communication. Chapters 1.2 through 1.6 will each be devoted to a single principle.

Foundations of Human Communication

CHAPTER OUTLINE

CHAPTER OBJECTIVES

After studying this chapter, you should be able to

1. List five fundamental principles of communication.

2. Define communication and explain why it is an important course of study.

3. Describe three criteria that can be used to determine whether communication is competent.

4. Compare and contrast communication as action, interaction, and transaction.

5. Identify five characteristics of communication.

6. Define and describe communication in interpersonal, group, and presentational communication situations.

Good communication is as stimulating as black coffee and just as hard to sleep after.

Anne Morrow Lindbergh

Jean Dubuffet, Visage rouge et visage bleu (red face and blue face) from the series "Le Metro," gouache on paper, 1943. Photo: Philippe Migeat. CNAC/MNAM/Dist. Reunion des Musees Nationaux/Art Resource, NY. © 2007 Artists Rights Society (ARS), New York/ADAGP, Paris.

Communication is essential for life. Communicating is a fundamental aspect of being human. Even if you live in isolation from other people, you talk to yourself through your thoughts. Like life-sustaining breath, communication is ever-present in our lives. Understanding and improving how we communicate with others is a basic life skill.

Human communication is inescapable. Consider the number of times you have purposefully communicated with someone today, as you worked, ate, studied, shopped, or went about your daily duties. Most people spend between 80 and 90% of their waking hours communicating with others.[1] It is through the process of communication that we convey who we are, both to ourselves and to others; it is our primary tool for making our way in the world.

This book presents fundamental principles that undergird all aspects of communicating with others when both sending and receiving messages. In the course of our study of human communication, we will discuss a myriad of skills, ideas, concepts, and contexts. The number of terms, ideas, skills, and competencies that you'll encounter in this discussion can be overwhelming. To help you stitch together the barrage of ideas and information, we will organize our study around five fundamental communication principles. Together, these five principles will provide a framework for our discussion of the importance and pervasiveness of human communication.

Principle One: Be aware of your communication with yourself and others.
Principle Two: Effectively use and interpret verbal messages.
Principle Three: Effectively use and interpret nonverbal messages.
Principle Four: Listen and respond thoughtfully to others.
Principle Five: Appropriately adapt messages to others.

These five principles distill decades of research as well as the wisdom of those who have taught communication during the past century. We don't claim that everything you need to know about communication is covered by these five principles. They do, however, summarize considerable knowledge about the communication process and what constitutes effective and ethical communication. This book examines each fundamental principle in the context of three prevalent communication situations:

• interpersonal interactions
• group and team communication
• presentational speaking

Our goal is to present both classic and contemporary research conclusions about the role and importance of communication in our lives. In addition to discussing live, face-to-face human communication, we will highlight the increasing importance of technology in our communication with others in a feature called Technology and Communication that will appear throughout the book.

Before we elaborate on the five fundamental communication principles, it is important to provide some background for our study of communication. The purpose of this first chapter is to provide that background. We will define communication, discuss why it is important to study, examine various models of or perspectives on communication, identify characteristics of human communication, and distinguish interpersonal, group, and presentational speaking situations.

Communication Defined

Communication is one of those words that seems so basic you may wonder why it needs to be formally defined. Yet scholars who devote their lives to studying communication don't always agree on its definition. One research team counted more than 126 published definitions.[2]

In its broadest sense, **communication is the process of acting on information**.[3] Someone does or says something, and others think or do something in response to the action or the words as they understand them.

Communication is not unique to humans. It is possible, for example, for you to act on information from your dog. She barks; you feed her. This general definition also suggests that your dog can act on information from you. You head for the pantry to feed her; she wags her tail and jumps in the air, anticipating her dinner. Although researchers study communication between species as well as communication systems used by particular animal species, these fields of study are beyond the scope of this book. The focus of our study is human communication: people communicating with other people.

To refine our definition of communication, we can say that **human communication is the process of making sense out of the world and sharing that sense with others by creating meaning through the use of verbal and nonverbal messages**.[4] Let's look at the key components of this definition.

- *Communication is about making sense.* We make sense out of what we experience when we begin to interpret what we see, hear, touch, smell, and taste with sensations, feelings, thoughts, and words. Identifying patterns and structure in what we experience is a key part of making sense out of what happens to us. Although we often think that "making sense out of something" means rationally and logically interpreting what we experience, we also make sense through intuition, feelings, and emotions.[5]
- *Communication is about sharing sense.* We share what we experience by expressing to others and to ourselves what we experience. We typically use words to express our thoughts, but we also use music, art, clothing, and a whole host of other means to convey what we are thinking and feeling to others.
- *Communication is about creating meaning.* It's more appropriate to say that meaning is *created* through communication rather than sent or transmitted. To say that we send or transmit messages is to imply that what we send

is what is received. In human communication, however, what is expressed by one person is rarely interpreted by another person precisely as intended. In reality, meaning is *co-created* by both the speaker and the listener. By this we mean that all individuals who are involved in the communication process shape how a message is understood by drawing on their own experiences while attempting to make sense out of the message. Meaning is created in the heart and mind of both the message source and the message receiver, based on such things as the characteristics of the message, the situation, and the perceptions and background of the communicators.

- *Communication is about verbal and nonverbal messages.*   One way we communicate is by using words that trigger meaning in others symbolically. **Symbols are words, sounds, gestures, or visual images that represent thoughts, concepts, objects, or experiences**. The words on this page are symbols that you use to derive meaning that makes sense to you.

  Not all symbols are verbal; some are nonverbal. You use gestures, posture, facial expression, tone of voice, clothing, and jewelry to express ideas, attitudes, and feelings. Nonverbal messages primarily communicate emotions—our likes and dislikes, whether we're interested or uninterested, and our feelings of power or lack of power.

Some scholars assert that *all* human behavior is really communication. When you cross your arms while listening to your friend describe her day, she may conclude that you're not interested in what she's talking about. But it could just be that you're cold. While all human expression has the potential to communicate a message (someone may act or respond to the information they receive from you), this does not mean you *intentionally* are expressing an idea or emotion. Presenting information to others does not mean communication has occurred: Information is not communication. "But I told you what to do!" "It's there in the memo. Why didn't you do what I asked?" "It's in the syllabus." These exasperated communicators assumed that if they sent a message, someone would receive it. However, communication does not operate in a simple, linear, what-you-send-is-what-is-received process. People don't always accurately interpret the messages we express—and this unprofound observation has profound implications. One reason we have communication courses, academic departments that focus on communication, and people who earn Ph.D.s in communication is because of the challenge we encounter in understanding one another.

Because of the ever-present potential for misunderstanding, communication should be *other-oriented*—it should acknowledge the perspective of others, not just the creator of the message. Communication that does not consider the needs, background, and culture of the receiver is more likely to be misunderstood. We'll emphasize the importance of considering others or considering your audience throughout each volume. Knowing something about the experiences of the person or persons you're speaking to can help you communicate more effectively and appropriately.

Human communication is complex and varied. It also emerges in many different forms: face-to-face conversations, speeches, radio and television programs, e-mail, Web sites, letters, books, and articles.

Communication Competence

What does it mean to communicate competently? Does it mean you are able to present a well-delivered speech? Or that you are able to carry on a brilliant conversation with someone? Is the fact that you are usually asked to chair a committee meeting because you are so organized evidence of your communication competence? Being a competent communicator is more than just being well liked, glib, able to give polished presentations, or able to interact smoothly with individual people or in groups and teams. Although it is difficult to identify core criteria that define competent communication in all situations, we think certain goals of communication serve as measures of competence regardless of the setting. We suggest the following three criteria:[6]

- The message should be understood as the communicator intended it to be understood.
- The message should achieve the communicator's intended effect.
- The message should be ethical.

The Message Should Be Understood

A primary goal of any effective communication transaction is to develop a common understanding of the message from both the sender's and the receiver's perspectives. You'll note how the words *common* and *communication* resemble each other. We acknowledge the challenge of communicating with others; differences in culture, language, experience, gender, education, and background all are sources of misunderstanding. One of the aims of the principles we discuss in this book is to create clarity of expression and a common understanding.

Message clarity is missing in the following headlines that have appeared in local U.S. newspapers:

Panda Mating Fails: Veterinarian Takes Over
Drunks Get Nine Months in Violin Case
Include Your Children When Baking Cookies
Police Begin Campaign to Run Down Jaywalkers
Local High School Dropouts Cut in Half

Meanings are fragile, and messages can be misunderstood. An effective message is one that the receiver understands.

The Message Should Achieve Its Intended Effect

When you communicate intentionally with others, it is for a specific purpose: to achieve a goal or to accomplish something. Because different purposes require different strategies for success, being aware of your purpose can enhance the probability of your achieving it.

Typical goals of speaking in public are to inform, to persuade, or to entertain. In small groups we often communicate to solve problems and make decisions. In our interpersonal relationships we interact to build trust, develop intimacy, or just enjoy someone's company. Thus, another criterion for judging the effectiveness of communication is to gauge whether the intent of the message is achieved.

Whether you are attempting to close a sale, get a date, give directions to the mall, or tell a joke, you should consider your goal. The purpose of our communication with others is not always to give or receive something tangible. Sometimes it is simply to make human contact, to establish a relationship, or just to be with someone. But one way to assess whether your communication was effective, regardless of the purpose, is to determine whether the outcome you sought is the outcome you got.

The Message Should Be Ethical

Communication can be used to achieve good or bad objectives. A message that is understood and achieves its intended effect but that manipulates listeners, unfairly restricts their choices, or uses false information may be effective, but it is not appropriate or ethical. **Ethics are the beliefs, values, and moral principles by which we determine what is right or wrong**. Ethics and ethical behavior have long been considered critical components of human behavior in a given culture.

Philosophers have debated for centuries whether there is such a thing as a universal moral and ethical code.[7] British author and scholar C. S. Lewis suggests that there is a universal ethical code that serves as the basis for interpreting the "goodness" or "badness" of human behavior; evidence for such a code can be found, says Lewis, in the teachings of cultures throughout the world and through time.[8] In their book *Communication Ethics and Universal Values*, communication scholars Clifford Christians and Michael Traber make the following claim: "Every culture depends for its existence on norms that order human relationships and social institutions."[9] What are these universal norms—these beliefs and behaviors that describe what is normal, appropriate, or inappropriate? Christians and Traber suggest there are three universal cultural norms: (1) the value of truth, (2) respect for another person's dignity, and (3) the expectation that innocent people should not suffer harm.[10]

Scholars and philosophers who suggest that a universal code of ethics exists do not claim that people in all cultures always behave in ways that are true to universal standards. Proponents of a universal ethical code do suggest that a universal moral code is the ideal basis for evaluating what is right and wrong behavior, including communication behavior.

All religions of the world have a moral code that provides guidance for how people should treat others.[11] The Ten Commandments serve as ethical guidelines for those who adhere to Judeo-Christian ethical principles. In Christianity the Golden Rule—"Do unto others what you would have others do unto you"—is a fundamental value. Buddhism teaches a similar value: "One should seek for others the happiness one desires for oneself." Hinduism asks adherents to live by the precept "Do nothing to others which would cause pain if done to you." Judaism teaches, "What is hateful to you, do not do to others." Islam suggests, "No one of you is a believer until he desires for his brother that which he desires for himself." The underlying ethic of how to treat others can clearly be seen across most of the world's religions.[12]

Our purpose is not to prescribe a specific religious or philosophical ethical code, but rather to suggest that humans from a variety of cultures and traditions have sought to develop ethical principles that guide their interactions with others.

Philosophy and religion are not the only realms that focus on ethical behavior. Most professions, such as medicine, law, and journalism, have explicit

The Dalai Lama teaches an ethical code that provides guidance for successful communication whether or not you believe in the Tibetan Buddhist religion.

codes of ethics that identify appropriate and inappropriate behavior. The National Communication Association has developed a Credo for Communication Ethics to emphasize the importance of being an ethical communicator:

> Ethical communication is fundamental to responsible thinking, decision making, and the development of relationships and communities within and across contexts, cultures, channels, and media. Moreover, ethical communication enhances human worth and dignity by fostering truthfulness, fairness, responsibility, personal integrity, and respect for self and others.[13]

Echoing the wisdom offered by others, we suggest that competent communication is grounded in an other-oriented ethical perspective that is fundamental to all human interactions.

For most people, being ethical means being sensitive to others' needs, giving people choices rather than forcing them to behave a certain way, keeping private such information as others wish to remain private, not intentionally decreasing others' feelings of self-worth, and being honest in presenting information. Unethical communication does just the opposite: It forces views on others and demeans their integrity.

Being honest is a key element of ethical communication. If you knowingly withhold key information, lie, or distort the truth, then you are not communicating ethically or effectively. For example, after Paul missed the test in his communication class, he mournfully told his professor that his grandmother had died and he had to attend the funeral. Paul's professor allowed him to make up the test. Paul's professor understood the message, so Paul achieved the effect he wanted. Paul's grandmother, however, is alive and well. According to our criteria for effective communication, Paul's dishonesty made his communication inappropriate and unethical.

Throughout each volume we will offer opportunities for you to examine ethical issues in a feature called Ethics and Communication.

Why Study Communication?

Why are you here? No, we don't mean "Why do you exist?" or "Why do you live where you do?" What we mean is, "Why are you taking a college course about communication?" Perhaps the short answer is, "It's required." Or maybe your advisor, parent, or friend encouraged you to take the course. If it is a required course, what's the rationale for that requirement? And required or not, what can a systematic study of human communication do for you?

Communication touches every aspect of our lives. To be able to express yourself to other people is a basic requirement for living in a modern society. From a practical standpoint, most of you will make your living with your minds rather than your hands.[14] Even if you do physical labor, you will need communication skills to work with others. When you study communication, you are

Ethics *and* Communication

What Are the Sources of Your Ethical Views?

Many people think that success means achieving what they want to achieve. Success is often equated with acquiring money, power, position, and influence. But when communicating with others, we've suggested, we achieve success if the communication message is understood as intended, achieves its intended effect, and satisfies a third criterion: It is ethical. Success is based not only on the communication outcome, but also on the methods and approaches used to communicate. If you lie, knowingly withhold key information, or use force to achieve your communication goals, then your message has not been successful, even if you are understood perfectly and you get what you want.

The question of who gets to decide what constitutes ethical behavior is one that arises often. Ethics are the beliefs, values, and moral principles by which we determine what is right or wrong. But where do your ethical beliefs, values, and principles come from? What are the sources of your sense of what is right and wrong?

Use the checklist below to identify the key sources of your ethical views.

INSTRUCTIONS: First, rate the influence of each factor listed below on a scale of from 1 (a minor influence on your ethical beliefs and practices) to 5 (a major influence on your ethical beliefs and practices).

_____ Grandparents
_____ Other family members (e.g., brothers, sisters, aunts, uncles)
_____ Friends
_____ Parents

_____ The Internet
_____ Government officials and public figures
_____ Laws and the legal system
_____ Music
_____ Works of art
_____ Sacred and inspired writing (e.g., the Bible)
_____ Religious beliefs
_____ Clergy and religious leaders
_____ Fiction and poetry
_____ TV and radio
_____ Newspapers and magazines
_____ Teachers
_____ Other sources

After you have rated the sources of influence, circle the sources of ethical influence that you rated the highest. (Perhaps you rated several sources a 5.) Of those items you circled, rank-order the top three. Assign a rank of 1 to the most important ethical influence, a 2 to the second most important, and a 3 to the third most important.

- What connection can you make between the sources of ethical influence in your life and the way you communicate with others?
- Can you think of specific ways in which the sources of your ethical beliefs and practices have directly influenced your communication with others?

Often we are unaware of the underpinnings of our ethical beliefs. This activity invites you to consciously examine the link between the sources of your perceptions of what is right and wrong and your communication behavior toward others.

developing leadership skills. "The art of communication," says author Daniel Quinn, "is the language of leadership."[15]

Although the value of being a competent communicator is virtually undisputed, there is evidence that many people struggle to express themselves clearly or to accurately understand messages from others. One study estimated that

On the Web

Most colleges and universities offer courses in communication and allow students to major or minor in communication, speech communication, or communication studies. The study of human communication may also be among the offerings of a department that focuses on mass communication, speech communication, and theatre. Students who select communication as a major or a minor pursue a wide variety of careers and professions, including business, law, government, education, and social services.

There are several professional academic communication organizations that offer a wealth of resources, information, and ideas about human communication. Chances are that the instructor for your communication course is a member of one or more of these organizations. The following Web sites offer you a panoramic view of the communication discipline from an academic perspective.

www.natcom.org is the Web address for the National Communication Association.

http://facstaff.uww.edu/wca is the Web address for the World Communication Association.

www.icahdq.org is the Web address for the International Communication Association.

www.americancomm.org is the Web address for the American Communication Association.

www.cios.org/encyclopedia/comlinks/websites.htm is a comprehensive Web site that lists dozens of Web sites on a variety of communication topics.

one-fifth of the students in the United States were not successful with even elementary communication tasks; in addition, more than 60% of the students could not give clear oral directions for someone else to follow.[16] When leaders in major corporations were asked to specify the most important skills for workers to have, 80% said listening was the most important work skill; 78% identified interpersonal communication skill as the next most important. However, the same leaders said only 28% of their employees had good listening skills and only 27% possessed effective interpersonal communication skills.[17] In support of these leaders' observations, another national study found that adults listen with 25% accuracy.[18] In addition to lacking communication skill, there is also evidence that the majority of adults are fearful of speaking in public; about 20% of the population is acutely apprehensive of presentational speaking.[19]

Aren't some people just born to be better communicators than others? If so, why should you work to develop your communication skill? Just as some people have more innate musical talent than others, there is evidence that some people may have an inborn biological ability to communicate with others.[20] This does not mean you should not work to develop your communication ability. Throughout each volume we will offer ample evidence that if you work to improve your skill, you will be rewarded by enjoying the benefits of enhanced communication competence. What are these benefits? Read on.

To Improve Your Employability

Regardless of your specific job description, the essence of what you do when working at any job is to communicate; you talk, listen, relate, read, and write, whatever your job title. People who can communicate effectively with others are in high demand. As noted by John H. McConnell, CEO of Worthington Industries, "Take all the speech and communication courses you can because the world turns on communication."[21] McConnell's advice is supported by research as well as by personal observations. As shown in Table 1.1.1, a survey of personnel managers revealed that they consider communication skills the top factor in helping graduating college students obtain employment.[22]

In addition to the practical, work-related rationale, enhancing your communication skill can significantly improve the quality of relationships with others in a variety of situations.

TABLE 1.1.1
Factors Most Important in Helping Graduating College Students Obtain Employment[23]

Rank/Order	Factors/Skills Evaluated
1	Oral communication (speaking) skills
2	Written communication skills
3	Listening ability
4	Enthusiasm
5	Technical competence
6	Work experience
7	Appearance
8	Poise
9	Resume
10	Part-time or summer employment
11	Specific degree held
12	Leadership in campus/community activities
13	Recommendations
14	Accreditation of program activities
15	Participation in campus/community activities
16	Grade-point average
17	School attended

To Improve Your Relationships

We don't choose our biological families, but we do choose our friends. For unmarried people, developing friendships and falling in love are the top-rated sources of satisfaction and happiness in life.[24] Conversely, losing a relationship is among life's most stressful events. Most people between the ages of 19 and 24 report that they have had from five to six romantic relationships and have been "in love" once or twice.[25] Understanding the role and function of communication can help unravel some of the mysteries of human relationships. At the heart of a good relationship is good communication.[26]

Virginia Satir, a pioneer in family enrichment, described family communication as "the largest single factor determining the kinds of relationships [we make] with others."[27] Learning principles and skills of communication can give us insight into why we relate to other family members as we do. Our early communication with our parents had a profound effect on our self-concept

WATCH

and self-worth. According to Satir, people are "made" in families. Our communication with family members has shaped how we interact with others today.

Many of us will spend as much or more time interacting with people in our places of work as we do at home. And although we choose our friends and lovers, we don't always have the same flexibility in choosing those with whom or for whom we work. Increasing our understanding of the role and importance of human communication with our colleagues can help us better manage stress on the job as well as enhance our work success.

To Improve Your Health

Life is stressful. Research has clearly documented that the lack or loss of close relationships can lead to ill health and even death. Having a social support system—good friends and supportive family members—seems to make a difference in our overall health and quality of life. Good friends and intimate relationships with others help us manage stress and contribute to both physical and emotional health. For example, physicians have noted that patients who are widowed or divorced experience more medical problems, such as heart disease, cancer, pneumonia, and diabetes, than do married people.[28] Grief-stricken spouses are more likely than others to die prematurely, especially around the time of the departed spouse's birthday or near their wedding anniversary.[29] Terminally ill patients with a limited number of friends or social support die sooner than those with stronger ties.[30] Without companions and close friends, our opportunities for intimacy and stress-managing communication are diminished. Studying how to enrich the quality of our communication with others can make life more enjoyable and enhance our overall well-being.

So again, we ask the question: Why are you here? We think the evidence is clear: People who are effective communicators are more likely to get the jobs they want; have better quality relationships with friends, family, and colleagues; and even enjoy a healthier quality of life.

Communication Models

Communication researchers have spent a considerable amount of time trying to understand precisely how communication takes place. In the course of their study, they have developed visual models that graphically illustrate the communication process.

By reviewing the development of communication models, you can see how our understanding of communication has evolved over the past century. Early models viewed communication as a transfer or exchange of information, but this view evolved to include a more interactive, give-and-take approach.

Communication can improve the quality of life for people of any age.

Researchers' understanding then progressed even further to today's view that communication is a process in which meaning is co-created simultaneously among people. The three models of the communication process that we show here begin with the simplest and oldest perspective and then move to more contemporary models.

Communication as Action: Message Transfer

"Did you get my message?" This simple sentence summarizes the communication-as-action approach to human communication. In this model, communication takes place when a message is sent and received. Period. Communication is a way of transferring meaning from sender to receiver. In 1948, Harold Lasswell described the process as follows:

Who (sender)
Says what (message)
In what channel
To whom (receiver)
With what effect[31]

Figure 1.1.1 shows a simplified representation of the communication process developed by communication pioneers Claude Shannon and Warren Weaver, who viewed communication as a linear input/output process consisting of a source, a message, a channel, a receiver, and noise. Today, although researchers view the process as more complex, they still define most of the key components in this model in basically the same way that Shannon and Weaver did.

FIGURE 1.1.1
A Model of Communication as Action

Source: From *The Mathematical Theory of Communication*. Copyright 1949, 1998 by the Board of Trustees of the University of Illinois. Used with permission of the University of Illinois Press.

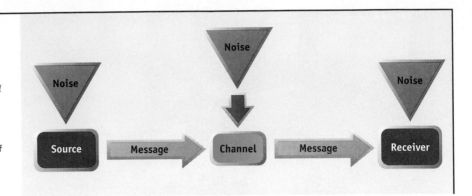

Source   The **source** of communication is the originator of a thought or an emotion, who expresses ideas or feelings and puts a message into a code that can be understood by a receiver. Translating ideas, feelings, and thoughts into a code is called **encoding**. Vocalizing a word, gesturing, and establishing eye contact are means of encoding our thoughts into a message that can be decoded by someone. **Decoding, the opposite process of encoding, is a process of interpreting ideas, feelings, and thoughts that have been translated into a code.**

Receiver   The **receiver** is the person who decodes the message and attempts to make sense out of what the source encoded. Think of a TV station as a source broadcasting to a receiver (your TV) that picks up the station's signal. In human communication, however, there is something in between the source and the receiver: We filter messages through past experiences, attitudes, beliefs, values, prejudices, and biases.

Message   **Messages** are the written, spoken, and unspoken elements of communication to which we assign meaning. You can send a message intentionally (talking to a friend before class) or unintentionally (falling asleep during class); verbally ("Hi. What's up?"), nonverbally (a smile and a handshake), in written form (a book), or through any number of electronic channels.

Channel   **A message is communicated from sender to receiver via some pathway called a channel.** With today's technological advances, we receive messages from a variety of channels. With your phone, the Internet, or a fax transmission, the communication channel may be a telephone line. Cellular telephones use a wireless channel. Ultimately, communication channels correspond to your senses. When you call your mother on the telephone, the message is conveyed via an electronic channel that activates auditory cues. When you talk with your mother face to face, the channels are many. You see her: the visual channel. You hear her: the auditory channel. You may smell her perfume: the olfactory channel. You may hug her: the tactile channel.

Noise **Noise is interference, either literal or psychological, that hinders the accurate encoding or decoding of a message**. Noise keeps a message from being understood and achieving its intended effect. Without noise, all of our messages would be communicated with considerable accuracy. But noise is always present. It can be literal—the obnoxious roar of a gas-powered lawn mower—or it can be psychological, such as competing thoughts, worries, and feelings that capture our attention. Instead of concentrating on your teacher's lecture, you may start thinking about the chores you need to finish before the end of the day. Whichever kind it is, noise gets in the way of the message and may even distort it. Communicating accurate messages involves minimizing both literal and psychological noise.

It may appear that scholars have neatly identified the components of communication, such as source, message, channel, receiver, and noise, and can prescribe precisely what is needed to make communication effective. While the communication-as-action approach is simple and straightforward, it has a key flaw: Human communication rarely, if ever, is as simple a matter as "what we put in is what we get out." Others cannot automatically know what you mean just because you think you know what you mean. Although by Lasswell's and Shannon and Weaver's time communication scholars had already begun identifying an array of key elements in the communication process, the action approach overlooked their complexity.

Communication as Interaction: Message Exchange

The communication-as-interaction perspective uses the same elements as the action model but adds two new ones: feedback and context. **Feedback is the response to the message.** Without feedback, communication is less likely to be effective. When you order your pepperoni pizza and the server says in response, "That's a pepperoni pizza, right?" he has provided feedback to ensure that he decoded the message correctly.

Think of a Ping-Pong game. Like Ping-Pong balls, messages bounce back and forth. We talk; someone listens and responds; we respond to this response. This perspective can be summarized using a physical principle: For every action there is a reaction.

Feedback can be intentional (applause at the conclusion of a symphony) or unintentional (a yawn as you listen to your uncle tell his story about bears again); verbal ("That's two burgers and fries, right?") or nonverbal (blushing after being asked for a date).

A second component recognized by the interaction perspective is **context—the physical, historical, and psychological communication environment.** All communication takes place in some context. As the cliché goes, "Everyone has to be somewhere." The literal or psychological "somewhere" of communication is the context. A conversation with your good friend on the beach would likely differ from one the two of you might have in a funeral home. Context encompasses not only the physical environment but also the number of people present, their past relationship with the communicators, the

FIGURE 1.1.2
A Model of Communication as Interaction
Interaction models of communication include feedback as a response to a message sent by the communication source and place the process in a context.

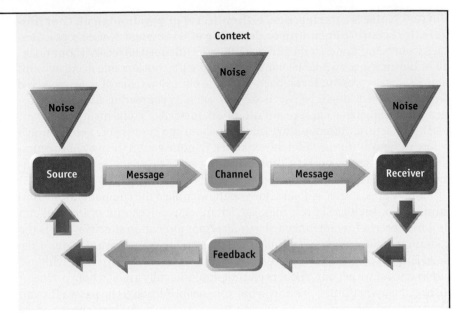

communication goal, and the culture in which the communicators are steeped. The psychological context includes the impact of what is going on in the minds of the communicators; the speaker's and listener's personalities and styles of interacting with others influence how messages are understood.

The communication-as-interaction model, as shown in Figure 1.1.2, is more realistic than the communication-as-action model, but it still has limitations. Although it emphasizes feedback and context, it does not quite capture the complexity of the communication process if the communication takes place *simultaneously*. The interaction model of communication still views communication as a linear, step-by-step process. But in many communication situations, both the source and the receiver send and receive messages at the same time.

Communication as Transaction: Message Creation

The communication-as-transaction perspective, which evolved in the 1960s, acknowledges that when we communicate with another, we are constantly reacting to what our partner is saying and expressing. Most scholars today view this perspective as the most realistic model of communication. Although it uses such concepts as action and interaction to describe communication, in this model, all of the interaction is simultaneous. As Figure 1.1.3 indicates, we send and receive messages concurrently. Even as we talk, we are also interpreting our partner's nonverbal and verbal responses. Transactive communication also occurs within a context, and noise can interfere with the quality and accuracy of our encoding and decoding of messages.

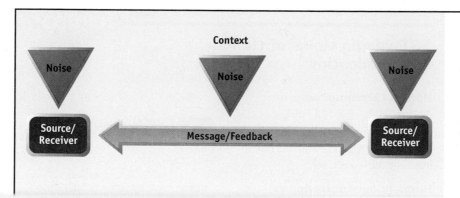

FIGURE 1.1.3
A Model of Communication as Transaction
The source and the receiver of a message experience communication simultaneously.

As we send messages, we monitor the degree to which the other person understands each message. We mutually define the symbols we use. If one partner misunderstands a message, both can work to clarify the meaning. For example, if I ask you to hand me the book off my desk and you hand me a pad of paper, we have failed to create a shared meaning. I might then say, "No, not

Components of the Human Communication Process

Term	Definition
Source	Originator of an idea or emotion
Receiver	Person or group toward whom a source directs messages and who decodes the message
Message	Written, spoken, and unspoken elements of communication to which we assign meaning
Channel	Pathway through which messages pass between source and receiver
Noise	Any literal or psychological interference with the clear encoding or decoding of a message
Encoding	Translation of ideas, feelings, and thoughts into a code
Decoding	Interpretation of ideas, feelings, and thoughts that have been translated into a code
Context	Physical, historical, and psychological communication environment
Feedback	Verbal and nonverbal responses to a message

RECAP

An Evolving Model of Human Communication

Human Communication as Action

Human communication is linear, with meaning sent or transferred from source to receiver.

Human Communication as Action

Human Communication as Interaction

Human communication occurs as the receiver of the message responds to the source through feedback. This interactive model views communication as a linear sequence of actions and reactions.

Human Communication as Interaction

Human Communication as Transaction

Human communication is simultaneously interactive. Meaning is created based on mutual, concurrent sharing of ideas and feelings. This transactive model most accurately describes human communication.

Human Communication as Transaction

the pad of paper, the red book next to the phone"; you then would hand me the book. Your action would require me to explain and be more specific. We would not simply transfer or exchange meaning; we would create it during a communication transaction.

One research team says that communication is "the coordinated management of meaning" through episodes during which the message of one person influences the message of another.[32] Technically, only the sender and receiver of those messages can determine where one episode ends and another begins. We make sense out of our world in ways that are unique to each of us.

Communication Characteristics

Now that we have defined communication, noted its importance, and seen how our understanding of it evolved over the last half of the 20th century, we turn our attention to describing how it works by examining the characteristics of communication. The following characteristics are evident when communication occurs: Communication is inescapable, irreversible, and complicated; it emphasizes content and relationships; and it is governed by rules.

Communication Is Inescapable

Opportunities to communicate are ubiquitous—they are everywhere. Even before we are born, we respond to movement and sound. With our first cry, we begin the process of announcing to others that we are here. And once we make contact with other humans, we communicate and continue to do so until death. Even though many of our messages are not verbalized, we nonetheless intentionally, and very often unintentionally, send them to others. As we noted earlier, some communication scholars question whether it is possible to communicate with someone unintentionally. What experts do agree on is this: Communication with others plays an ever-present role in our life. We spend most of our waking hours sending messages to or interpreting messages from others.[33] Even as you silently stand in line at a supermarket checkout line, your lack of eye contact with others waiting in line suggests you're not interested in striking up a conversation. Your unspoken messages may provide cues to which others respond. Even when you don't intend to express a particular idea or feeling, others may try to make sense out of what you are doing—or not doing. Remember: People judge you by your behavior, not your intent.

Communication Is Irreversible

"Disregard that last statement made by the witness," instructs the judge. Yet the clever lawyer knows that once her client has told the jury that her husband gave her a black eye during an argument, the client cannot really "take back" the message. In conversation we may try to modify the meaning of a spoken message by saying something like, "Oh, I really didn't mean it." But in most cases, the damage has been done. Once created, communication has the physical property of matter; it can't be uncreated. As the helical model in Figure 1.1.4 suggests, once communication begins, it never loops back on itself. Instead, it continues to be shaped by the events, experiences, and thoughts of the communication partners. A Russian proverb nicely summarizes the point: "Once a word goes out of your mouth, you can never swallow it again."

Communication Is Complicated

Pick up any newspaper this morning, and you will see that there is conflict brewing or erupting in some part of the world. Perhaps there is conflict and disagreement in your own home or in a relationship with someone you care about. Communicating with others is not simple. If it were, we would know

FIGURE 1.1.4
A Helical Model of Communication

Interpersonal communication is irreversible. This helical model shows that communication never loops back on itself. Once it begins, it expands infinitely as the communication partners contribute their thoughts and experiences to the exchange.

Source: F. E. X. Dance, *Human Communication Theory* (Holt, Rinehart and Winston, 1967), 294. Permission of Frank E. X. Dance.

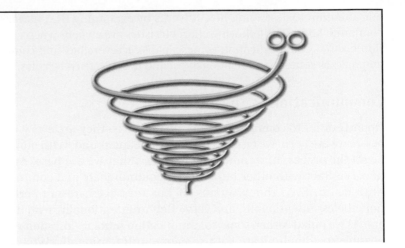

how to reduce dramatically the number of misunderstandings and conflicts in our world. This book could also offer you a list of simple techniques and strategies for blissful management of your communication hassles. You won't find that list in this book or any other credible book. Human communication is complicated because of the number of variables and unknown factors involved when people interact. To illustrate the complexity of the process, communication scholar Dean Barnlund has suggested that whenever we communicate with another person, there are really at least six "people" involved: (1) who you think you are; (2) who you think the other person is; (3) who you think the other person thinks you are; (4) who the other person thinks he or she is; (5) who the other person thinks you are; and (6) who the other person thinks you think he or she is.[34] Whew! And when you add more people to the conversation, it becomes even more complicated.

Life is not only complicated, it's also uncertain. There are many things we do not know. We seek information about such everyday things as the weather or about such questions as what others may think about us. Several communication theorists suggest that we attempt to manage our uncertainty through communication.[35] In times of high uncertainty (when there are many things we do not know) we will communicate more actively and purposefully so as to manage our uncertainty. For example, we are likely to ask more questions, seek information, and listen intently when we are uncertain.

Adding to the complexity of communication and the problem of our own uncertainty is the fact that messages are not always interpreted as we intend them. Osmo Wiio, a Scandinavian communication scholar, points out the challenges of communicating with others when he suggests the following maxims:

1. If communication can fail, it will.
2. If a message can be understood in different ways, it will be understood in just the way that does the most harm.

3. There is always somebody who knows better than you what you meant by your message.
4. The more communication there is, the more difficult it is for communication to succeed.[36]

Although we are not as pessimistic as Professor Wiio, we do suggest that the task of understanding each other is challenging.

Communication Emphasizes Content and Relationships

What you say—your words—and how you say it—your tone of voice, amount of eye contact, facial expression, and posture—can reveal much about the true meaning of your message. If one of your roommates loudly and abruptly bellows, "HEY, DORK! CLEAN THIS ROOM!" and another roommate uses the same verbal message but more gently and playfully suggests, "Hey, dork. Clean this room," both are communicating a message aimed at achieving the same outcome. But the two messages have different relationship cues. The first shouted message suggests that your roommate may be grumpy and frustrated that the room still harbors the remains of last night's pizza party, while roommate number two's more calmly expressed request suggests he or she may be less frustrated and simply wants the room tidied up a bit.

The content of communication messages is the new information, ideas, or suggested actions that the speaker wishes to express. The relationship dimension of a communication message is usually more implied; it offers cues about the emotions, attitudes, and amount of power and control the speaker feels toward the other.[37]

Another way of distinguishing between the content and relationship dimensions of communication is to consider that the content of a message refers to *what* is said. The relationship cues are provided in *how* the message is communicated. For example, when you read a transcript of what someone says, you can get a different meaning than you would if you actually heard the person's words.

THE FAR SIDE® BY GARY LARSON

© 1988 FarWorks, Inc. All Rights Reserved/Dist. by Creators Syndicate.

"The wench, you idiot! Bring me the *wench*!"

WATCH

The rules of both formal and informal play often call for a high five between teammates or friends.

Communication Is Governed by Rules

When you play Monopoly, you know that there are explicit rules about how to get out of jail, buy Boardwalk, or pass "Go" and get $200. The rules are written down. When you play a game with others, there may even be some unwritten rules, such as "When you play Monopoly with Grandpa, always let him buy Boardwalk. He gets grumpy as a bear before breakfast if he doesn't get to buy it." There are also rules that govern how we communicate with others. Most of the rules are imbedded in our culture or discussed verbally rather than written in a rulebook.

According to communication researcher Susan Shimanoff, **a rule is a "followable prescription that indicates what behavior is obligated, preferred, or prohibited in certain contexts."**[38] The rules that help define appropriate and inappropriate communication in any given situation may be explicit or implicit. For a class, explicit rules are probably spelled out in your syllabus. But your instructor has other rules that are more implicit. They are not written or verbalized because you learned them long ago: Only one person speaks at a time; you raise your hand to be called on; you do not pass notes.

Communication rules are developed by those involved in the interaction and by the culture in which the individuals are communicating. Most people learn communication rules from experience, by observing and interacting with others.

Communicating with Others: Three Situations

The five communication principles operate whenever people communicate, regardless of the number of people present or the content of their messages. The three classic situations to which communication researchers apply these principles are interpersonal communication, group communication, and presentational communication.

Each of the next five chapters is devoted to one of the five principles we've identified and relates these principles to the three most typical unmediated communication situations you will experience. By *unmediated,* we mean those communication encounters that do not involve some kind of *medium* such as

and Communication

Diversity

Principles for a Lifetime: Principles for All Cultures?

We've suggested that our five principles for a lifetime constitute a framework for all human communication. Again, let's review the five principles:

Principle One: Be aware of your communication with yourself and others.

Principle Two: Effectively use and interpret verbal messages.

Principle Three: Effectively use and interpret nonverbal messages.

Principle Four: Listen and respond thoughtfully to others.

Principle Five: Appropriately adapt messages to others.

The question is "How applicable are these five principles for a lifetime to communication in a variety of cultures?" Culture is the learned system of knowledge, behavior, attitudes, beliefs, values, and norms that is shared by a group of people. People who were born and raised in Asian countries, for example, have different cultural expectations than do people who were born and raised in North America. But do these five communication principles apply to *all* people everywhere, despite cultural differences and a wide variety of cultural traditions and backgrounds in the world? Is it true that all people should be aware of their communication, use and interpret verbal and nonverbal messages, listen and respond thoughtfully, and appropriately adapt their messages to others?

We're not suggesting that all cultures use and interpret verbal or nonverbal messages the same way (principles two and three)—there are obvious differences from one culture to another in language and use of nonverbal cues. But we are suggesting that in all cultures, the use and interpretation of verbal and nonverbal messages is important in determining whether communication is effective. We are also not saying that people from all cultures adapt messages in the same way (principle five). There are clear cultural differences in the way people choose to adapt messages to others. But do people in all cultures adapt messages to others in some way, even though the interpretation of the adapted message varies from culture to culture? We suggest that these five fundamental principles may provide a common framework for talking about communication in a variety of cultures. Do you agree or disagree with this statement?

In your communication class there are undoubtedly people from a variety of cultural backgrounds. Perhaps some of your classmates grew up in countries other than your own. Respond to the following questions, and then compare your answers with those of your fellow students.

1. How applicable are the five communication principles to your cultural experience?

2. Do any of the communication principles *not* apply in your culture?

3. Can you think of another fundamental communication principle that is not included in our list of five? If so, what is it?

4. Do you agree that these communication principles apply to all people?

the telephone, the Internet, TV, fax, or another type of technology; any communication that involves such technology is *mediated communication.* Most of the research conclusions about interpersonal, group, and presentational situations are based on communication that takes place live and in person. So we'll spend most of our discussion focusing on how communication is expressed and interpreted when people are face to face. There is a growing collection of research findings, however, that is helping us understand how the Internet and other technological tools are affecting our communication. When appropriate, we'll offer some ideas and suggestions for interacting with others via mediated settings.

We now turn our attention to introducing these three contexts of communication: interpersonal, group, and presentational communication.

Interpersonal Communication

Interpersonal communication is a special form of human communication that occurs when two people interact simultaneously and attempt to mutually influence each other, usually for the purpose of managing relationships. At the heart of this definition is the role of communication in developing unique relationships with other people.[39]

For many years communication scholars considered any two-person interaction interpersonal communication. Today interpersonal communication is defined not by the number of people who communicate but by the quality of communication that occurs when we express and interpret verbal and nonverbal messages. Interpersonal communication occurs not just when we interact with someone, but when we treat the other person as a one-of-a kind human being.

Impersonal communication occurs when we treat people as objects or when we respond to their roles rather than to who they are as unique people. Based on this definition, asking a server for a glass of water at a restaurant is impersonal rather than interpersonal communication. If you strike up a conversation with the server—say you discover it's her birthday, or you discover that you both know the same people—your conversation moves from impersonal to interpersonal. We're not suggesting that impersonal communication is unimportant or necessarily inferior or bad. Competent communicators are able to interact with others in a variety of situations.

Another attribute of interpersonal communication is that the communication is simultaneous. Both people are communicating at the same time, and there is mutual influence—both persons are reacting or involved in the process. Interpersonal communication is not a one-sided monologue; it's a dialogue in the sense that all communicators are influenced and meaning is created simultaneously.[40] Interpersonal communication reflects the characteristics of the transactional model of communication that we discussed earlier.

A final attribute, and among the most important, is that interpersonal communication is the fundamental means we use to manage our relationships. A relationship is an ongoing connection we make with others through interpersonal communication. To relate to someone is to give and take, listen and respond, act and react. When we talk about a good or positive relationship with someone, we often mean that we are "together" or "in sync." In an effective relationship, the individuals involved feel that their verbal and nonverbal messages are understood and that there is a relational harmony based on a common understanding between the communicators. We will apply the five principles of human communication to interpersonal communication in Chapters 2.1 and 2.2.

Group Communication

Each of us belongs to a gang of some type; it's just that some gangs are more socially acceptable than others. Comparisons between a rambunctious street gang and the local PTA may seem a stretch. But even though the street gang and the PTA have radically different objectives, both share similarities of function and form that make them **a group: a collection of people who have common goals, who feel they belong to the group, and who influence each other.**

Human beings are social, collaborative creatures. We do most of our work and play in groups. And today's globe-shrinking technology makes it possible for people to be linked with others in virtual groups even when they are in different physical locations. One focus of this book is the communication that occurs in groups—how we make sense out of our participation in groups and share that sense with others. We define **small group communication** as **the verbal and nonverbal message transactions that occur among from three to about fifteen people who share a common goal, who feel a sense of belonging to the group, and who exert influence on each other.**[41]

We engage in interpersonal communication when we interact with another person.

A group must have at least three people; **a two-person interaction is referred to as a dyad.** What is the upper limit on the number of people for meaningful group discussion? Some scholars say fifteen, others say more.[42] The bigger the group, the less influence each person has on the group and the greater the chance that subgroups or splinter factions will emerge.

Our definition of group communication includes the notion that in order to be considered a group, people need a common goal—something that members all would agree is the reason for the group's existence. Group members also have a sense of belonging to the group. A collection of travelers waiting for the subway may have a common goal of catching the train, but they probably don't see themselves as belonging to a group with a single goal of going to the same place. Members of a small group need to have a sense of identity with the group; they should sense that it is their group.

Here's another attribute of a small group: Group members exert influence on one another. Each person potentially influences the actions and responses of others. Even if a group member sits like a lump and says nothing, this nonverbal behavior exerts an influence. Each group member, by virtue of being a member of the group, has the potential to exert leadership on the group. To lead is to influence.

What's the difference between a group and a team? Although some people use the two terms interchangeably, we see a distinction. A **team is a coordinated group of individuals intentionally organized to work together to achieve a specific, common goal.** To us, a team is more highly structured and organized than a group. Team members have clearly defined roles, duties, and responsibilities. Think of a sports team. Team members have assigned roles and well-thought-out assignments. Team members don't just show up and mill around and do what comes their way. They are focused. Teams also have clearly defined rules and explicit expectations for team operations. Their goals are well defined and measurable. And they coordinate their work efforts as they collaborate to achieve their well-articulated goals. In Chapters 3.1 and 3.2, we will discuss more thoroughly the five communication principles for a lifetime as they apply to groups and teams.

Presentational Communication

For many people, speaking in public is a major source of anxiety. **Presentational communication occurs when a speaker addresses a gathering of people to inform, persuade, or entertain.** In this book we will focus on applying the principles of communication when informing and persuading listeners.

Of the three contexts in which the principles we present in this book are applied, this context has the distinction of being the one that has been formally studied the longest. In 333 BC, Aristotle wrote his famous *Rhetoric*, the first fully developed treatment of the study of speech to convince an audience. He defined rhetoric as the process of discovering the available means of persuasion in a given situation. In essence, **rhetoric is the process of using symbols**

to persuade others. Today many communication departments have several courses that focus exclusively on how to persuade others, design and deliver both informative and persuasive messages, and evaluate the messages of others. Although we have certainly advanced in our understanding of informing and persuading others in the past two millennia, much of what Aristotle taught has withstood the tests of both time and scholarly research.

Our focus in Chapters 4.1 through 4.5 is on basic strategies for designing and delivering a speech to others. As with interpersonal and group communication, we will discuss presentational communication through the perspective of the five principles that anchor our study. Effective presentational speakers are aware of their communication and how they interact with their audience. They also effectively use, interpret, and understand verbal and nonverbal messages; listen and respond to their audience; and adapt their message to their listeners.

There is a wealth of information on and strategies for each of these three communication contexts. Most communication departments offer separate courses on these three areas. Our challenge is to present fundamental principles that illuminate all applications of human communication. Being aware of how you interact with others, monitoring your verbal and nonverbal messages, listening and responding thoughtfully, and adapting your messages to others will serve you well whether you are talking with a friend, participating in a meeting, or giving a speech.

Are interpersonal, group, and presentational communication the only contexts in which communication takes place? The answer is no—communication takes place in a variety of situations. One of the most prominent forms of communication in our lives involves the media. As we noted earlier, **mediated communication is any communication that is expressed via some channel other than those that are used when we communicate in person.** Some physical medium, such as a wire, a cable, a phone line, a telephone, a TV set, a computer, or some other technology, carries the messages between sender and receiver. The channel of communication is not only physical but also electronic, in the form of the signal coming into your TV set, your phone, or your computer. **Mass communication occurs when a mediated message is sent to many people at the same time.** A TV or radio broadcast is an example of mass communication. As we noted earlier in this chapter, our focus in this book is on unmediated communication. This is not meant to suggest that mass communication is not important, only that it is beyond the scope of this book. At some colleges and universities, mass communication is a focus of study in a separate department; at other colleges and universities, the study of mass communication is included in the same department that studies all human communication.

In the chapters ahead we will analyze the five principles of communication for a lifetime as they apply to the three typical unmediated communication situations—interpersonal, group, and presentational communication. Our primary goal is to help you better understand your communication and improve your ability to communicate with others for the rest of your life.

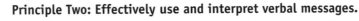

FOR A LIFETIME: Enhancing Your Skills

Aware

Principle One: Be aware of your communication with yourself and others.

- Be aware of your intrapersonal communication.
- Be conscious of how your own "self-talk" has an impact on your communication with others and your overall communication behavior.

Verbal

Principle Two: Effectively use and interpret verbal messages.

- Use clear and precise words to explain ideas and concepts to others.
- Make a concerted effort to accurately interpret the words of others.

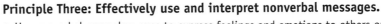

Nonverbal

Principle Three: Effectively use and interpret nonverbal messages.

- Use nonverbal, unspoken cues to express feelings and emotions to others or to modify the explicit verbal message you are communicating to others.
- Make a conscious effort to accurately decode the nonverbal messages of others.

Listen and Respond

Principle Four: Listen and respond thoughtfully to others.

- Be other-oriented by taking special care to listen to both the verbal and the nonverbal messages of others.
- Be deliberate in how you provide feedback to those to whom you are listening.

Adapt

Principle Five: Appropriately adapt messages to others.

- Use your listening and nonverbal communication skills to help you appropriately adjust both your message and how you communicate it to others.
- Make ethical choices about how to best formulate a message and respond to others to achieve your communication goals.

SUMMARY

Communication is essential for life. At its most basic level, communication is the process of acting on information. Human communication is the process of making sense out of the world and sharing that sense with others by creating meaning through verbal and nonverbal messages. It is important to learn about communication, because being a skilled communicator can help you obtain a good job and enhance the quality of your relationships, as well as improve your physical and emotional health. Early models viewed human communication as a simple message-transfer process. Later models evolved to view communication as interaction and then as simultaneous transaction. Key components of communication include source, receiver, message, channel, noise, context, and feedback.

Communication has five characteristics: It is inescapable; it is irreversible; it is complicated; it emphasizes content and relationships; and it is governed by rules.

Five principles are fundamental to good communication. First, be aware of your communication with yourself and others. Being mindful of your communication is important to help you improve your communication. Second, effectively use and interpret verbal messages. Words are powerful and influence our thoughts, our actions, and our relationships with others. Third, effectively use and interpret nonverbal messages. Unspoken cues provide important information about our emotions, feelings, and attitudes. Fourth, listen and respond thoughtfully to others. Being able to interpret accurately the messages of others enhances comprehension and relational empathy. Fifth, appropriately adapt messages to others. It is important to adapt messages to others to enhance both understanding and empathy.

These five principles are applicable to the most common communication contexts: interpersonal, group, and presentational communication. Interpersonal communication is a special form of communication that occurs when two people interact simultaneously and mutually influence each other, usually for the purpose of managing relationships. Small-group communication is interaction among a small group of people who share a common purpose or goal, who feel a sense of belonging to the group, and who exert influence on the others in the group. Presentational communication occurs when a speaker addresses an audience for the purpose of informing, persuading, or entertaining.

DISCUSSION AND REVIEW

1. Define the term *communication*. Compare and contrast this definition with the text's definition of *human communication*.
2. Why is it important to study communication?
3. Compare and contrast communication as action, interaction, and transaction.
4. What are characteristics of communication?
5. Identify the five fundamental principles of communication.
6. Discuss how the five principles of communication apply to interpersonal, group, and presentational communication contexts.

PUTTING PRINCIPLES INTO PRACTICE

1. Working alone or with a team of your classmates, develop one or more original models of communication. Include all of the elements that describe how communication works. You could develop a model for each of the three communication situations that we presented in this chapter (interpersonal, group, presentational speaking). Your model could be a drawing or you could use objects (like tinker toys or other building toys) to illustrate the communication process. Explain your model to the class.

2. In this chapter we noted that communication is complicated. There are really six "people" involved in a conversation that seemingly involves just two people. Choose a partner and try to verbalize your impressions about the six people involved in your exchanges with that person.

3. To get better acquainted with other members of a small group, try this ice-breaker activity. Tell three things about yourself, one of which is not true. Other group members should guess which one of the three things you have disclosed is false. The purpose of this activity is not to teach you how to lie or be unethical, but to assess the power and sometimes inaccuracy of the impressions we make on others. After all group members have made their guesses, provide the correct information. Discuss how you form first impressions and the role these impressions play in your communication with others.

4. In a small group, take turns introducing yourself to other class members. Consider the following ideas as ways to tell other classmates about yourself.
   • What does your name mean to you?
   • Describe what you do best and what you wish you did better.
   • Draw or symbolize your "lifeline." Show the high points and low points of your life, perhaps using simple drawings or symbols to illustrate your life hopes, joys, concerns, and goals.
   • If you could be someone other than yourself, who would you be? Why?

After you have all introduced yourselves, discuss the interaction you've had according to the characteristics of communication included in the chapter. For example, how was your discussion guided by rules?

Chapter 1.1   *Practice Test*

MULTIPLE CHOICE.   Choose the *best* answer to each of the following questions.

1. The effectiveness of our communication is *not* judged by the degree to which
   a. the receiver understands the message correctly.
   b. we achieve our goals in the situation.
   c. the receiver agrees with our message.
   d. we communicate an ethical message.

2. Most contemporary communication scholars agree that the _____ model of communication is the most realistic model.
   a. linear
   b. transactional
   c. interactional
   d. encoded

3. The pathway through which messages pass between source and receiver is the

   a. source.
   b. channel.
   c. receiver.
   d. context.

4. Susan arrives late for her date with Richard. He jumps from his chair and sarcastically says, "Glad you're here!" The relationship aspect of this message is communicated primarily by
   a. the words Richard said.
   b. Richard's sarcastic tone of voice.
   c. the time indicated on Richard's watch.
   d. b and c.

5. Telling the cashier at the gas station how much you owe and then paying her is an example of
   a. interpersonal communication.
   b. personal communication.
   c. team communication.
   d. impersonal communication.

6. Feedback and context are two distinguishing characteristics of which model of communication?

   a. communication as action

   b. communication as mediation

   c. communication as transaction

   d. communication as interaction

7. According to a recent study, which of the following do business leaders consider the most important communication skill for workers to have?

   a. presentational communication

   b. small group problem solving

   c. conflict management

   d. listening

8. Julie goes over in her mind what she wants to say during her upcoming job interview. This is an example of

   a. intrapersonal communication.

   b. interpersonal communication.

   c. impersonal communication.

   d. presentational communication.

9. Which of the following is *not* a distinction between a team and a group?

   a. A team is more highly structured than a group.

   b. Team members have assigned roles.

   c. Groups are more focused than teams.

   d. Groups have less-well-defined goals than teams.

10. A small group requires at least

    a. two members.

    b. three members.

    c. four members.

    d. five members.

11. According to the communication-as-action model, noise can impact all of the following *except*

    a. the source.

    b. the channel.

    c. the receiver.

    d. the feedback.

12. The meaning of a message is

    a. created in the heart and mind of the sender.

    b. created in the heart and mind of the receiver.

    c. co-created by both the sender and the receiver.

    d. determined solely by the symbols used.

13. Which of the following is a true statement about symbols?

    a. Effective communicators focus more effort on encoding messages.

    b. The words and symbols we use have power.

    c. Symbols are the things they represent.

    d. Words cannot hurt us.

14. Even though Phillip and Tim agreed to end their argument with each other by "starting over as if it had never taken place," each still felt angry toward the other. Phillip and Tim have failed to realize that

    a. communication is inescapable.

    b. communication is irreversible.

    c. communication involves content and relationship.

    d. communication is governed by rules.

15. When there is a contradiction between your verbal message and your nonverbal message,

    a. your verbal message is more believable than your nonverbal one.

    b. your nonverbal message is more believable than your verbal one.

    c. your verbal and nonverbal messages are equally believable.

    d. your verbal and nonverbal messages are equally unbelievable.

16. Which of the following is *not* suggested by Christians and Traber as a universal cultural norm?

    a. the value of truth

    b. respect for another person's dignity

    c. using language that doesn't offend others

    d. there should be no harm to innocent people

17. Maria and Jordan are working together to plan an event for their service fraternity. While they are talking, Maria keeps worrying about how

much Jordan likes her. Which type of noise is Maria experiencing?

a. physical

b. literal

c. psychological

d. physiological

18. According to one scholar, "the largest single factor determining the kinds of relationships [we make] with others" is

a. intrapersonal communication.

b. family communication.

c. the quality of our friendships.

d. our ability to communicate competently.

19. During times of high uncertainty, we attempt to manage our uncertainty by

a. listening more and communicating less.

b. communicating about the same as usual, but a little more slowly.

c. communicating more actively and purposefully.

d. paying more attention to verbal messages than nonverbal messages.

20. Aiden and Celeste are discussing a new business proposal. Aiden reviews the elements of the proposal one at a time. Celeste holds her response until he has finished speaking and then tells Aiden her thoughts on the element he has just explained. This interaction best reflects which model of human communication?

a. communication as action

b. communication as interaction

c. communication as reaction

d. communication as transaction

TRUE/FALSE.   Indicate whether the following statements are *true* or *false*.

1. T or F   Communication rules are learned through trial and error.

2. T or F   Human communication is about transmitting our sense of the world to others.

3. T or F   Your emotional well-being may be influenced by how you communicate with others.

4. T or F   The purpose of communication may be to simply make contact with someone else.

5. T or F   As long as others understand your message and you accomplish your objective, your communication is considered to be effective.

6. T or F   Any two-person interaction is interpersonal communication.

7. T or F   A person sitting silently on a city bus and not looking at anyone else is not communicating.

8. T or F   Impersonal communication is any communication that is expressed via some channel other than in a live and in-person situation.

9. T or F   Presentational communication has been formally studied longer than interpersonal or small group communication.

10. T or F   Different communication models reflecting the ways people communicate have evolved over the years.

FILL IN THE BLANK.   Complete the following statements.

1. A dyad is a _____-person interaction.

2. The act of giving meaning to the symbols shared by another is _____.

3. A _____ indicates the behavior that is appropriate in a given situation.

4. Your thoughts and emotions are examples of _____ communication.

5. Using symbols to influence or persuade others is called _____.

6. Our _____ cues usually tell others how to interpret what we are saying.

7. _____ communication occurs when two people simultaneously interact with each other.

8. The _____ shares a message that can be understood by the receiver.

9. Any element of communication to which we assign meaning is a _____.

10. Impersonal communication is characterized by treating people as _____.

Self-Awareness and Communication

CHAPTER OUTLINE

CHAPTER OBJECTIVES

After studying this chapter, you should be able to

1. Discuss the importance of self-awareness in the process of improving one's communication skills.

2. Define attitudes, beliefs, and values as they relate to self-concept development.

3. Name and briefly describe the three types of selves, according to James's research.

4. Describe the four factors that affect the development of self-concept.

5. Describe Stewart's four characteristics of identity.

6. Explain the difference between self-concept, self-image, self-esteem, and self-worth.

7. Describe how gender, social comparisons, self-expectations, and self-fulfilling prophecies affect one's self-esteem.

8. Provide examples of positive self-talk, visualization, and reframing that demonstrate the connection between these techniques and the enhancement of self-esteem.

9. Define perception and explain its three stages.

10. Discuss three ways to enhance your perceptual accuracy.

A person who buries his head in the sand offers an engaging target.

Mabel A. Keenan

Marc Chagall, The Painter, 1976. Scala/Art Resource, NY. © 2007 Artists Rights Society (ARS), New York/ADAGP, Paris.

D o you have your own Web site? Many of you have designed a personal Web page as part of a class project or simply because you wanted a way to communicate who you are to people across the globe. Did you include a photo of yourself on the site? What information about you would someone who visited your site learn?

If you do not have your own Web page, you've probably had other opportunities to communicate who you are, perhaps by writing a self-exploratory essay as part of your college application process. Some of you have no doubt placed personal ads in your local or campus newspaper. What did you choose to focus on as you described yourself—physical attributes? personality characteristics? intellectual abilities? What information did you leave out, either because you're not proud of those aspects of yourself, you didn't think anyone would be interested, or you were concerned about privacy?

Still others of you have likely visited the Web site of an Internet dating service, such as eharmony.com, which asks you a battery of questions about yourself. Your responses are analyzed across multiple personality dimensions and your profile can be matched with compatible potential partners who also use the service.[1]

Activities such as designing a personal Web site, writing an essay about yourself, crafting a personal ad, or responding to dating service questions rely on a central, important element: awareness. Stephen Covey, author of the best-selling book *The Seven Habits of Highly Effective People,* describes self-awareness as that which "allows us to stand apart and examine even the way we 'see' ourselves—our self-paradigm, the most fundamental paradigm of effectiveness. It affects not only our attitudes and behaviors, but also how we see other people."[2]

Figure 1.2.1 presents the model introduced in the Introduction—our "communication principles for a lifetime" model. You will no doubt become

FIGURE 1.2.1
Communication Principles for a Lifetime

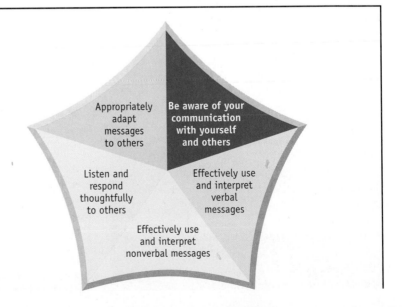

quite familiar with this model and its five principles as you read this book. As we said in the Introduction, these integrative principles provide the foundation for effective communication in various contexts that you encounter throughout your life. In this chapter we explore the first principle: *Be aware of your communication with yourself and others.* Developing self-awareness involves being conscious not only of the present moment, but also of who you are (your self-concept), your value in this life (your self-esteem), and your perception of yourself and others.

Self-Awareness: How Well Do You Know Yourself?

Have you ever been standing in a line at the grocery store checkout and felt something brush past your legs? You look down and realize that a small child has crossed your path, no doubt on the way to the candy display. The child has no real awareness of what has occurred—that she or he has inadvertently touched a stranger while attempting to satisfy a goal. But you, as an adult, are aware. Moments of self-awareness arrive at different times for different people, and self-awareness is a never-ending process. You don't reach a point where you've "maxed out" your self-awareness. This fascinating process of understanding your own existence continues throughout life.

Social psychologists have categorized self-awareness into three types or dimensions.[3] The first is **subjective self-awareness, an ability that humans and animals have to differentiate themselves from their social and physical environment**. We see ourselves as being different and apart from the physical world and from other beings in it. A second category, which humans and only a few animals (primates) possess, is **objective self-awareness, the ability to be the object of one's own attention, to be aware of one's state of mind, to realize that one is thinking and remembering.** The final awareness state is **symbolic self-awareness, a unique human ability to develop a representation of oneself and communicate that representation to others through language.** This last form of awareness holds the most interest for those of us who study communication.

One framework, attributed to Abraham Maslow, helps explain the process of becoming self-aware; it has also been used to explain the attainment of communication skill. The framework suggests that people operate at one of four levels:

Ballet has become second nature to this skilled dancer because he has worked hard to reach that level of competence.

1. *Unconscious incompetence.*   We are unaware of our own incompetence. We don't know what we don't know.
2. *Conscious incompetence.*   At this level, we become aware or conscious that we are not competent; we know what we don't know.
3. *Conscious competence.*   We are aware that we know or can do something, but it has not yet become an integrated skill or habit.
4. *Unconscious competence.*   At this level, skills become second nature. You know or can do something but don't have to concentrate to be able to act on that knowledge or draw on that skill.

To better understand how this framework operates, let's use conversation skills as an example. Suppose Janie is a poor communicator but doesn't realize it, so she is at level 1 when it comes to interacting with other people. Either Janie hasn't thought about developing interaction skills or she actually believes herself to be a good conversationalist. Then Janie starts becoming more self-aware and realizes that her style of talking with people isn't winning her any friends. She's unsure about how to fix this problem, but she is conscious that she has some deficits in this area (level 2). She sets out to improve her communication skills by taking a class, purposefully working on how she talks with people and soliciting honest feedback from people with whom she interacts. Janie develops an improved interaction style and is now at the level of conscious competence. Once these skills are fully integrated into Janie's behavior with people, so she doesn't have to strive to communicate effectively, she will have reached level 4, unconscious competence. Almost any skill can be described in terms of these four levels. It is also possible to be at one level with one skill and another level with another skill. For example, you may be skilled at meeting new people but less skilled at managing conflict.

People can experience moments of heightened self-awareness and significant personal growth. Taking a communication course like the one you're enrolled in can spark such a moment. In this course, you will be challenged to think long and hard about your answers to the question "Who am I?" You'll be encouraged to survey what you believe about yourself and to think about the role such aspects as your gender, race or ethnicity, nationality, sexual orientation, and social class play in your view of self. You'll be challenged to consider how you communicate with others, how you are shaped and affected by those with whom you interact, and how you can use your powers of communication. But the key beginning point is awareness. Before attempting to communicate who you are to others, you must first be aware of yourself.

QUICK REVIEW

VISUAL LITERACY

Self-Concept: Who Are You?

Aware

If someone were to say to you, "Who are you?" how would you respond? You might start with basic demographic information like your age and where you're from; perhaps you would describe yourself in relation to groups and organizations to which you belong. Or you might talk about yourself according to various roles you assume, like "I'm a student at State" or "I'm so-and-so's daughter (or son)." Whatever answer you give will be incomplete, because you can't really convey the totality of who you are to others. But it's an interesting place to begin, considering just how you would answer the "Who am I" question.

Psychologist Karen Horney defines **self** as **"that central inner force, common to all human beings and yet unique in each which is the deep source of growth."**[4] Your "Who am I" responses are also part of your **self-concept—your identity, your subjective description of who you think you are, how you see you as a person.**[5] Some people use the term *self-image* synonymously with self-concept, but we want to avoid confusion over these terms. We subscribe to a more narrow meaning for the term self-image, in that **self-image is your view of yourself in a particular situation or circumstance.**[6] That view changes from situation to situation. For example, you may be extroverted in chemistry class but not at a party where you don't know too many people. You may become very nervous when giving a presentation but are quite comfortable communicating with people one on one. You have several self-images, because they change as the situation changes. These different self-images are part of the larger component we call self-concept. The self-concept is the way we *consistently* describe ourselves to others; it is deeply rooted and slow to change.

Self-Concept Components

Who you are is also reflected in the attitudes, beliefs, and values that you hold. **An attitude is a learned predisposition to respond to a person, object, or idea in a favorable or unfavorable way.** Attitudes reflect what you like and what you don't like. If you like sports, spaghetti, and history, you hold positive attitudes toward these things. You were not born with a fondness for sports; you learned to like them just as some people learn to enjoy the taste of exotic foods.

Beliefs are the way in which you structure your understanding of reality—what is true and what is false. Most of your beliefs are based on previous experience. You trust that the sun will rise in the morning and that you will get burned if you put your hand on a hot stove.

Values are enduring concepts of good and bad, right and wrong. Your values can be difficult to identify because they are so central to who you are. But knowing what you value in your life is part of this principle of self-awareness that we focus on in this chapter. When you go to the supermarket, you may spend a few minutes deciding on whether to buy chocolate or vanilla ice cream, but you probably do not spend much time deciding whether you will steal the ice cream or pay for it, because you value honesty over dishonesty. Other values may reflect your sense of loyalty, patriotism, justice and fairness, and love and caring for others. Our values are instilled in us by our earliest connections with others; for almost all of us, our parents are the first influences on our development of values. Of the three elements, attitudes are the

RECAP

Self-Concept Components

Component	Definition	Dimensions	Example
Attitude	Learned predisposition to respond favorably or unfavorably toward something	Likes–Dislikes	You like ice cream, scented candles, and tennis.
Belief	The way in which we structure reality	True–False	You believe your parents love you.
Value	Enduring concept of right and wrong	Good–Bad	You value honesty and truth.

most superficial and likely to change; values are more at the core of a person and least likely to change. We consider attitudes, beliefs, and values again in our discussion of persuasion in Chapter 4.5.

One or Many Selves?

Shakespeare's famous line "To thine own self be true" suggests that you have a single self to which you can be true. But do you have just one self? Or is there a more "real you" buried somewhere within? "I'm just not myself this morning," sighs Sandy, as she drags herself out the front door to head for her office. If she is not herself, then *who is she?* Most scholars conclude that we have a core set of behaviors, attitudes, beliefs, and values that constitute our self—the sum total of who we are. But our *concept* of self can and does change, depending on circumstances and influences.

Perhaps the most enduring and widely accepted framework for describing who you are was developed by the philosopher William James. He identified three components of the self: the material self, the social self, and the spiritual self.[7]

The Material Self   Perhaps you've heard the statement, "You are what you eat." The material self goes a step further by suggesting, "You are what you have." **The material self is the element of self reflected in all of the tangible things you own: your body, your possessions, your home.**

One element of the material self receives considerable attention in our culture: the body. Do you like the way you look? Most of us would like to change something about our appearance. Research has determined that in the United States, women experience more negative feelings about their bodies than men and experience significant self-esteem loss as a result.[8] Many women hold images of very thin women, such as supermodels, as ideals and develop dissatisfaction with their own bodies in comparison. Women's dissatisfaction with their bodies has markedly increased over the past 25 years.[9] However, research also shows that men are not immune to body dissatisfaction, in that they compare their own bodies with ideal male bodies displayed in the media and are concerned about what others want and expect them to look like.[10] When there is a discrepancy between our desired material self and our self-concept, we may respond to eliminate the discrepancy. We may try to lose weight, get a nose job, or acquire more hair. The multibillion-dollar diet industry is just one of many that profit from our collective desire to change our appearance.

We also attempt to keep up with the proverbial Joneses by wanting more expensive clothes, cars, and homes. By extension, what we own becomes who we are. The bigger, better, more "high-tech," and more luxurious our possessions, we may subconsciously conclude, the better *we* are.

The Social Self   **Your social self is your concept of self as developed through your personal social interactions with others.** William James believed that you have as many social selves as you have people who recognize you and that you change who you are depending on the friend, family member, colleague, or acquaintance with whom you are interacting. For example, when you talk to your best friend, you are willing to "let your hair down" and reveal more thoughts and feelings than you might in a conversation with your communication professor, your parents, or your boss. Each relationship that you

WATCH

RECAP

William James's Dimensions of Self

Dimension	Definition	Examples
Material Self	The physical elements that reflect who you are	The self you reveal through your body, clothes, car, home
Social Self	A variety of selves that change in situations and roles, reflected in your interactions with others	Your informal self interacting with friends; your formal self interacting with your professors
Spiritual Self	Introspections about values, morals, and beliefs	Belief or disbelief in God; regard for life in all its forms

Technology *and* Communication

Exploring Self-Concept through Computer-Mediated Communication

Technology, particularly through the advances of computers and the Internet, allows us to explore our self-concepts in ways not possible to previous generations. Perhaps long-distance pen pals experienced something similar, in that they could choose which aspects of themselves to highlight in letters to someone they would never meet. But the ease with which the Internet enables us to experiment with expressions of our self-concepts to others online makes this a fascinating area of study.

One person who has conducted extensive research into online communication is Annette Markham, author of *Life Online: Researching Real Experience in Virtual Space*. Markham examines how online users communicate their sense of self in CMC (shorthand for computer-mediated communication) versus RL (real life).[11] In one online interview, Markham asked a user to compare his CMC and RL selves. His response was that he was "more confident online, because I'm a better editor than writer/speaker. I do well when I can backspace." Markham agreed with the user regarding the luxury of being able to edit one's online communication, saying that she liked the backspace key for its "ability to correct everything you say and therefore are." Markham recounts one particularly interesting exchange with a user named Sherie, who felt much more confident and expressive online. Sherie explained:

> i choose to exist as myself in language online. i don't try to come up with other personae, so it feels more like being me than i sometimes feel offline. offline one often finds oneself in certain social roles that one must maintain; student, teacher, family member, etc. . . . i don't like my appearance all that much, and so i don't like myself in flesh all that much. i think myself in language is more communicative of who i am. eloquence makes me beautiful online.

Who is to say which is more real for an avid computer user—the online self or the offline self? As we delve more and more into what computers can do for us, and what they do *to* us, we will no doubt continue to question the real versus virtual self. Perhaps these selves aren't distinct; perhaps the online persona is merely an extension or facet of the real person. Should it be cause for concern when people feel positive self-esteem only when they are online? Or should we be glad that people have an outlet that allows them to feel good about themselves?

have with another person is unique because you bring to it a unique social self. This means that you are multifaceted, not false with people, because you have different selves in relation to different people.

The Spiritual Self   **Your spiritual self consists of all your internal thoughts and introspections about your values and moral standards.** It is not dependent on what you own or with whom you talk; it is the essence of who you *think* you are and of your *feelings* about yourself. It is a mixture of your spiritual beliefs and your sense of who you are in relationship to other forces in the universe. It is your attempt to understand your inner essence, whether you view that essence as consciousness, spirit, or soul. Your spiritual self is the part of you that attempts to answer the question, "Why am I here?"

The self-concept we develop through communication with our family stays with us throughout our lives.

How the Self-Concept Develops

Some psychologists and sociologists have advanced theories that suggest we learn who we are through four basic means: (1) our communication with other individuals, (2) our association with groups, (3) roles we assume, and (4) our self-labels.

Communication with Others   A valued colleague of ours often says, when he teaches communication courses, that every time you lose a relationship you lose an opportunity to see yourself. What he means is that we don't come to know and understand ourselves in a vacuum. We learn who we are by communicating with others, receiving their feedback, making sense out of it, and internalizing or rejecting all or part of it, such that we are altered by the experience. For example, let's say you like to think of yourself as a real comedian. Now think about it for a moment: How would you know you were funny if it were not for others laughing at humorous things you say or do? Sure, you can crack yourself up, but the real test of whether you're funny or not is how others react to you.

In 1902, scholar Charles Horton Cooley first advanced the notion that we form our self-concepts by seeing ourselves in a figurative looking glass: We learn who we are by interacting with others, much as we look into a mirror and see our reflection.[12] Like Cooley, George Herbert Mead, author of *Mind, Self, and Society,* also believed that our sense of who we are is a consequence of our relationships with others.[13] So when we form new relationships and sustain the old ones, we gain opportunities to know ourselves better.

Interpersonal communication scholar John Stewart describes four characteristics of the self or one's identity.[14] First, identities are multidimensional and changing. Human beings are complex. Some of a person's aspects are stable,

and Communication

Ethics

Cyber Selves

One of the values most people hold dear is honesty—a critical dimension in successful relationships. From interpersonal communication texts to self-help advice columns to *The Oprah Winfrey Show,* all stress the importance of honesty in conveying who you are to others. But are there any grey areas when it comes to honesty in an Internet interaction?

Whether you're in a chat room or e-mailing someone you met in cyberspace, the potential for identity exploration is very real. You can become anyone you want to be through cyber-communication, altering your sex, age, race, looks, nationality, and occupation as you describe them to others in order to explore alternate identities. People you communicate with on the Net can alter their identities too, so you

never really know who you're talking to unless you move on to another context, like a face-to-face encounter.

In Chapter 1.1 we suggested three essential attributes of competent communication, the third of which was "The message should be ethical." The question is, Is it ethical to alter your identity in cyberspace—to purposefully communicate a false impression of yourself to another person over the Internet? What if the receiver of your communication believes that you are representing yourself truthfully? Is the exercise of altering your identity, of trying a different self on for size, and communicating a false sense to another person a breach of ethics? Is it wrong, or is it in a grey area in which it isn't a breach of ethics as long as no one gets hurt?

such as his or her genetic profile or ethnicity, but most aspects of the self are constructed and therefore fluid, meaning that identity changes because of circumstances and, primarily, our interactions and relationships with others.

Second, identity involves responsiveness to others. We do not form our sense of self in a vacuum. We come to know ourselves and construct our identities through communication with others. A third characteristic is that identities develop in both past and present relationships. Who you are today is greatly a function of your family background and relationships. Those early messages you received, nicknames you were given, and the ways family members related to you significantly influenced your view of self. While family relationships often remain important in our lives, these primary relationships may be replaced or de-emphasized, as present relationships with friends, romantic partners, classmates, and coworkers shape the self-concept and help to construct identity.

Finally, Stewart suggests that identities can be avowed and ascribed. **An avowed identity is one you personally assign to yourself and act out** such as student, athlete, friend, and so forth. **An ascribed identity is assigned to you by others,** and you may or may not agree with the assignment. For example, a classmate may deem you an "overachiever," but you think your hard work and dedication to your studies make you a good student—an achiever, but not necessarily an over-achiever. Avowed and ascribed identities shift and are negotiated through our interactions with others.

Association with Groups   I'm a native New Yorker. I'm a soccer player. I'm a rabbi. I'm a real estate agent. I'm a member of the Young Democrats. Each of these self-descriptive statements answers the "Who am I" question by citing identification with a group or organization. Our awareness of who we are is often linked to who we associate with. How many of these kinds of group-associated terms could you use to describe yourself? Religious groups, political groups, ethnic groups, social groups, study groups, and occupational and professional groups play important roles in shaping your self-concept. Some of these groups we are born into; others we choose on our own. Either way, group associations are significant parts of our identities.

As you no doubt are aware, peer pressure is a powerful force in shaping attitudes and behavior, and adolescents are particularly susceptible to it. But adolescents are not alone in allowing the attitudes, beliefs, and values of others to shape their expectations and behaviors. Most adults, to varying degrees, ask themselves, "What will the neighbors think? What will my family think?" when they are making choices.

Assumed Roles   A large part of most people's answers to the "Who am I" question reflects roles they assume in their lives. Mother, aunt, brother, uncle, manager, salesperson, teacher, spouse, and student are labels that imply certain expectations for behavior, and they are important in shaping self-concept.

Gender asserts a powerful influence on the self-concept from birth on. As soon as they know the sex of their child, many parents begin associating their children with a gender group by adhering to cultural rules. They give children sex-stereotypical toys, such as catcher's mitts, train sets, or guns for boys, and dolls, tea sets, and "dress-up" kits for girls. These cultural conventions and expectations play a major role in shaping our self-concept and our behavior.[15] Research indicates that up until the age of three, children are not acutely aware of sex roles. Between the ages of three and five, however, behaviors reflecting masculine and feminine roles begin to emerge (as encouraged by parents), and they are usually solidified between the ages of five and seven.[16] Research shows that by the time we reach adulthood, our self-concepts are quite distinguishable by gender, with men describing themselves more in terms of giftedness, power, and invulnerability; and women viewing themselves in terms of likability and morality.[17]

Self-Labels   Although our self-concept is deeply affected by others, we are not blank slates for them to write on. The labels we use to describe our own attitudes, beliefs, values, and actions also play a role in shaping our self-concept. Where do our labels come from? We interpret what we experience; we are self-reflexive. **Self-reflexiveness is the human ability to think about what we're doing while we're doing it.** We talk to ourselves about ourselves. We are both participants and observers in all that we do. This dual role encourages us to use labels to describe who we are.

When you were younger, perhaps you dreamed of becoming a rocker or a movie star. People along the way may have told you that you were a great musician or a terrific actor, but as you matured, you probably began observing yourself more critically. You struck out with a couple of bands; you didn't get the starring role in a local stage production. So you self-reflexively decided that you were not, deep down, a rocker or an actor, even though others may have labeled you as "talented." Sometimes, through this self-observation, we may experience a period of depression or disillusionment because who we thought we were does not pan out, and we confront the need to change. However, we may also discover strengths that encourage us to assume new labels.

RECAP

How the Self-Concept Develops

Communication with Others	The self-concept develops as we communicate with others, receive their feedback, make sense out of it, and internalize or reject all or part of it.
Association with Groups	We develop our self-concept partly because of and through our identification with groups or organizations.
Assumed Roles	The self-concept is affected by roles we assume, such as son or daughter, employee, parent, spouse, student.
Self-Labels	The terms we use to describe our attitudes, beliefs, values, and actions play a role in shaping the self-concept.

QUICK REVIEW

Self-Esteem: What Is Your Value?

It may sound crass to consider a person's *value*, but we do this every day. **Our assessment of our value as a person, reflected in our perception of such things as our skills, abilities, talents, and appearance, is termed self-esteem.** Closely related to your self-concept, or your *description* of who you are, is your self-esteem, your *evaluation* of who you are. The term **self-worth is often used interchangeably with self-esteem.** As Gloria Steinem describes it, in her book *Revolution from Within: A Book of Self-Esteem,* "It's a feeling of 'clicking in' when that self is recognized, valued, discovered, *esteemed*—as if we literally plug into an inner energy that is ours alone, yet connects us to everything else."[18]

While the self-concept pertains to one's enduring identity, self-esteem pertains more to one's current state of mind or view of self. Self-esteem can fluctuate because of relatively minor events, such as getting a lower grade on a paper than one expected, or major upheavals, such as the break-up of an important relationship. Self-esteem can rise or fall within the course of a day; sometimes just a look from someone (or someone's failure to notice you) can send you into a tailspin and make you feel your value as a person is diminished. Or a certain level of self-esteem can last for a while—you may have a series of months or even years that you look back on and think, "Yeah; I felt pretty lousy about myself in those days. Glad that period is over." Researchers have identified four factors that provide clues about the fluctuating nature of self-esteem.

Gender

In Chapter 1.6 we provide a more extensive discussion of the role of sex and gender in the communication process. Research reveals that sex and gender have an impact on one's self-esteem. Before exploring that impact, let's first clarify our use of the terms *sex* and *gender*, because many people use them interchangeably, and that can lead to confusion. One meaning for the term **sex is the biological/physiological characteristics that make a person male or female.** In another usage, sex can refer to sexual activity. The term used most often in this book is *gender*. In its most specific sense, gender refers to psychological and emotional characteristics of individuals that cause them to be masculine, feminine, or androgynous (having a combination of both feminine and masculine traits). Defined broadly, **gender is a cultural construction that contains psychological characteristics but also includes your sex (being female or male), your attitudes about**

On the Web

Self-esteem is such a pervasive and important topic that there is even a national association devoted to its study. The National Association for Self-Esteem (NASE) is an organization whose purpose is, as described on its Web site, "to fully integrate self-esteem into the fabric of American society so that every individual, no matter what their age or background, experiences personal worth and happiness." The Web site for NASE offers links to books, tapes, and CDs, as well as seminars, conferences, and educational programs on topics associated with self-esteem, such as parenting strategies that help foster positive self-esteem in children. Check out the Web site at

www.self-esteem-nase.org

appropriate roles and behavior for the sexes in society, and your sexual orientation (to whom you are sexually attracted).[19] Because the term *gender* is more broad and all-inclusive, it's our preferred term in this book.

Research that has primarily focused on the development of self-esteem in childhood and adolescence documents ways that boys' self-esteem develops differently from girls'. In a patriarchal (or male-dominated) culture, such as that of the United States, women and girls suffer loss of self-esteem to a much greater degree than men and boys.[20] A survey of 3,000 schoolchildren, conducted by the American Association of University Women, showed that self-esteem decreases between elementary grades and high school, but this decrease is significantly more pronounced in girls.[21] Myra and David Sadker, authors of the book *Failing at Fairness: How America's Schools Cheat Girls*, explain how boys experience a "self-esteem slide," while girls' self-esteem loss is a "free fall."[22]

The difference in self-esteem levels seems to pertain to such factors as boys feeling better able to do things than girls. A related factor is the reinforcement boys receive from participating in athletics, which helps them cope with changes in their bodies better than girls. But this trend has begun to change, as we witness rising participation in and appreciation for women's athletics.[23] In the summer of 1999, over 90,000 people—the largest audience to ever attend a women's sporting event—jammed a California stadium to see the U.S. women's soccer team defeat the team from China in the finals of the women's World Cup. The event drew over 4 million television spectators worldwide.[24] More professional teams for women—as well as college, university, and school teams—are being established and gaining momentum, as we continue to recognize the impact of athletic accomplishment on people's self-esteem.

Supportive relationships with friends can help young girls overcome feelings of low self-esteem.

Social Comparisons

A process called **social comparison, in which we measure ourselves against others, is one way we become more aware of ourselves and derive our sense of self-worth.**[25] I'm good at playing basketball (because I'm part of a winning team); I can't cook (because others cook better than I do); I'm good at meeting people (whereas most people seem to be uncomfortable interacting with new people); I'm not handy (but my dad can fix anything). Each of these statements implies a judgment about how well or badly you can perform certain tasks, with implied references to how well others perform the same tasks. A belief that you cannot fix a leaky faucet or cook like a chef may not in itself lower your self esteem. But if there are *several* things you can't do or *many* important tasks that you cannot seem to master, these shortcomings may begin to color your overall sense of worth. If it seems like you're a "jack of all trades, master of none" and everyone else is a "master," your self-esteem may suffer as a result.

One powerful social comparison that contributes to self-esteem loss in girls and women is fueled by images of physical attractiveness in the media.

Diversity *and* Communication

Self-Esteem and Ethnicity

Studies have shown that sex and gender affect self-esteem, but what other factors influence people's levels of self-esteem? Might people's ethnic or racial identity affect the way they value themselves? Research shows a positive correlation between self-esteem level and attachment to racial or ethnic groups.[26] More simply put, the more people feel committed to and positive about their ethnic group, the higher their levels of self-esteem tend to be. People who have negative attitudes about their ethnicity, who are unclear about their identification with a particular racial or ethnic group, or who are uncommitted to their racial or ethnic group tend to have lower levels of self-esteem. Additionally, people's views of their own ethnic group have more of an impact on self-esteem than other people's views, meaning that the way you identify with and view your own ethnicity has more effect on your self-esteem than the way another person views your ethnic group. All of these findings were less

pronounced for persons who self-identified as white, which supports other studies showing that Caucasians often do not view "whiteness" as a racial or ethnic identity.

Granted, it's easy to blame the media for society's ills as well as individual people's problems. But mediated messages are so pervasive, accessible, and influential that studies are determining a link between exposure to ads, films, TV, and Internet sources and diminished self-esteem among females. Mass media create and reinforce for consumers notions of what is considered physically attractive, and achieving that media-driven standard is next to impossible for most people.

So pervasive is the drive for physical beauty in U.S. culture that popular (and, some argue, disturbing) television programming capitalizes on this drive and on viewers' insecurities. *The Swan* and *Extreme Makeover* are but two examples of prime-time television shows that have aired in recent years, in which contestants or selected "ugly ducklings" are put through extreme physical transformations in very short time spans. These transformations often include painful nose jobs, chin implants, breast enlargements, liposuction, laser skin treatments, and rigorous short-term body-sculpting regimens. The climax of these shows occurs when contestants' "new and improved" faces and bodies are revealed to family and friends or to panels of judges who award prizes.[27]

One line of research has found that females of a wide range of ages—from pre-adolescents through college students—compare their own physical attractiveness to that of models in ads. When they perceive that they don't measure up, they often experience the "model trap." This trap is a continual cycle of viewing physically "perfect" models, hating them, then growing to like them, love them, followed by efforts to emulate them, failing in those efforts, resenting them again, and repeating the cycle.[28]

While this form of mediated social comparison has had a greater effect on females' than on males' self-esteem, advertisers have begun to target male consumers, too—so social comparisons to male models, and resulting self-esteem loss among males, are on the rise. In an analysis of *Men's Health* magazine, author Michelle Cottle explores increasing media attention being paid to male desires for physical beauty and effects on self-esteem. She explains, "With page after page of bulging biceps and Gillette jaws, robust hairlines and silken skin, *Men's Health* is peddling a standard of male beauty as unforgiving and unrealistic as the female version sold by those dewy-eyed pre-teen waifs draped across the covers of *Glamour* and *Elle*."[29]

It can be self-defeating to take social comparisons too far, to cause your self-esteem to suffer because you compare yourself unfairly or unrealistically to others. The wiser approach is to compare yourself to your friends and neighbors, people you know and who are similar to you in many ways, rather than to people who are obviously not like you. Expecting to be as wealthy as Microsoft Chair Bill Gates is unrealistic for most of us, so it's unwise to compare your income to his. You might, however, compare how much you make at your job with the incomes of others who have similar positions or abilities comparable to yours. A healthy sense of self-worth is derived in part from the conclusions we draw from realistic, fair comparisons.

Self-Expectations

Another factor that affects your self-esteem is an estimation of how well you accomplish your goals. **Self-expectations are goals we set for ourselves about how we believe we ought to behave and what we ought to accomplish**, such as losing weight, developing a "buff" body, making better grades, being appointed or elected to an important office in an organization, graduating by a certain time, and acquiring wealth by a certain age. Self-esteem is affected when you evaluate how well you measure up to your own expectations. For instance, if you expect to receive all A's this semester and you don't achieve that, it's likely that your self-esteem will be affected negatively. You may have to readjust your goals and expectations, or just become more determined to achieve the straight-A goal next semester.

Some people place enormous expectations on themselves, probably because their parents had enormous expectations for them when they were growing up. We wish people who are stressed out all the time could give themselves a break, because they place such unrealistic, high demands on themselves. The popular achievement gurus will tell you that setting high goals is a good thing, that you will not accomplish much if you set easily attainable goals. But we are suspicious of that advice; we see too many people whose self-esteem is low because they place such pressure and unrealistic demands on themselves. When they can't live up to those demands, they feel guilty and begin to see themselves as failures. A downward trend involving expectation, failure, guilt, and low self-esteem is hard to reverse.

Self-Fulfilling Prophecy

A concept related to the creation of self-expectations is the **self-fulfilling prophecy, the idea that what you believe about yourself often comes true because you expect it to come true.** If you think you'll fail a math quiz because you have labeled yourself inept at math, then you must overcome not only your math deficiency but also your low expectations of yourself. If you hold the self-perception that you're pretty good at conversation, then you're likely to act on that assumption when you approach a conversation with someone. Your conversations, true to form, go well, thus reinforcing your belief in yourself as a good conversationalist.

Your level of self-esteem also affects the kinds of prophecies you make about yourself and colors your interpretation of events.[30] Persons with high self-esteem tend to anticipate or predict successes for themselves; they are then reinforced when they experience those successes. Conversely, persons with low self-esteem tend to interpret their successes as flukes; they attribute an achievement to luck rather than to their own efforts. Successes can enhance your self-esteem, but if you are in a downward spiral of low self-esteem, you may not recognize your own achievements to let them have a positive effect on your self-esteem.

Factors Affecting Self-Esteem

Sex Differences	In male-dominated cultures, females suffer self-esteem loss to a much greater degree than men and boys, primarily as a result of males' feeling better able to do things than females.
Social Comparisons	Judgments about how well or poorly you can perform certain tasks compared to others can be self-defeating and can cause self-esteem to suffer.
Self-Expectations	Your estimation of how well you perform in comparison to your own goals or self-expectations has a profound impact on self-esteem.
Self-Fulfilling Prophecies	What you believe about yourself often comes true because you expect it to come true.

QUICK
REVIEW

Communication and the Enhancement of Self-Esteem

WATCH

We know the damage low self-esteem can do to a person—it can limit her or his ability to develop and maintain satisfying relationships, to experience career successes and advancement, and to create a generally happy and contented life. But in recent years, teachers, psychologists, self-help gurus, clergy members, social workers, and even politicians have suggested that many of our societal problems stem from our collective feelings of low self-esteem. Our feelings of low self-worth may contribute to our choosing the wrong partners; becoming addicted to drugs, alcohol, sex, or gambling; experiencing problems with eating and other vital activities; and opting, in too many cases, for death over life. So we owe it to society, as well as ourselves, to develop and work to maintain a healthy sense of self-esteem, as an integral part of the process of becoming more self-aware.

While no simple list of tricks can easily transform low self-esteem into feelings of being valued and appreciated, you can improve how you think about yourself. One thing is clear from research about self-esteem: Communication is essential in the process of building and maintaining self-esteem.[31]

Engage in Positive Self-Talk

Intrapersonal communication refers to how you take in information or stimuli in your environment and make sense out of it.[32] It also involves communication within yourself—self-talk, or what some

scholars term "inner speech."[33] Your self-concept and level of self-esteem influence the way you talk to yourself about your abilities and skills. The reverse is also true, in that your inner dialogue has an impact on both your self-concept and your level of self-esteem. One of your authors recalls a snow-skiing experience. After several unsuccessful tries to manage an archaic ski-lift contraption (not your simple chair lift), she was determined to reach the top of the slope (just so she could fall down it). She remembers actively talking to herself throughout the climb to the top, willing herself not to fall off the lift, and feeling exhilarated upon achieving even this small piece of the process. The "You can do this" self-talk helped her keep focused on the task at hand and provided positive reinforcement of her self-concept.

Although becoming your own cheerleader may not enable you to climb metaphorical mountains quite so easily, there is evidence that self-talk, both positive and negative, is related to the building and maintaining of one's self-concept.[34] Realistic, positive self-talk can have a reassuring effect on your level of self-worth and therefore your interactions with others. Conversely, repeating negative messages about your lack of skill and ability can keep you from trying and achieving.

Positive self-talk is important in all forms of communication. When you communicate with someone, you probably also carry on an inner dialogue as you process what the other person is saying and doing and how you want to respond. In group meetings, self-talk enables group members to process the interaction. If the communication is excited or even heated, positive self-talk can motivate you to engage in the interaction, possibly offering disagreement with members' ideas. Another example of a situation that calls for positive self-talk is one that is challenging to most people—the presentational speaking context. Comedian Jerry Seinfeld commented a few years back that the number-one fear among Americans was of public speaking; people were more afraid of it than of death (which was number six). He joked that people would rather be in the coffin at a funeral than have to deliver the eulogy, or speech of tribute to the deceased.

Most speakers experience feelings that range from mild activation (feeling "jazzed" or "up" for the event) to debilitating, blinding fear. But don't worry—there are only a very few people at the upper end of the anxiety scale. When you make a presentation, you definitely need positive self-talk. You can create a negative self-fulfilling prophecy by telling yourself, "I can't do this; I won't be able to get through it. This speech is going to be lousy, and I'm going to fall flat on my face. My topic is lame; the audience will be bored and think I'm pathetic." Over years of teaching presentational speaking, we know that some students tell themselves just those kinds of negative messages.

But others have learned the power of getting "psyched" for presentations, just as an athlete would get psyched for a game or a performer for a show. These people harness the power of positive self-talk to get themselves "pumped" for a good outcome. When they hear negative messages creeping into their heads and creating self-doubt, they quash those messages before they have a chance to take hold. In any situation—from a mild challenge to the most pressure-filled circumstance you can envision—if you hear yourself start to say in your head, "I'm not sure I can do this" or "This isn't going to go well," stop right there and rephrase those statements. There's no need to completely turn the statement around ("This will be easy; a piece of cake") because you might not believe it. But simply tone down the negativity and say, "I can get through this; I'll be just fine. I CAN do this; I'll survive." While positive self-talk is not a substitute for preparation and effort, it can keep you on track by helping you focus and, ultimately, achieve your goal.

Visualize

Visualization—a method of enhancing self-esteem in which one imagines oneself behaving in a certain way—takes the notion of self-talk one step further. Besides just telling yourself that you can achieve your goal, you can actually try to "see" yourself conversing effectively with others, performing well on a project, or exhibiting some other desirable behavior. Because the United States is such a visual culture, most of us have no trouble visualizing elaborate scenarios in our heads.

Research suggests that an apprehensive public speaker can manage her or his fears by visualizing positive results.[35] In fact, visualization reduces anxiety as well as negative self-talk or the number of debilitating thoughts that enter a speaker's consciousness.[36] If you are one of the many people who fears making presentations, try visualizing yourself walking to the front of the room, taking out your well-prepared notes, delivering a well-rehearsed and interesting presentation, and returning to your seat to the sound of applause from your audience. This visualization of positive results enhances confidence and speaking skill. The same technique can be used to boost your sense of self-worth about other tasks or skills. If you're nervous about a date, for example, visualize each step of the date (as realistically as you can). Think through what you might talk about on the date and how the night will progress. This mental rehearsal will help reduce your anxiety. In addition, visualizing yourself interacting or performing well can help you change long-standing feelings of inadequacy.

Reframe

The process of redefining events and experiences, of looking at something from a different point of view, is termed reframing. When a movie director gets different "takes" or shots of the same scene, she or he is striving to get the best work possible. The director alters small details, like camera angles or actor movements, to get yet another look or vision for a scene. Just like that movie director, you can reframe your "take" on events or circumstances that cause you to lose self-esteem.

Here's an example: If you get a report from your supervisor that says you should improve one area of your performance, instead of engaging in self-talk that says you're terrible at your job, reframe the event within a larger context. Tell yourself that one negative comment does not mean you are completely a bad employee.

Of course, you shouldn't leave negative experiences unexamined, because you can learn and profit from your mistakes. But it is important to remember that our worth as human beings is not contingent on a single *anything*—a single grade, a single failed relationship, a single response from a prospective employer, or a single play in a football game. Looking at the big picture—at the effect this one event will have on your whole life, on society, on history—places negative experiences we all have in realistic contexts.

Develop Honest Relationships

The suggestion that you develop honest relationships may sound like the latest advice from Dr. Phil, but it is actually harder to accomplish than it sounds. Think about it: How many people are in your life who really give you the straight scoop about yourself? How many people are so solid in their relationship with you that they can tell you the things that are the hardest to hear, things that no one else would dare tell you? Most of us can count the number of those people on one hand. That doesn't mean we aren't honest with the many friends and acquaintances we have in our lives, but most of us really trust only a select few enough to deal with the tough stuff.

Having at least one other person who will give you honest feedback and help you objectively reflect on your virtues and vices can be extremely beneficial in fostering healthy, positive self-esteem. As we noted earlier, other people play a major role in shaping our self-concept and self-esteem. You don't want to find yourself at a point where you're oblivious to the feedback of others. That kind of attitude can make you unrealistic and rigid, unable to adjust to life's changing circumstances. Most people who reject or overlook significant others' feedback end up isolated and with low self-esteem.

Surround Yourself with Positive People

Related to the development of honest relationships is a suggestion about the people you choose to associate with the most in your life. If you want to improve your self-esteem and to develop a more positive outlook, it's better to surround yourself with people who tend to have higher levels of self-esteem than with people who will bring you down. Granted, sometimes you don't have a choice; you get assigned a roommate in college, you end up with an instructor's choice of lab or study partner, and you rarely get to choose the people you work with. So we are not suggesting that you disassociate yourself from people who have low self-esteem, because that's unrealistic. Plus, we all suffer from bouts of low self-esteem at some time or another. People with low self-esteem need to be around uplifting people—those whose positive self-regard will rub

On the Web

Some people are outgoing, others are shy. Extroverted, introverted—it takes all kinds. But shy people often struggle with self-esteem issues because it seems as though everyone around them can carry on conversations or give presentations with no problem. It's hard when you feel you have a lot to say but not the means or the confidence to say it. You probably won't be surprised to find that there are several Web sites devoted to just these kinds of problems. Two sites we visited offer particularly helpful insight into the problems of shyness and lack of self-confidence:

www.mapfornonprofits.org
www.managementhelp.org/prsn_wll/prsn_wll

off on them. What we mean is that it is hard enough to actively work on your self-esteem without constantly being around people with negative attitudes. Engaging in "pity parties" can lead to wallowing in poor self-esteem, which makes it doubly hard to alter that downward course. If you don't have a choice and must be around someone with low self-esteem, you can try to immunize yourself from his or her negativity—possibly by attempting to change a negative subject of conversation into a positive one.

As an example, we know an elderly woman, Hazel, who was in good enough health to be able to help the Meals on Wheels organization deliver food to shut-ins in her town. Hazel often talked about how sour many of the people on her route were, how their attitudes had "gone south" because of poor health, limited options, and fading hope. She felt that her main purpose wasn't to deliver a hot meal but to extend the gift of her positive outlook. She often told us about how many complaints she heard in the course of one day, but she was determined to stay optimistic and to offer hope to those she visited. One time Hazel described what she viewed as a personal triumph. The most sour person on her route—a woman with very low self-esteem and a cranky disposition, one who never did anything but gripe to Hazel when she visited—began to "thaw." One day when Hazel delivered her meal, the woman actually greeted her at the front door and seemed genuinely glad to see Hazel. She complained less often as she slowly began to enjoy the warm glow of Hazel's sunny disposition and empathic responses. Hazel felt that the woman's self-esteem had begun to improve, that her outlook on life had begun to change.

So this is what we mean by surrounding yourself with positive people whenever you feel a loss of self-esteem. Misery may love company, but misery gets old quickly and can degenerate into permanent low self-esteem, sometimes without your realizing it's happening.

Lose Your Baggage

Not making the team. Getting passed over for a key promotion at work. Seeing a long-term relationship end. Feeling like a failure. We've all had experiences that we would like to undo or get a second chance at, so that we could do it differently or so that we would *be* different. We all carry around experiential or psychological "baggage," but the key question is, How much space does that baggage take up within your self-concept? To phrase this another way: How negatively is your self-esteem affected by your baggage?

Individuals with low self-esteem tend to lock on to events and experiences that happened years ago and tenaciously refuse to let go of or move past them. Looking back at what we can't change only reinforces a sense of helplessness. Constantly replaying negative experiences only serves to make our sense of self-worth more difficult to repair. As Stephen Covey explains, with regard to his Highly Effective Habit #2, "Begin with the End in Mind," self-awareness leads us to an exploration of our values. The way we are living, our "script" as Covey terms it, may not be in harmony with our values, but we have the power to change. As Covey puts it, "I can live out of my imagination instead of my memory. I can tie myself to my limitless potential instead of my limiting past. I can become my own first creator."[37]

If you were overweight as a child, you may have a difficult time accepting that who you are today is not determined by pounds you carried years ago. A traumatic or defining experience in the past has a serious impact on your self-concept; it will probably always remain a part of you. But it doesn't have to affect your current level of self-esteem. Becoming aware of changes that have occurred in your life can assist you in developing a more realistic assessment of your value. It's important to take mental inventory of experiences in your past and then decide to let go of and move past those experiences that cause your present-day self-esteem to suffer.

RECAP

Strategies for Enhancing Self-Esteem

Engage in Positive Self-Talk	If you want positive results, talk positively to yourself. If you are self-critical and negative, you may set yourself up for failure. Rephrase doubts and negative thoughts into positive, uplifting encouragement.
Visualize	In anticipation of a significant event, picture how you want the event to go, as a mental rehearsal. If you feel anxious or nervous, visualize success instead of failure.
Reframe	Try to look at experiences and events, especially those that can cause you to lose self-esteem, from a different point of view. Keep the larger picture in mind, rather than focusing on one isolated, negative incident.
Develop Honest Relationships	Cultivate friends in whom you can confide and who will give you honest feedback for improving your skills and abilities. Accept that feedback in the spirit of enhancing your self-esteem and making yourself a wiser, better person.
Surround Yourself with Positive People	Associating with persons with high self-esteem can help you enhance your own self-esteem and develop a more positive outlook.
Lose Your Baggage	Dump your psychological and experiential baggage from the past: Work to move beyond the negatives of your past, so that you focus on the present and relieve your self-esteem of the burden of things you cannot change.

QUICK REVIEW

The Perception Process

This chapter focuses on the principle of awareness—developing greater understanding and skill by becoming more cognizant of yourself, others, and communication. In the first part of this chapter, we discussed self-concept (how we perceive ourselves) and self-esteem (how we value ourselves). We continue now by exploring how we perceive ourselves and our communication with others, as well as the many ways in which we perceive other people and their communication. But just what is perception?

On the most basic level, **perception is the arousal of any of our senses.** A sound travels through the air, vibrates in the eardrum, activates the nerves, and sends a signal to the brain. A similar sequence of events takes place when we see, smell, feel, or taste something. So perception begins with the process of attending to stimuli in the environment. The process of perception also includes structuring and making sense out of information provided by the senses. You come out of a building and see wet pavement and puddles of water, hear thunder, smell a fresh odor in the air, and feel a few drops of water on your head. You integrate all those bits of information and conclude that it is raining and has been for a while.

Perceiving people, however, goes beyond the simple processing of sensory information. We try to decide what people are like, making judgments about their personalities, and we give meaning to their actions by drawing inferences from what we observe.[38] When you meet someone new, you notice certain basic attributes, like the person's sex, general aspects of physical appearance, the sound of her or his voice, whether or not he or she smiles, uses a friendly tone of voice, has an accent, and so forth. You also attend to specific details that the person communicates, verbally and nonverbally. Once you've chosen these stimuli to pay attention to, you then categorize the information into some sort of structure that works for you. Finally, you attempt to make sense out of your structured perceptions; you assign meaning to what you have perceived. Let's examine each of these three stages in the perception process.

Stage One: Attention and Selection

You are watching a group of parents at a playground with their children. The kids are playing, running around, laughing, and squealing, as children will do. You view the activity, hear the noise, feel the heat of the day on your skin, and perhaps smell hot dogs cooking on a grill. They smell so good you can almost taste them. After a moment, one of the parents who was sitting and chatting with other parents jumps up and runs over to comfort his or her child who has fallen down and is crying. You were watching the action but didn't see the particular incident and didn't register the child's cry amidst all the noise. But the child's parent did. How did this happen?

The ability of parents to discern their own child's voice from a chorus of voices is one of the mysteries of human nature, but it also exemplifies the first stage of perception. Our human senses simply cannot process all of the stimuli that are available at any given moment, so we select which sensations make it through to the level of awareness and ignore or filter out the rest. The activities of **attention (the act of perceiving stimuli in your environment)** and **selection (the act of choosing specific stimuli in your environment to focus on)** constitute the first stage of the perception process. Have you ever listened to music in the dark, so you could eliminate visual sensations and focus only on what you were hearing? Have you ever watched TV with the sound turned off, just so you could enjoy the visual images without the "static" of sound? This is a particularly helpful strategy during televised sporting events, when the announcers continue talking over every bit of the action. (We believe this to be the original motivation for the development of the remote control's mute button.) What we're doing in those instances is selecting what we will and will not attend to.

Here's another example: Imagine a parent in a grocery store, pushing a cart with a small child sitting in it. The child wants something, so she or he says, "Mommy, I want this." When there's no reaction from the mother, the child repeats the statement, "Mommy, I want this." If there's still no response, the child will likely say the statement over and over again, increasing the volume and stressing different words each time, as in "Mommy, I WANT this." What's amazing to the casual observer is the way the parent can tune out the child's request. Sometimes, the child will repeat the phrase so many times that you want to intervene and say, "Hey, your kid's talking to you; get that thing for him (her)." But the parent has heard the child's voice many times before, so she or he finds it easy to choose not to attend to that particular stimulus.

This selectivity can also cause us to fail to perceive information that is important.[39] Jack and Jill are having an argument; Jack is so absorbed in making his points that he fails to see that Jill is crying. By selecting certain stimuli, we sometimes miss other clues that might be important, that might help us better understand what is happening and how to respond.

Stage Two: Organization

After we select stimuli to attend to and process, we start **organization** by **converting information into convenient, understandable, and efficient patterns that allow us to make sense of what we have observed**. Organization makes it easier for us to process complex information because it allows us to impose the familiar onto the unfamiliar and because we can easily store and recall simple patterns.

Look at the three items in Figure 1.2.2. What does each of them mean to you? If you are like most people, you will perceive item A as a horseshoe, item B as the word *communication*, and item C as a circle. Strictly speaking, none of those perceptions is correct. For item A, you see a pattern of dots that you label a horseshoe because a horseshoe is a concept you know and to which you attach various meanings. The item really isn't a horseshoe; it could be an inverted U. It's actually a set of dots. But rather than processing a set of dots, it's much easier to organize the dots in a way that refers to something familiar.

FIGURE 1.2.2
What Do You See?

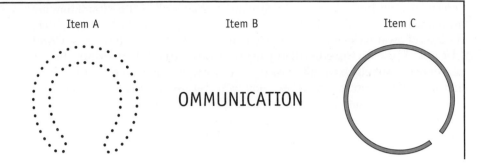

Item A   Item B   Item C

OMMUNICATION

For similar reasons, we organize patterns of stars in the sky into various constellations with shapes, like the Big and Little Dippers.

In Figure 1.2.2, items B and C reveal our inclination to superimpose structure and consistency on what we observe. This tendency leads us to create a familiar word from the meaningless assemblage of letters in item B and to label the figure in item C a circle, even though a circle is a continuous line without any gaps. **The perpetual process of filling in missing information is called closure,** and it applies to our perceptions of people as well. When we have an incomplete picture of another human being, we impose a pattern or structure, classify the person on the basis of the information we do have, and fill in the gaps.

Perhaps you've sat in an airport or busy shopping mall watching people and tried to guess what they did for a living, what their personalities were like, or what their backgrounds were. Maybe you saw people you guessed were wealthy, hotheads, teachers, losers, athletes, loners, or surfer dudes. As you looked at people's clothing and saw how they walked or behaved, you made inferences about them. You superimposed some structure by using a general label and filling in the gaps in your information. This activity can get you into trouble, of course, but we'll save that discussion until the end of the chapter, when we focus on the problem of stereotyping.

Stage Three: Interpretation

Once we have organized stimuli, we begin the process of **interpretation** by **attaching meaning to what is attended to, selected, and organized**. We attach meaning to all that we observe. In some cases, the meanings are fairly standardized, as they are for language, for example. But others are much more personalized. If you shake someone's hand and it feels like a wet, cold fish, what is your reaction and interpretation? If you notice someone you don't know staring at you from across a room, what thoughts go through your head? If a toddler is crying in a room full of people and a woman comes over and picks the child up, what do you assume about the woman? These examples all illustrate how we impose meaning on what we observe to complete the perceptual process.

Of course, our interpretations can be inaccurate or off-base; we may perceive a situation one way, when in fact something entirely different is occurring. For example, the final scene in the movie *Swingers* is hilarious because it illustrates the faulty nature of human interpretation. Two of the "swinging" male characters are sitting in a booth at a diner. One of them thinks that a woman several booths away is making eyes at him. She appears to be making flirtatious facial expressions and mouthing something which he interprets as a come-on. He's just about to make his move when he realizes that the woman is looking across her table at a baby in a portable carrier, positioned in the opposite side of the booth, and she's cooing and making faces at the child.

RECAP

The Perception Process

Term	Explanation	Examples
Perception	The arousal of any of our senses	Tasting spicy food; hearing the sound of laughter; smelling smoke
Attention and Selection	The first stage in the perception process, in which we perceive stimuli and choose which ones to focus awareness on	Watching TV in your room while hearing giggling and laughter, and ignoring the TV show in order to eavesdrop on the giggler
Organization	The second stage in the perception process, in which we structure stimuli into convenient and efficient patterns	Realizing that the laughter is coming from your younger sister, who's on the phone
Interpretation	The final stage in the perception process, in which we assign meaning to what we have perceived	Deciding that your sister is talking on the phone to her boyfriend, because she only laughs like that when she talks to him

Communication and the Enhancement of Perceptual Accuracy

Our perceptions of others affect the way we communicate, just as others' perceptions of us affect the way they communicate with us. We continually modify the topics, language, and manner in which we communicate according to perceptions—ours and theirs.

"Of course I care about how you imagined I thought you perceived I wanted you to feel."

Patrick sees Maria at a party and thinks she is attractive; Maria is nicely dressed and seems to be enjoying herself, laughing occasionally at a story someone is telling. Patrick thinks, "This might be someone I want to get to know," so he works his way over to join the conversation of Maria and the group she's sitting with. Maria notices Patrick coming over, because she checked him out too. However, not too long after joining the group, Patrick attempts to tell a humorous story, hoping to get a positive reaction from Maria. Instead, he gets a cold stare from her, as though she didn't understand or appreciate his attempt at humor. Maria walks away from the conversation thinking that Patrick is rude, while Patrick decides that Maria is not as attractive as he first thought. In this example, the man and woman both formed perceptions based on minimal information. They then experienced each other in the form of a brief conversation, and that bit of communication significantly altered their original perceptions. This process happens often in daily life.

The goal in the perception process is to form the most accurate perceptions you can, because then you have better, more reliable information on which to act. So what can you do to improve your ability to form accurate perceptions? We offer three suggestions.

Increase Your Awareness

We've made this topic—awareness—our first of five communication principles for a lifetime, and we've done so for a reason. As we discuss in the next two chapters, developing your skills in perceiving and then decoding others' verbal and nonverbal communication is critical as you strengthen existing relationships and establish new ones.

Exercise your senses, especially your sense of hearing. Work at really listening to people—fully listening, without interrupting them to put in your two cents' worth. Try to be more verbally and nonverbally aware, meaning monitor how you communicate with others and how people respond to you. If you don't like the responses you're getting from people, it may be time for a change in *your* behavior, not theirs. You also want to monitor the verbal and nonverbal cues others exhibit. Pay attention to contextual cues, such as where an interaction is taking place, the time of day, the perceived moods of those interacting, and any physical or psychological barriers that impede the communication exchange. Learn from your mistakes, rather than repeat them.

The last thing anyone wants to be is a "communication clod," the kind of person who never notices things unless they're on fire. Communication clods seem to be in their own worlds, rarely acknowledging that others exist, rarely pausing to perceive what's going on in the world around them. We suspect that all of us have known people like this. And we are all capable of clodlike behavior from time to time, but you just don't want "communication clod" to be what comes to mind when people think of you.

Avoid Stereotypes

"She's a snob." "He's a nerd." "They're a bunch of dumb jocks." All of these statements reflect **stereotypes, which are generalizations we apply to persons because we perceive them to have attributes common to a**

Do you make any assumptions about these people based on their outfits and behavior? Should you?

particular group.[40] Social psychologist Douglas Kenrick and his colleagues suggest that "Stereotyping is a cognitively inexpensive way of understanding others: By presuming that people are like other members of their groups, we avoid the effortful process of learning about them as individuals."[41]

What comes to mind when you hear the term *redneck?* (Maybe you think of the comedian Jeff Foxworthy, who has a repertoire of "you might be a redneck" jokes.) Do you associate with the term such qualities as being backward, ultra-conservative, or out of touch with what's happening in the world? If you perceive someone to have these qualities and you consider that person a redneck, then you have just invoked a stereotype.

First, let's examine the positive or functional aspects of stereotypes. They emerge from our human nature to simplify and categorize stimuli in our environment, which we described as components of the perception process. Further, they serve as a baseline of information. If you know nothing else about a person other than she or he is a "northerner," for instance, then you can think about commonly held characteristics of other persons you've met from the northern part of the United States and go from there. But obviously, there's a serious downside.

Have you ever taken a class and, from day one, felt that the teacher pegged you a certain way? The teacher perceived you to be a slacker or uninterested in the course topic, on the negative side, or a straight-A student or future Ph.D., on the positive side. The bottom line is that no one likes to be treated as a stereotype because it's limiting and impersonal. You can also feel pressure to try to live up to a stereotype, such as "All Asian students are exceptionally bright." Stereotypes are often degrading, as in age-old references to dumb blondes, bad women drivers, and dirty old men. Many of the worst stereotypes are related to gender, race/ethnicity, age, and physical appearance.

Scholars have been studying stereotypes for a couple of decades; some of this research explores the ways we try to inhibit stereotypical thoughts before they have a chance to affect our behavior.[42] For example, if you grew up hearing family members invoke stereotypes about different racial groups, you may decide as an adult that you will not follow suit—that inflicting racial stereotypes is inappropriate. However, because it's part of your upbringing and ingrained in you, your first thoughts may be stereotypical when you encounter someone from a racial group other than your own. You have to assert mental control to suppress the stereotypical thoughts. But researchers have found that this suppression actually has the opposite effect than desired, in that stereotypical thoughts are highly likely to reappear subsequently with even stronger intensity, what the researchers term a "rebound effect."[43] So it may be better never to let stereotypes form into expectations, rather than trying to rid ourselves of harmful stereotypical thinking after the fact.

In Chapter 1.3, we explore language that reveals stereotypical thoughts. In Chapter 1.6, when we discuss the skill of adapting communication to our listeners, we revisit the topic of stereotypes. For now, just remember that there's nothing inherently wrong with a stereotype, as a baseline of information. But the rigid way we enforce a stereotype, the expectations we form based on the stereotype, and our ensuing communication toward the stereotyped person are problematic.

Check Your Perceptions

You can check the accuracy of your perceptions and attributions indirectly and directly, so that you increase your ability to perceive things and people and respond to them effectively. **Indirect perception checking involves an intensification of your own perceptual abilities to seek additional information to either confirm or refute your interpretations of someone's behavior.** If you suspect that your romantic partner wants to end your relationship, for instance, you are likely to look for cues in his or her tone of voice, eye contact, and body movements to confirm your suspicion. You will probably also listen more intently and pay attention to the language your partner chooses to use. The information you gain is "checked" against your original perceptions.

Direct perception checking involves asking straight out whether your interpretations of a perception are correct. You can accomplish this in two ways: asking people directly for their interpretations of their own actions or asking other observers for their "take" on a situation (going to a third or outside party). Asking people directly is often more difficult than asking a third party for an interpretation. For one thing, we don't like to admit uncertainty or suspicions to others; we might not trust that they will respond honestly. And if our interpretations are wrong, we might suffer embarrassment or anger. But asking someone to confirm a perception shows that you are committed to understanding his or her behavior. If your friend's voice sounds weary and her posture is sagging, you may assume that she is depressed or upset. If you ask "I get the feeling from your tone of voice and the way you're acting that you are kind of down and depressed; what's wrong?" your friend can then either provide another interpretation ("I'm just tired; I had a busy week") or expand on your interpretation ("Yeah, things haven't been going very well . . ."). Your observation might also be a revelation: "Really? I didn't realize I was acting that way. I guess I am a little down."

We have found over our years as professors that perception checking with our colleagues, as well as with family members and trusted friends, is an invaluable tool, particularly when emotions are involved. It can be very helpful to discuss situations with other people, to get their input as to what happened, why it happened, how they would feel about it if it happened to them, and what you might do about it. This is especially advisable in work settings, when the wisdom of someone else's perceptions can save you professional embarrassment or prevent you from losing your job because of an emotional or rash reaction. So we

On the Web

Galen Bodenhausen, a social psychologist at Northwestern University, and his international group of colleagues and students have developed a Web site based on their years of research into stereotyping and social perception. The site describes major ongoing research efforts sponsored by their organization, the Social Cognition Laboratory. It also provides links to publications and classroom instruction on the topic, so you can view syllabi from courses devoted to the study of stereotyping and perception. Here's the address:

www.psych.northwestern.edu/folks/bodenhausen/research.htm

highly advocate seeking out the wise counsel of trusted colleagues. The "Can I run something by you?" strategy gives you a broader perspective and a basis of comparison.

PRINCIPLES FOR A LIFETIME: Enhancing Your Skills

Aware

Principle One: Be aware of your communication with yourself and others.

- Becoming aware of yourself, as you develop your self-concept, involves communicating with others, associating with groups with whom you identify, assuming social roles, and selecting self-labels that describe who you are.
- Inventory yourself for any negative self-fulfilling prophecies that can be detrimental to your self-esteem.
- Engage in positive intrapersonal communication, or self-talk, because a heightened awareness of how you talk to yourself can help you enhance self-esteem.
- Develop your perceptual abilities by becoming more aware of yourself and others.

SUMMARY

This chapter is devoted to the first communication principle for a lifetime: *Be aware of your communication with yourself and others.* Self-awareness is a process that continues throughout life, as we perceive and come to understand our own existence in the social world. The way we view ourselves is termed self-concept, which includes our attitudes, beliefs, and values. William James viewed the self as containing three components: The material self includes our bodies and those tangible possessions that give us identity. The social self is the part that engages in interaction with others. The spiritual self consists of thoughts and assumptions about values, moral standards, and beliefs about forces that influence our lives.

The self-concept develops through our interactions with other people and the groups with which we associate. The roles we assume are important in our view of self; they provide labels for who we are.

Self-concept, or who you think you are, and self-esteem, your evaluation of your self-worth, affect how you interact with others. Your gender has an effect on your self-esteem. When you compare yourself to others, especially others who are different from you, your self-esteem can be affected either positively or negatively. Your view of your own worth is also affected by those expectations or goals you set for yourself and how close you come to achieving them. You may set a goal for yourself that ends up creating a self-fulfilling prophecy. You may believe something about yourself and act in a way that reinforces that belief, and the cycle continues.

It is difficult to alter your self-esteem, but various techniques can prove helpful: engaging in positive self-talk, visualizing success instead of failure, avoiding inappropriate comparisons with others, reframing events and relationships from a different perspective, developing honest relationships with others, surrounding yourself with uplifting people, and letting go of the past by losing old baggage.

This chapter also pointed out that perception is the process of taking in stimuli through our senses, and it involves three components: attention and selection, organization, and interpretation. Our perceptions of others affect how we communicate, and how others perceive us affects how they communicate with us. If you want to increase your powers of perception, so that you develop greater sensitivity and awareness, you first need to pay greater attention to things and people around you. Observe with more detail over time, so that you take in more data. Second, when you're in the organizing stage of perception, avoid imposing stereotypes on people or trying to fit them into rigid categories, such that you expect certain behavior and exert pressure on individuals to behave as expected. Finally, conduct indirect and direct perception checks to determine the accuracy of your "take" on people and situations.

DISCUSSION AND REVIEW

1. Why is self-awareness critical to the development of communication skill? How can you tell a self-aware communicator from those who are not self-aware?

2. What makes up the material self? The social self? The spiritual self?

3. What is the difference between your self-concept and your self-image? Between your self-concept and your self-esteem?

4. Do you believe that your gender and your self-esteem are related? Why or why not?

5. Have you known or do you know someone who has experienced a self-fulfilling prophecy? How did this affect your or the person's communication and general behavior?

6. If you lost some self-esteem because of an event, circumstance, or person's actions, which of the techniques in this chapter would help you regain your self-esteem?

7. Imagine that you're attending a sporting event. Describe how the three stages of perception affect the way you process the action.

8. Think of occasions when you've directly checked your perceptions with others. Did the perception checks change your perspective?

PUTTING PRINCIPLES INTO PRACTICE

1. On a sheet of paper write down major things you know to be true of yourself. For example, you might start with your values and write down, "I am an honest person." Include positive and negative attributes that you're aware of in your personality. After you've generated as many items as

possible, review the list and see if it encapsulates your self-concept.

2. Have you ever needed the power of positive self-talk and visualization to get you through a particular experience? (For example, probably everyone has had a nerve-racking first date experience.) What kind of self-talk is helpful in such a situation? How can visualization help increase your self-confidence in a high-pressure situation such as a first date?

3. With a small group of classmates, venture outside the building where your class meets and conduct a perceptual experiment. Watch people passing by on their way to classes or as they leave campus. Decide as a group to focus on certain individuals and then discuss your differing perceptions of them. How do you each perceive the physical appearance of people you see? What clues do their nonverbal behaviors give about their personalities? Do you invoke any stereotypes as you discuss different people?

4. Generate statements that reveal common stereotypes about people in the following groups. Try to generate stereotypes that reflect positive as well as negative perceptions. We provide a couple of examples, just to get you started. Then focus on the damage that stereotypes can do to someone's self-esteem. Also, think about how your communication with someone from each group might be affected by stereotypes.

Group	Positive Stereotype	Negative Stereotype
elderly	Old people are wise.	Old people can't fend for themselves.
women	Women are naturally more loving and nurturing than men.	Women are terrible drivers.
men		
blondes		
overweight people		
people of Irish descent		
athletes		
southerners		
politicians		
environmentalists		
tax accountants		
librarians		
professors		

Chapter 1.2   *Practice Test*

MULTIPLE CHOICE.   Choose the *best* answer to each of the following questions.

1. The perception process consists of which of the following stages?

   a. attention and selection, organization, interpretation

   b. organization, visualization, interpretation

   c. attribution, organization, selection

   d. attention and selection, reframing, closure

2. Javier says, "I knew I wouldn't get that job. Obviously, I messed up the interview because the interviewer didn't say she would call me back. Why did I even apply? Plus, my skills aren't what they are looking for anyway." Javier's explanation for not getting the job illustrates

a. the influence of social roles.

b. a self-fulfilling prophecy.

c. reframing.

d. stereotypes.

3. "When I see our apartment is really messy, with your clothes thrown all over and dirty dishes stacked up in the sink, I don't know if you are so busy with school that you haven't had time to clean up or if you are hoping that I will clean up after you. What is the reason?" This statement is an example of

a. indirect perception checking.

b. intrapersonal communication.

c. self-talk.

d. direct perception checking.

4. "I have had a hard time this semester because I have had to work many hours each week in addition to going to school. Even though it's been difficult, I realize now that I have the ability to juggle many different tasks simultaneously. So, this semester has really increased my confidence in my ability to succeed." This statement is an example of

a. attention and selection.

b. visualization.

c. reframing.

d. organization.

5. "Why should I talk to the professor about my grade on the test? Professors never listen to students anyway." This statement is an example of

a. a self-fulfilling prophecy.

b. stereotyping.

c. negative self-talk.

d. social comparison.

6. Looking through your closet to find the "perfect" outfit for your job interview is an example of being influenced by your

a. material self.

b. social self.

c. spiritual self.

d. emotional self.

7. Stacy can remember her parents telling her they were Republicans before she even knew what the word *Republican* meant. To this day, Stacy tends to vote Republican in every election. Stacy's self-concept is being influenced by her

a. assumed role.

b. self-label.

c. communication with others.

d. association with groups.

8. Measuring your self-worth in relationship to others who are similar to you is

a. a self-fulfilling prophecy.

b. self-expectation.

c. visualization.

d. social comparison.

9. When you are aware that you are thinking about and remembering things, you are experiencing

a. subjective self-awareness.

b. objective self-awareness.

c. conscious self-awareness.

d. symbolic self-awareness.

10. Learning to get over negative experiences that happened in your past is an example of

a. self-talk.

b. reframing.

c. losing baggage.

d. visualization.

11. Ed and Amanda are walking through the mall. Ed doesn't realize that Amanda has stopped to look in the Sharper Image and continues to walk and talk as if Amanda were still beside him. Ed's misperception is being influenced most by his

a. attention and selection.

b. awareness.

c. organization.

d. interpretation.

12. Jorge rushes to clear the dishes from the dinner table because he knows *Monday Night Football* is coming on in three minutes. Jorge's behavior is being influenced most by his

a. attitude.

b. belief.

c. value.

d. none of the above

13. After making a monster dunk, Shaquille O'Neal flashes his college fraternity's "sign." At that point, Shaq's self-concept is being influenced by his

a. assumed role.

b. self-label.

c. communication with others.

d. association with groups.

14. When he got to second grade, Jaden decided he didn't want his dad walking him into school anymore. Jaden experienced a change in his

a. material self.

b. social self.

c. spiritual self.

d. emotional self.

15. Before each shot, Michelle Wie looks down the fairway and imagines exactly where her golf ball will land. This is an example of

a. self-talk.

b. reframing.

c. losing baggage.

d. visualization.

16. The fact that our identities are assigned by ourselves and others and that they are negotiated through our communication with others reflects which characteristic of identity?

a. Identities are multidimensional and changing.

b. Identity involves responsiveness to others.

c. Identities develop in past and present relationships.

d. Identities can be avowed and ascribed.

17. Marie and Andrea are having lunch, and Marie says, "One of the things that I love about you is that you are such an optimist." With respect to Andrea's identity, being an "optimist" is a(n) _____ characteristic.

a. avowed

b. ascribed

c. multidimensional

d. responsive

18. According to your textbook, suppressing stereotypical thoughts

a. is effective in helping to increase your perceptual accuracy.

b. can overcome biases learned from family and friends during childhood.

c. can make those thoughts stronger in the long run.

d. is impossible because stereotypes are originally based on facts.

19. Kaitlyn suspected that her best friend, Alondra, wanted to break up with her boyfriend. Kaitlyn paid close attention to how Alondra complained about him, avoided his phone calls, and was late getting ready for dates with him, but did not say anything to Alondra about it. What method was Kaitlyn using to check her perception of Alondra?

a. direct perception checking

b. active perception checking

c. indirect perception checking

d. avoidant perception checking

20. Self-awareness itself is not unique to human beings. Other animals also possess self-awareness. Which type of self-awareness is uniquely human?

a. objective self-awareness

b. symbolic self-awareness

c. sympathetic self-awareness

d. subjective self-awareness

TRUE/FALSE.   Indicate whether the following statements are *true* or *false*.

1. T or F   Your self-concept can be changed.

2. T or F   One strategy for increasing the accuracy of your perceptions is to become a better listener.

3. T or F   Comparing yourself to others is one way to elevate your self-worth.

4. T or F Between elementary school and high school, the self-esteem of boys decreases more than the self-esteem of girls.

5. T or F The way others communicate with us influences our level of self-esteem.

6. T or F Objective self-awareness is the ability to see one's self as an object, separate from the rest of the physical environment.

7. T or F Most aspects of the self are stable, but some aspects remain fluid and change often.

8. T or F Ascribed identities are those assigned to you by others and with which you agree.

9. T or F In the perception process, interpretation refers to filling in missing information.

10. T or F According to your book's authors, *self-concept* and *self-image* refer to "your subjective description of who you think you are and how you see yourself as a person" and can be used interchangeably.

FILL IN THE BLANK.   Complete the following statements.

1. Your personal and subjective description of who you are is your _____.

2. A(n) _____ is revealed in your tendency to respond to something in a positive or negative way.

3. A(n) _____ identity is one that you choose and act out.

4. Taking an experience and defining it from a different point of view is _____

5. _____ are generalizations you make about someone based on his or her group membership.

6. Your feelings for what is good, bad, right, and wrong are your _____.

7. Your sense of what is true and not true determines your _____.

8. _____ is your measure of your value as a person.

9. The ability to develop a representation of your self and share it with other people is _____ self-awareness.

10. The organizational process of filling in missing information is known as _____.

Understanding Verbal Messages

CHAPTER OUTLINE

Why Focus on Language?

The Nature of Language

The Power of Words

Confronting Bias in Language

Using Words to Establish Supportive Relationships

Summary

CHAPTER OBJECTIVES

After studying this chapter, you should be able to

1. Describe the relationship between words (symbols) and meaning.
2. Explain the difference between denotative and connotative meanings people develop for words.
3. Explain the difference between concrete and abstract meanings of words.
4. Define culture-bound words and context-bound words.
5. Identify four primary ways in which words have power.
6. Describe the major ways in which biased language reveals attitudes about race, ethnicity, nationality, and religion.
7. Provide examples of language that reflects bias related to gender and sexual orientation.
8. Explain how biased language reveals attitudes about age, class, and ability.
9. Explain the difference between supportive and defensive ways to relate to others.

The difference between the right word and the almost right word is the difference between lightning and the lightning bug.

Mark Twain

Adolf Fenyes, Brother and Sister. National Gallery, Budapest/ET Archive, London/SuperStock, Inc.

"yo will u plz help me? i can't make my dude get that i like him"
"i want 2 b yur friend bc yur funny"

If you understand the two sentences above, you probably do a lot of online chatting (instant messaging) or e-mailing, so you're familiar with and comfortable using a form of shorthand that makes computer-mediated communication faster. These adaptations of the English language are becoming more popular in everyday communication; for example, successful pop star Avril Lavigne titled one of her hit songs "Sk8rboi." However, parents and teachers alike have become concerned about the effects of such language shortcuts on students' writing ability and communication skills in general. Not only are words shortened, often by the omission of vowels, but numbers are substituted for letters, grammar rules are ignored, and standard punctuation and capitalization all but disappear. Some college professors of English composition courses have found it necessary to "un-teach Internet-speak," because students transfer online language shorthand to their written work.[1] A persistent use of slang may be fine when instant messaging with friends, but when it becomes such a habit that it slips into other written or oral communication—especially at inappropriate moments (like calling a potential boss at a job interview "dude")—then you've got a problem. When it comes to different uses of language, the key is to be able to develop "code-switching" abilities, meaning that you use more standard or formal language when appropriate (as in college papers, professional resumés, and job interviews) and relegate the shortcuts

The late Barbara Jordan, former Congresswoman from Texas, recognized that language can be a powerful tool to help us exert influence and enhance our relationships.

**FIGURE 1.3.1
Communication
Principles for a
Lifetime**

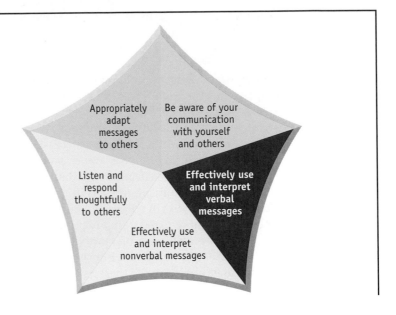

Appropriately
adapt
messages
to others

Be aware of your
communication
with yourself
and others

Listen and
respond
thoughtfully
to others

**Effectively use
and interpret
verbal
messages**

Effectively use
and interpret
nonverbal messages

and "slanguage" to informal online chats, e-mail, and conversations with friends who translate.[2]

Before diving into our discussion of language, let's review for a moment. Figure 1.3.1 depicts our five core principles of communication. In Chapter 1.2, where we discussed the first of our five principles for a lifetime, we explored ways to become more aware of yourself and your perceptions of things and people with whom you come into contact. An important step in this process of coming to know and understand yourself better is an honest, insightful examination of how you talk. How do you come across when meeting someone new? When talking with your best friends? What kind of communicator do your closest friends and family members think you are? How would they describe the way you talk?

Consider this: What you say is who you are. That may sound like a strong statement, but it is true that the words you use reveal who you are. Granted, you communicate with more than your words. Your background, culture, values, experiences, and the way you express yourself nonverbally reveal who you are as well. But as we explore the power of words, we challenge you to think about the incredible tool you have at your disposal: verbal communication. Take an inventory of your use of language as you read this chapter. Do you use language that accurately and effectively represents to other people who you are? Do some areas need improvement? Because of the tremendous potential of verbal communication—its power to reveal the self, to make and break relationships and careers, and to shape cultures—we've chosen to make this one of our five key principles for a lifetime.

Why Focus on Language?

On occasion, we do stop to consider the effects of our language on others—usually when we're attempting to persuade or we've said something that has injured or angered someone else. We've all been in situations that made us wish we could get a conversational second chance or a "take two." But it's important to keep in mind that every time we speak, every time we use language, we are revealing our thoughts, our very selves to others—no matter how inane, superficial, or emotion-laden the conversation.

One of our main messages in this chapter is this: *Words are powerful.* They affect your emotions, thoughts, actions, and relationships. They affect how you are perceived by others. In fact, recent interviews with employers revealed their concern about college graduates' lack of language skills, attributed to growing up in a culture that is more a visual one, which stresses nonverbal cues, than an oral one, which stresses language.[3] Their concern is that students' verbal skills, including both speaking and writing, are underdeveloped. This is clearly a negative trend, in light of other research that has determined that one's ability to use words to effectively participate in conversation with others is a key component in judgments about one's competence as a communicator. In this study, people who talked less in conversation were perceived by others as being less interpersonally skilled, compared to people who comfortably and actively engaged in conversation.[4] If you better understand the nature and power of language, if you attend to your use of language and work to use words with forethought and skill, you can exert great influence and enhance your relationships.

Our second main theme in this chapter is this: *You choose language.* You do not use language involuntarily, in the way that your knee might jerk when rapped with a doctor's mallet as an involuntary reflex to a stimulus. You choose the language you use—even if you make that choice in the split second it takes your brain to select a symbol (word) to communicate your thought or impulse. At times we go into "default mode," choosing language we've chosen before. We are prone to patterns in our language because, as humans, we prefer regularity. We also choose particular words because we like them, they've worked well for us in the past, or we grew up with those words and have used them for many years. But pattern and history can breed too much comfort, preventing you from asking yourself, "Is this the best way to say this? Should I say this another way?" You have an incredible wealth of words from which to choose, and the power to make choices that allow you to communicate who you are to others in the most effective way possible.

On the Web

So you decide that your vocabulary needs a bit of expansion. Where do you turn? To the dictionary you got as a high school graduation present? To reruns of *South Park?* For a Web site that will expand your capacity for English through its creative plays on words, visual puzzles, and innovative approaches to crosswords and word searches, try

www.puzzability.com

For a site that offers anagramming and such services as A.Word.A.Day e-mails, try

wordsmith.org

Our goal in this chapter is to help you improve your ability to choose and use words effectively, as well as to interpret the verbal communication of others. To accomplish that goal we explore the nature of language, the power of words, and ways to expose subtle and not-so-subtle bias in language—bias that can inhibit your ability to present yourself to others in a manner you desire. Finally, we examine the role of verbal communication in establishing supportive relationships.

The Nature of Language

A **language is a system of symbols (words or vocabulary) structured by grammar (rules and standards) and syntax (patterns in the arrangement of words) common to a community of people.** Australian communication scholar Dale Spender explains that language is "our means of ordering, classifying, and manipulating the world. It is through language that we become members of a human community, that the world becomes comprehensive and meaningful, that we bring into existence the world in which we live."[5] That last phrase is particularly important, because it suggests that the very words we use help create our world.

One supposition about language relates to this notion of creating existence. Two language researchers, Edward Sapir and Benjamin Lee Whorf, developed what has come to be known as the Sapir–Whorf Hypothesis.[6] This hypothesis suggests that human language and thought are so interrelated that thought is actually rooted in and controlled by language. One implication of the supposition is that you cannot conceive of something for which you have no word. As a fascinating illustration of what we mean by this, take the case of a speech therapist visiting an Indian tribe. When he noticed that very few Indians in the tribe stuttered, he also discovered that their language had no word for stuttering. He concluded that few people in the tribe had this affliction because it never entered their minds as a possibility.[7]

Words dictate and limit the nature of our reality. To extend the theory further, one could argue that the quality of one's language reflects the quality of one's thought. More simply, your verbal communication reveals how you think and what you think about. This is only one explanation for how language and thought operate in human beings, but it is a provocative notion to consider that language has such a powerful influence on our everyday thinking processes.

People Use Words as Symbols

A **symbol is a word, sound, gesture, or visual image that represents a thought, concept, object, or experience.** Just as a flag is a symbol of a country, words are symbols that trigger thoughts, concepts, or feelings. For

and Communication

Words across the Country

Cultural diversity emerges because of the existence of co-cultures, or groups within a larger culture. The United States is a huge country, with many different co-cultures. Persons with disabilities, the elderly, Asian Americans, and gays and lesbians are examples of co-cultural groups within the larger United States culture. Another form of diversity that is less often researched and discussed results from regional differences. *Bypassing,* or differences in meanings or usages of certain words among persons from various regions of the country, is quite interesting to explore.

For example, one college student from Texas lived across the hall in a campus dormitory from a woman from Kansas. One night when the communal bathroom facilities stopped working, the Texan told the Kansan,

"Don't go down the hall right now—the commodes are stopped up." Later, the Kansan came by the Texan's room and said, "Why didn't you tell me the toilets weren't working?" They finally realized that the Kansan's meaning for the word *commode* was a small table built low to the ground; the Texan would never have used the term *toilet*. So the miscommunication had to do with a simple difference in meaning of one word.

Because we are such a mobile society now, you will no doubt encounter language differences as you move about the country or as you meet people from other areas who have moved to where you live. It's important to be aware of the potential for language differences right here in our own country, even if English is most Americans' first language.

instance, what comes to mind when you see or hear the word *poverty?* The word may conjure up in your mind's eye a homeless person begging for change on the street corner or televised images of starving children in third-world countries. Or perhaps you envisioned your own lighter-than-you'd-like wallet.

HOMEWORK

People Attach Meanings to Words

Now imagine that you use the word *poverty* in a conversation, in an effort to convey to the other person the concept or image in your mind. You know what you're thinking when you say the word; the challenge is for the other person to understand your thoughts behind your choice of word. In communication terms, this is the process of creating meaning. **The meaning of a word is a person's interpretation of that symbol—it is how the person makes sense of the symbol.** Meanings don't reside in the words themselves but in the ways in which communicators use the words. You attach a meaning to the word *poverty*, the symbol you choose in conversation; your listener creates meaning for the word when he or she attempts to interpret what you've said. Words aren't the culprits in communication problems; the meanings people create for words lead to successful or problematic communication.

When the speaker's and the receiver's meanings do not correspond because the same words mean different things to different people, a communication problem called bypassing arises. For example, have you

HOMEWORK

ever found yourself at odds with someone because you had a different sense of what it meant to arrive "early" or "late" to an event? For some, getting there "early" means arriving at least a half an hour before the event begins; for some, "early" means right on time. Being "late" can mean different things to different people as well. Some heated arguments can be boiled down to a simple difference in meaning.

People Create Denotative and Connotative Meanings for Words

EXPLORE

As we have said, language is a vehicle through which we share with others our sense of the world and who we are. Through language we convert our experience into symbols and then use the symbols to share that experience. But as you learned in Chapter 1.1, the process of symbol sharing through language is not just a simple process of uttering a word and having its meaning clearly understood by another. Messages convey both content and feelings. So people create meanings for language on two levels: the denotative and the connotative.

The **denotative meaning of a word is the restrictive or literal meaning of a word.** For example, one dictionary defines *apartment* as "a room or suite of rooms used as a residence."[8] This definition is a literal, or denotative, definition of the word *apartment;* it describes what the word means in U.S. culture.

By contrast, **the connotative meaning of a word conveys feelings; people create personal and subjective meanings for words**. Using the example above, to you, the word *apartment* might mean a comfortable place to relax at the end of the day or a setting in which to entertain friends. To others, though, the word *apartment* might engender feelings of guilt (if the apartment hasn't been cleaned in a while) or feelings of dread (if apartment rent is draining the wallet or relationships with roommates leave something to be desired). Clearly, the connotative level of language is more individual. While the denotative or objective meaning of the word *apartment* can be found in any dictionary, your subjective response to the word is probably not contained there.

People Convey Concrete and Abstract Meanings through Words

Meanings for words can be placed along a continuum from concrete to abstract. **A word's meaning is concrete if we can experience what the word refers to (the referent) with one of our senses**—if we can see it, touch it, smell it, taste it, or hear it. If we cannot do these things with the referent—**if it cannot be perceived or experienced with one of the senses—then the word's meaning is abstract.** In general, the more concrete the language, the easier it is for others to understand. The more abstract a word, the more difficult it is to understand or agree on a meaning. For example, the word *patriotism* is abstract because we cannot hear or taste patriotism. But a word that suggests a demonstration of patriotism, such as *voting,* is more concrete, because we can physically perform the act of voting. It's wise to minimize the use of abstract words when you're trying to clarify a message. Concrete terms help make a message more clear.

Meanings Are Culture Bound

Culture is a learned system of knowledge, behavior, attitudes, beliefs, values, rules, and norms that is shared by a group of people and shaped from one generation to the next.[9] The meaning of a word, just like the meaning of any symbol, can change from culture to culture. To a European, for example, a *Yankee* is someone from the United States; to a player on the Boston Red Sox, a *Yankee* is an opponent; and to an American from the South, a *Yankee* is someone from the North. A few years ago, General Motors sold a car called a *Nova.* In English, *nova* means "bright star," and in Latin, *nova* means "new"— both appropriate connotations for a car. In Spanish, however, the spoken word *nova* sounds like the words *no va,* which translates "It does not go." As you can imagine, this name was not a great sales tool for the Spanish-speaking market.

Meanings Are Context Bound

A lot of people quoted in the media can be heard to say later, when questioned or interviewed, "My comments were taken out of context." We now have a term for a short statement that summarizes the essence of a longer message—the "sound bite." When you lift only a small piece of the greater text of what people have said, you take their words out of context. This practice can confuse and misrepresent a speaker's original message. Your English or communication teacher has undoubtedly cautioned you that taking something out of context changes its meaning. The meanings people attach to symbols are affected by situations. The statement "That car is really bad" could mean that the car is a piece of junk or, in contemporary slang, a really great car. We need to know the context in order to decipher a communicator's specific meaning.

> ## RECAP
>
> ### The Nature of Language
>
> - People use words as *symbols.* Symbols represent something else.
> - People create *meanings* for words. Meaning is a person's interpretation of a symbol.
> - Words have both *denotative* and *connotative* meanings. The denotative meaning is a restrictive, or literal, meaning; the connotation is a personal and subjective meaning.
> - People convey *concrete* and *abstract* meanings through words. A word's meaning is concrete if we can experience what the word refers to with one of our senses; if not, then the meaning is abstract.
> - Meanings are *culture bound.* The meaning of a word can change from culture to culture.
> - Meanings are *context bound.* The situation or context for communication aids people as they attach meanings to symbols.

The Power of Words

We've all heard the old schoolyard chant "Sticks and stones may break my bones, but words can never hurt me." We don't know who first came up with that statement, but we imagine it to be someone who never experienced the sting of name-calling, the harmful effects of being labeled a "slow reader," or the legacy of an unfortunate family nickname. Words *do* hurt. They have the power to evoke a wide range of emotions in listeners. But words can also heal and inspire and transform the human spirit. Let's explore a few of the powerful attributes of words.

The Power to Create and Label Experience

How many diseases or medical conditions can you think of that are named after the person who discovered the condition? Some that come to mind include Alzheimer's, Parkinson's, and Tourette Syndrome. While you might not want your name associated with a disease, the point is that the name for a phenomenon labels the experience, thus making it more real. It also etches it into history. As the English language continues to evolve, so does the need to name and describe new phenomena. For example, the term *sexual harassment* did not emerge until the 1970s; it was generated by feminists who wanted a term to correspond to a very real behavior many people experienced in the workplace.[10] Words give us tools to create and understand our world by naming and labeling what we experience.

Words also give us symbolic vehicles to communicate our creations and discoveries to others. As another example, when you label something "good" or "bad," you use language to create your own vision of how you experience the world. If you tell a friend that the movie you saw last night was vulgar and obscene, you not only provide your friend with a film critique but also communicate your sense of what is appropriate and inappropriate.

One theorist believes that you also create your moods and emotional states with the words you use to label your feelings.[11] If you get fired from a job, you might say that you feel angry and helpless or liberated and relieved. The first response might lead to depression and the second to happiness. One fascinating study conducted over a 35-year period found that people who described the world in pessimistic terms when they were younger were in poorer

Studies show that people who describe their world in optimistic terms during their youth often enjoy good health in later life.

health during middle age than those who had been optimistic.[12] Your words and corresponding outlook have the power to affect your mental, emotional, and physical health.

The Power to Affect Thoughts and Actions

A line from a Shakespearean tragedy reads, "That which we call a rose by any other name would smell as sweet." Would it really? If the name for this fragrant flower were "aardvark," would it still be the flower of people in love? Can you imagine getting a delivery of a dozen long-stemmed red aardvarks?

Some of you who are reading this text may be old enough to remember a weight-loss product called Ayds. Ayds were small, brown, chewy squares that helped reduce one's appetite (or so the manufacturers claimed). You can guess why this product disappeared in the 1980s; if it is still on the market, it has certainly been renamed. Given what we now know about the threat of the deadly disease AIDS, who today would willingly ingest a product with a same-sounding name? Advertisers have long known that the way a product is labeled greatly affects the likelihood that consumers will buy it. So words affect the way we think about things and react to them.

Words not only have the power to affect how we think about and respond to something; they also affect policy and procedures. Consider the story about a young FBI agent who was put in charge of the supply department. In an effort to save money, he reduced the size of memo paper. One of the smaller sheets ended up on Director J. Edgar Hoover's desk. Hoover didn't like the small size and wrote on the narrow margin of the paper, "Watch the borders." For the next six weeks, it was extremely difficult to enter the United States from Canada or Mexico.

The Power to Shape and Reflect Culture

If an impartial investigator from another culture were to study a transcript of all of your spoken utterances last week, what would she or he learn about you

Technology *and* Communication

Minding Your Manners, Even on the Net

*I*f you have access to a computer, it's highly likely that you have used e-mail. It has become the communication channel of choice for many people, but there are some important differences between e-mail and other forms of communication.

In a column for the *Houston Chronicle*, Jim Barlow discusses e-mail etiquette that goes beyond the basic rules—like using all caps means you're shouting or being emphatic.[13] He stresses that, just as with other more personal forms of communication, we should take the time to think before we hit the reply button in response to an e-mail message. Because of the impersonality of e-mail, many people communicate electronically in ways they wouldn't dare in person. A couple of Barlow's suggestions relate to appropriate language; the first is to remember your manners:

> I've noticed over the years that people are often incredibly rude in e-mail. Ask yourself, would you say that in person? If the answer is no, then why are you sending it via e-mail? Over the years when I've gotten a nasty e-mail, I've sometimes

called the person and pleasantly asked if he or she realized just how insulting that message sounded after it was read aloud. A couple of times my correspondent said indeed, that was why it was sent. But for the most part, there was simply an embarrassed silence.

Barlow also discusses bandwidth, meaning the number of cues in a form of communication that help listeners discern meaning. Face-to-face conversation has the greatest bandwidth; e-mail has the least. Barlow contends that the greater the bandwidth, the better the understanding. So he suggests that complicated subjects are best discussed in person, with a full range of verbal and nonverbal cues. Telephone communication is the next-best medium for discussing complicated topics, and e-mail has the greatest potential for misunderstanding.

Because of the ease and dazzle of technology, we sometimes forget to select the channel of communication that will best serve our purposes. E-mail may be a highly expedient means of communicating, but it may not be the best of all possible choices.

and the culture in which you live? If you frequently used words like *CD* and *rollerblades*, the investigator would know that these things are important to you. But he or she might not know what you mean if these things are not also part of her or his culture.

You have grown up within a culture; you've learned the language of that culture. And the way you use the language, the words and meanings you choose as well as the way you interpret others' communication, has the effect of shaping your culture. For example, author Devorah Lieberman recounts a story of one of her students who was a professional translator of Japanese and English.[14] On one occasion when this student was translating for an American speaker to a Japanese audience, the speaker began with "humorous" anecdotes about his experiences in Japan. The translator's version of these anecdotes was "The speaker is telling phrases that are considered funny in English but not in Japanese. I will tell you when he is finished so that you can laugh."

Co-cultures (cultural groups within a larger culture) also develop unique languages of their own as a way of forging connections and enhancing solidarity. For example, some gays and lesbians have reclaimed the once derogatory term *queer* and altered its meaning so that it's now a term of pride. Perhaps you have seen or heard of the cable television show *Queer as Folk.* Gang languages and symbols are also means of establishing an identity unique from other groups. This principle can even extend to just two people in a romantic relationship who develop nicknames or other forms of language as secret codes. They don't dare use that language in the company of others; the privacy of the language and their shared experiences create a sort of microculture—a culture of two.

The Power to Make and Break Relationships

Probably all of us have had the experience of saying something foolish, ridiculous, or embarrassing to another person. It seems that one of life's cruel ironies is the potential for human beings to say things they later regret. But if you've ever said something so inappropriate that it cost you a relationship—either one that didn't get off the ground or one that ended because of what you said—then you know firsthand the power of words to make and break relationships. For example, people in love sometimes overstate things when they get emotional. That's understandable. But it's wise to try to avoid word barriers, such as **polarization—the tendency to describe things in extremes or opposites without any middle ground.** You might hear one romantic partner say to the other, "You either love me or you don't." These kinds of pronouncements can make people feel controlled, as though there are only two options and no compromise position. President George W. Bush was both praised and criticized for stating in his post–September 11, 2001, speech to Congress, "You're either with us or you're with the terrorists."

The Power of Words

Words . . .

- **create and label experience.** New experiences may lead to new words. For example, a personal connection that forms over the Internet can be called a "cybership"— a combination of the terms "cyberspace" and "relationship."

- **affect thoughts and actions.** Words influence how we think. For instance, product names are critical to audience response and sales success. The critically acclaimed film *The Shawshank Redemption* was a box office failure, which some attributed to the film's obtuse title.

- **shape and reflect culture.** Cultures change; language both creates and reflects the changing nature of culture.

- **make and break relationships.** Verbal communication creates opportunities for us to know and be known by others. It is a primary tool for establishing relationships and deepening them; it can also be the reason a relationship ends.

QUICK
REVIEW

Confronting Bias in Language

We don't want to sound like the "language police"—that is, we don't want to dictate to you how you ought to talk. But we have found that oftentimes insensitive or stereotypical language usage arises out of ignorance or a lack of education. Even well-meaning, educated people can communicate bias through the language they choose to use. Words that reflect bias toward members of other cultures or groups can create barriers for listeners. In addition, such language ignores the fact that the world is constantly changing.

Also, this is not a lesson in how to be "P.C." The term *political correctness* with regard to language is an unfortunate contemporary label for something communication instructors have taught for decades—the use of language that doesn't exclude or offend listeners. In the following pages, we explore a few categories of language that illustrate the constant evolution of verbal communication and represent areas in which we can all heighten our sensitivity.

Biased Language: Race, Ethnicity, Nationality, and Religion

EXPLORE

Think about whether you have ever said or overheard someone say the following:

"I got a great deal on a car; the sticker price was a lot higher, but I jewed the dealer way down."
"You can't have that back, you Indian giver!"
"She's a real Bible banger."
"He doesn't have a Chinaman's chance to make the team."
"That divorce settlement gypped me out of what's rightfully mine!"

That last statement tends to puzzle people more than the others. It includes the term *gypped,* which is derived from the word for the nomadic cultural group

Ethics and *Communication*

Ebonics or "Standard" English?

*I*n the late 1990s, a controversy arose over the teaching of and tolerance for ebonics in schools. *Ebonics* is a word coined to refer to what used to be referred to as "Black English," meaning different pronunciations of existing words and the development of slang among members of African American communities. Some argued that ebonics went against "standards" of "correct" pronunciation and use of English; they felt it should neither be taught in public schools nor tolerated as a proper way of speaking. Proponents of ebonics, like the Reverend Jesse Jackson, pointed to the use of such language as an indicator of cultural pride and an expression of individuality. What is your view of ebonics? Do you believe that a "standard" form of English should be taught and used in schools and in society in general? If so, whose "standard" should be *the* standard?

known throughout the world as gypsies. The stereotype relates to being suckered or cheated out of what one is due.

What would your impression be of a person who made one of these statements? The language used in each of these examples demonstrates an insensitivity to members of other cultures and groups. Such language reflects **a word barrier known as allness, which occurs when words reflect unqualified, often untrue generalizations that deny individual differences or variations.** It's important to continue to educate yourself and monitor your speech so that you are not, even unconsciously, using phrases that depict a group of people in a negative, stereotypical fashion.

Is Supreme Court Justice Clarence Thomas black or African American? Is someone of Mexican or Spanish descent Mexican American, Hispanic, Latina, or Chicano? Given the power of words, the terms we use to refer to ethnic groups directly reflect perceptions of culture and identity. If you use the wrong word, you may be labeled politically incorrect or worse, a bigot.

THE FAR SIDE®   By GARY LARSON

In the mid 1990s, the U.S. Bureau of Labor Statistics surveyed 60,000 households, asking people what ethnic labels they preferred. More than 44% of those then referred to as black by the government preferred the term *black*, while 28% preferred *African American*. Twelve percent preferred *Afro-American*, and a little over 9% had no preference. In another ethnic category, *Hispanic* was the choice of 58% of those currently labeled Hispanics, rather than such terms as *Latino* or *of Spanish origin*. The survey also reported that the label *American Indians* was the term of choice for slightly less than half of the respondents, while 37% preferred *Native American*. Most of those currently designated as white preferred that term, although 16% liked the term *Caucasian* and a very small percentage liked the term *European American*.[15]

A sensitive communicator keeps abreast of linguistic changes and adopts the designations currently preferred by members of various ethnic groups. Sometimes students ask why this continued flexibility is so important—and the question arises out of both a resistance to change and a general wish that language (and other things in life) were simpler. Consider this: What if you really liked your first name but didn't like a nickname or a shortened version of it? And what if someone you worked with never got your name right, if she

On the Web

Here's an interesting Web site to check out:

www.yforum.com

This is the site for the National Forum on People's Differences, described as a no-holds-barred question-and-answer opportunity. Users can ask questions—either as postings or in a real-time chat format—that would be impolite or too embarrassing to ask in a face-to-face or telephone format. Examples of questions that have been posted on the site include: "What do retired people do all day?" "Is it disrespectful for a straight person to go to a gay bar?" "Why do Muslim women cover their hair?" "Is it considered offensive if a white person calls a black person 'black'?" It's interesting to observe the kinds of freedom the relative anonymity of the Internet provides.[16]

or he constantly used that more familiar or "playful" version of your name? You'd probably get irritated and try to correct the person. The principle is the same with ethnic and cultural designations. It's wise to allow members of a certain group to designate their own terms, then attempt to learn and become comfortable using those terms so that you reflect sensitivity as a communicator. Don't be afraid to ask directly, but sensitively, what term or terms are appropriate. A few years ago, a reader wrote to an African American columnist for the *Miami Herald*, asking for the appropriate term to use when referring to black people. Leonard Pitts addressed the dilemma in his column, explaining that part of the problem stems from his view that "race is not a scientific reality, but a social and cultural one." He advocated the evolution of vocabulary, no matter "how unwieldy, how imprecise, or how much of a PC pain in the backside." Pitts wrote of a saner world, in which such language obstacles would not be obstacles at all, because racial and ethnic differences would be minimized and thus would not command so much attention; the only term one would need to know to refer to another person would be the person's name.[17] Expressing a similar sentiment, celebrity Whoopi Goldberg was asked by an interviewer whether she preferred to be called black or African American. Her reply was, "Just call me Whoopi—that's what I prefer."

Biased Language: Gender and Sexual Orientation

Language that reveals bias in favor of one sex and against another is termed sexist or exclusive language, and it is more prevalent than you'd think. Decades of effort, spurred by the women's liberation movement in the 1960s, have raised the consciousness of American culture regarding exclusive language. But many people still do not alter their language to reflect and include both sexes. In addition, insensitivity or intolerance toward persons who are gay, lesbian, or bisexual is often reflected in heterosexist or homophobic language. **A person who uses heterosexist language speaks from an assumption that the world is heterosexual, as if romantic and sexual attraction to those of the same sex or to both sexes were simply not possible. Homophobic language more overtly denigrates persons of nonheterosexual orientations and usually arises out of a fear of being labeled gay or lesbian.** We briefly consider sexist and heterosexist forms of biased language below.

Language and the Sexes   Even though women now constitute over 50% of the U.S. population, to listen to the language of some people, you'd think it was still a man's world. Sexist language can reflect stereotypical attitudes or describe roles in exclusively male or female terms. Research indicates that exclusive language usage does the following: (1) maintains sex-biased perceptions, (2) shapes people's attitudes about careers that are appropriate for one sex but not the other, (3) causes some women to believe that certain jobs and roles aren't attainable, and (4) contributes to the belief that men deserve more status in society than women do.[18] Even dictionaries fall into patterns of describing women and men with discriminatory language.[19] Included in the *Oxford English Dictionary* definition for *woman* were (1) an adult female being, (2) female servant, (3) a lady-love or mistress, and (4) a wife. Men were described in more positive and distinguished terms: (1) a human being, (2) the human creation regarded abstractly, (3) an adult male endowed with many qualities, and (4) a person of importance of position.

The most common form of sexism in language is the use of a masculine term as though it were **generic, or a term to describe all people.** There are two primary ways that masculine-as-generic language typically appears in written and oral communication: in pronoun usage and in man-linked terminology.

Consistent evidence from research on sexist language shows that people—particularly in U.S. culture—simply do not tend to think in neuter. We think in male or female, which is another example of the polarization aspect of language discussed earlier. We don't tend to think of living entities as *it*, and we rarely use that pronoun to refer to them. When most people read or hear the word *he*, they think masculine, not some image of a sexless person.[20] Using generic masculine language, in essence, turns all persons into male persons.

Sexist language can be so deeply embedded in some persons' experience that it is used habitually, without much thought. For example, a student was giving a speech on how to project a winning, confident style on a job interview. The student said, "When you greet the boss for the first time, be sure to look him straight in the eye, give him a firm hand-shake, and let him know you're interested in the job." This language would be perfectly acceptable if the speaker were only describing a specific situation in which the job candidate was to meet a male boss. But his exclusive language choice only allowed for the possibility of a male boss, not a female boss, unless he meant the term *he* to stand for all persons—male and female bosses. In this case. What if the speaker had used only female pronouns, as in "look her straight in the eye, give her a firm handshake, and let her know you're interested in the job"? No doubt the exclusive female language would have drawn undue attention and perhaps distracted listeners. It is common for male terms to be used to refer to all persons, but less common for female language to serve as generic.

We don't know what you were taught in high school or in other college classes about generic language. Nevertheless, publishing standards today require the use of nonsexist language, which allows no masculine terms to stand for all persons. You'll notice that we use inclusive language in this text—because it reflects our value system and because our publisher requires it.

The solution to the problem of sexist language is not to replace all *he*s with *she*s, which would be an equally sexist practice. The point is to use terms that include both sexes so that your language reflects the contemporary world. If you want to refer to one person—any person of either sex—the most clear, grammatical, nonsexist way to do that is to use either *she or he, he/she,* or *s/he.*[21] Other options include (1) omitting a pronoun altogether, either by rewording a message or by substituting an article (*a, an,* or *the*) for the pronoun; (2) using *you* or variations of the indefinite pronoun *one;* or (3) using the plural pronoun *they.*[22]

Some college campuses are taking the pronoun issue even a step further. The Student Government at Smith College, a private women's college, recently voted to change the language of their Constitution. References to *she* and *her* were replaced by *the student,* in an effort to show sensitivity to students who identified themselves as transgender.[23] Transgender individuals do not view themselves in terms of standard cultural constructions of male or female, masculine or feminine. They contend that they have transcended societal confines of sex and gender, so standard references to *she, he, him,* and *her* do not apply to transgender people and could cause them to feel excluded. If you think the changes to the Smith College Student Government Constitution are really "out there," realize that several other colleges and universities are currently considering such linguistic innovations for their campus documents.

As with pronouns, research shows that masculine mental images arise when the term *man* is used, again rendering women invisible and reinforcing the male-as-standard problem.[24] Words such as Congress*man,* police*man,* and *man*kind ignore the fact that women are part of the workforce and the human race. Contrast these with *member of Congress* (or *senator* or *representative*), *police officer,* and *humankind,* which are gender neutral and allow for the inclusion of both men and women. Some progress in this area has been made to reflect changed attitudes toward women in the professional arena. Compare some

The gender-neutral term *firefighter* describes both of these people, whereas the sexist term *fireman* excludes the person on the right.

TABLE 1.3.1

Terms from the Past	Terms Used Today
stewardess	flight attendant
chairman	chair
fireman	firefighter
salesman	salesperson or clerk
mailman	mail carrier
female doctor or lady doctor	physician or doctor
girls at work or girl Friday	women at the office
Miss/Mrs.	Ms.
mankind	people, humans, or humankind

terms used in the past to describe workers to terms we now use (see Table 1.3.1).

A related issue concerns the generally accepted use of the phrase *you guys* as a generic reference. This language is not generic, since it includes the male term *guys*, but it is one of the most widely used, by both women and men, and unintentionally exclusive terms in everyday English. About using *you guys* to refer to a group of women, renowned author Alice Walker states, "I see in its use some women's obsequious need to be accepted, at any cost, even at the cost of erasing their own femaleness, and that of other women. Isn't it at least ironic that after so many years of struggle for women's liberation, women should end up calling themselves this?"[25]

Consciously remembering to use nonsexist, inclusive language brings several benefits.[26] First, inclusive language reflects inclusive attitudes. Your attitudes are reflected in your speech and your speech affects your attitudes. Monitoring your verbal communication for sexist remarks can help you monitor any sexist attitudes or assumptions you may hold. Second, using gender-inclusive language helps you become more other oriented, which will have a positive impact on your relationships. Consciously ridding your language of sexist remarks reflects your sensitivity to others. Third, inclusive language makes your speech more contemporary and unambiguous. If you use *he*, for example, how is a listener to know if you are referring to a male person or any person in general? And finally, inclusive language strengthens your style and demonstrates sensitivity that can empower others. By eliminating sexist bias from your speech, you affirm the value of all individuals with whom you interact.

Language and Sexual Orientation We realize that sexual orientation is one of the more difficult topics to discuss, mainly because people tend to hold strong opinions about it. But no matter your views about sexuality, it is vital to use sensitive, appropriate communication with whomever you encounter.

Just as you have learned to avoid racially charged terms that degrade and draw attention to someone's ethnicity, it's important to learn to avoid language that denigrates a person's sexual orientation and draws undue attention to this element of cultural diversity. One of your authors was quite taken aback a few years ago when she received a paper from a first-year student in which the derogatory term *fag* frequently appeared. You've no doubt heard this term, probably bantered about in high school, but its use can be a signal of homophobia—the fear of being labeled or viewed as gay or lesbian. Heterosexist language is more subtle; it often emerges through omission, meaning what is *not* said, rather than commission, or what *is* said. For example, have you ever heard an instructor in one of your classes give a dating example using two persons of the same sex? Most examples about relationships that you read or hear about in courses such as interpersonal communication or introduction to psychology reflect heterosexual romantic relationships. As another example, how often do you hear or use the term *partner* instead of *husband* or *wife?* The first term, *partner*, is inclusive of all forms of couples, while the latter terms, at least in most states, refer only to heterosexual marriage. These tendencies can communicate a heterosexist bias and suggest that other sexual orientations are inappropriate or nonexistent.

Biased Language: Age, Class, and Ability

"Just turn the car, grandpa!" Ever heard a driver say this in irritation, or said it yourself? Ever call an elderly person a "geezer" or an "old-timer"? Just as some people contend that Americans are hung up on gender and racial diversity, many believe that Americans are hung up on age. We live in a culture that glorifies youth and tends to put its elders "out to pasture." Age discrimination is a very real problem in the workforce—so much so that laws have been enacted to guard against someone's being denied professional opportunities because of age. Likewise, some older people may hold stereotypes of young people and may speak to them as though their youth exempted them from intelligence or responsible action. We recommend that you inventory your language for any terms that either show disrespect for elders or are patronizing or condescending to younger persons.

Another factor that influences language that has received research attention of late is socioeconomic class. Class distinctions typically are revealed in derogatory references to "blue-collar workers," "manual laborers," or "welfare recipients." Another class slur is the term "white trash." In the late 1990s, when Paula Jones filed a sexual harassment lawsuit against then-President Bill Clinton, she was called "white trash" and "trailer trash" as she was ridiculed in the press and in living rooms across the country. Avoid references that reveal a condescending or disrespectful attitude toward someone's education (or lack of it) and socioeconomic status.

Finally, an area of bias in language that most people became conscious of by the turn of the twenty-first century relates to ability. Some years ago, Helen

Keller was described as "deaf, dumb, and blind." Nowadays, the appropriate term for her inability to communicate vocally would be *mute*. Be careful that your language doesn't make fun of or draw attention to someone's physical, mental, or learning disability, such as calling someone a "cripple," "retard," or "slow reader." Research has found that when people with disabilities were called demeaning names, they were perceived as less trustworthy, competent, persuasive, and sociable than when they were described in positive terms.[27] The researchers warn against using derogatory language that is offensive to persons with disabilities. Also, scholars who research communication and disability recommend that you use the reference "persons with disabilities" rather than "disabled persons." The former language usage makes the person primary and the disability secondary; the emphasis is on a person, who just happens to have some form of disability. The latter usage emphasizes the disability over the human-ness of the person.[28]

RECAP

Confronting Bias in Language

Inventory your language for subtle and not-so-subtle indications of bias in several areas:

- *Race, Ethnicity, and Nationality.*   Avoid language that denigrates members of a racial or ethnic group; be careful not to overemphasize race or ethnicity or "mark" a person by using adjectives referring to national origin, as in "that Oriental student in my class."

- *Religion.*   Watch stereotypical language pertaining to religious affiliation, such as derogatory references to Jews, Muslims, or fundamentalist Christians, for example.

- *Gender.*   Include both sexes in your language, especially in your use of pronouns; avoid masculine generic pronouns and male-linked terms that exclude women.

- *Sexual Orientation.*   Be alert to the potential for heterosexism in your language—the assumption that everyone is heterosexual or that heterosexuality is the only possible orientation. Eliminate homophobic language that degrades and stereotypes gays, lesbians, bisexuals, and transgender individuals.

- *Age.*   Avoid calling too much attention to a person's age in your verbal communication. Be especially vigilant not to label or stereotype the elderly or to condescend to or glorify youth.

- *Class.*   Monitor references to socioeconomic differences, such as distinctions between blue-collar and white-collar workers.

- *Ability.*   Avoid verbal communication that draws attention to a person's physical, mental, or learning ability.

QUICK REVIEW

Using Words to Establish Supportive Relationships

As we said early on in this chapter, one reason verbal communication is important is because it has an impact on other people. Language is our primary tool for communicating who we are to others—for knowing them and being known by them. Relationships of all sorts bring life's greatest satisfactions, so the motivation for assessing and improving our verbal communication with others is obvious.

In our introductory communication classes, we often discuss **trigger words—those forms of language that arouse strong emotions in listeners**. One student, Travis, was immediately able to identify a word his wife used during arguments that really sparked his frustration and anger more than anything else. When Travis would make a point that would frustrate his wife —one for which she had no comeback—she would look at him, toss her hand in the air, and say, "Whatever." Perhaps this word triggers you too, because it punctuates a conversation; it acts as a dismissal of the other person and her or his point. Do you know what words trigger your emotions? These words or phrases can incite positive as well as negative feelings, but they acutely illustrate the power of words in the context of relationships. Certain uses of language can make us feel accepted and appreciated, or disrespected and hostile.

For over four decades, communication scholar Jack Gibb's research has been used as a framework for both describing and prescribing verbal behaviors that contribute to feelings of either supportiveness or defensiveness.[29] Gibb spent several years listening to and observing groups of individuals in meetings and conversations, noting that some exchanges seemed to create a supportive climate whereas others created a defensive one. Words and actions, he concluded, are tools we use to let someone know whether we support them or not. Thus Gibb defined **supportive communication** as **communication that uses language to create a climate of trust, caring, and acceptance**. The language used in **defensive communication,** in contrast, **creates a climate of hostility and mistrust**. When someone gets defensive, communication is seriously impeded. Think about times when your words made someone defensive and how hard you had to work (if you attempted it at all) to get the person to let the defenses down. In this section, we suggest ways to use verbal communication to create a supportive climate rather than an antagonistic one.

Describe Your Own Feelings Rather Than Evaluate Others

Most of us don't like to be judged or evaluated. Not only do we fear negative responses from others; we fear the potential that we will become defensive and say things we'll later regret. Criticizing and name-calling obviously can create relational problems, but so can our attempts to diagnose others' problems or weaknesses. As Winston Churchill declared, "I am always ready to learn, although I do not always like being taught."

One way to avoid evaluating others is to attempt to decrease your use of an accusatory *you*. Statements such as "You always say you'll call but you never do" or "You need to pick up the dirty clothes in your room" attack a person's sense of self-worth and usually result in a defensive reaction. Instead, use the word *I* to describe your own feelings and thoughts about a situation or event: "I find it hard to believe you when you say you'll call" or "I don't enjoy the extra work of picking up your dirty clothes." When you describe your own feelings instead of berating the receiver of the message, you take ownership of the problem. This approach leads to greater openness and trust because your listener is less likely to feel rejected or as if you are trying to control him or her.

Related to this point about description versus evaluation is the suggestion that you separate behaviors from persons in order to create a supportive climate. We probably all know people whose behaviors seem self-destructive, and we all do things from time to time that aren't in our own best interest. Maybe in reaction to getting dumped in a relationship that means a great deal to you, you call that person's answering machine 20 times, just to hear the voice recording. Maybe you indulge in self-defeating behavior like drinking too much, overeating (or the opposite, starving yourself), or driving around late at night with the music blasting, feeling sorry for yourself. In these critical moments, do people respond to you or to your behavior? A supportive response focuses on the behavior, not the person. A supportive response sounds something like this: "Here's what I see you doing; I'm still your friend and I care about you, but this behavior isn't healthy. How can I help you?" Responses that engender defensiveness might sound something like "You're really out of control," "You've become someone I don't recognize," and "Stop acting like this or I won't be able to be around you or be your friend." The supportive response doesn't characterize the person as the embodiment of his or her destructive behavior; it focuses only on the behavior, because that's what's happening at the moment. In religious circles, the advice goes "Hate the sin, love the sinner."

Solve Problems Rather Than Control Others

When you were younger, your parents gave you rules to keep you safe. Even though you may have resented their control, you needed to know that the stovetop was hot, when not to cross the street, and how dangerous it is to stick your finger in a light socket. Now that you are an adult, when people treat you like a child, it often means they are trying to control your behavior, to take away your options.

Most of us don't like to be controlled. Someone who presumes to tell us what's good for us instead of helping us puzzle through issues and problems to arrive at our own solutions or higher understanding is likely to engender defensiveness. In truth, we have little or no control over others. Open-ended questions such as "What seems to be the problem?" or "How can we deal with this issue?" create a more supportive climate than critical comments such as "Here's where you are wrong" and "You know what your problem is?" or commands such as "Don't do that!"

Be Genuine Rather Than Manipulative

To be genuine means honestly being yourself rather than attempting to be someone you are not. It also means taking a sincere interest in others, considering the uniqueness of each individual and situation, and avoiding generalizations or strategies that focus on your own needs and desires. A manipulative person has hidden agendas and her or his own concerns and interests most at heart. A genuine person has the other person's interests at heart and uses language to facilitate an open and honest discussion of issues and problems.

Empathize Rather Than Remain Detached from Others

Empathy, one of the hallmarks of supportive relationships, **is the ability to understand and actually feel or approximate the feelings of others and then to predict the emotional responses they will have to different situations.**[30] You work to put yourself in the other person's shoes, to experience as closely as you can what she or he is experiencing. The opposite of empathy is neutrality. To be neutral is to be indifferent or apathetic toward others. (Even when you express anger or irritation toward another, you are investing some energy in the relationship.) A statement that epitomizes this concept of neutrality is "I don't love you or hate you; I just *don't* you."

Remaining detached from someone when empathy is obviously called for can generate great defensiveness and damage a relationship. Here's an example: You're upset about an argument you just had with someone you're dating, so you seek the support and listening ear of a good friend. But that friend is in "party mode" or such a good mood that he or she chooses not to concentrate and listen to what's going on with you. Rather than engage in your situ-

Empathy, the ability to understand and experience the feelings of another, is a building block of a supportive relationship.

ation, your friend remains detached and blows off your concerns. In situations like this, most of us become defensive and frustrated, and the quality of our friendship may suffer. Empathy takes work, but it is a building block of a supportive relationship.

Be Flexible Rather Than Rigid toward Others

Some people are just *always* right, aren't they? (These people spend a lot of time alone, too.) Most people don't like someone who always seems certain that she or he is right. A "you're wrong, I'm right" attitude creates a defensive climate. This does not mean that you should have no opinions and go through life passively agreeing to everything. And it doesn't mean that there isn't a clear-cut right and wrong in a given situation. But instead of making rigid pronouncements, at times you may want to qualify your language by using phrases such as "I may be wrong, but it seems to me . . ." or "Here's something you might want to consider." Conditional language gives your opinions a softer edge that allows room for others to express a point of view; it opens the door for alternatives. Declarations tend to shut the door. Again, there are times when equivocation is not an appropriate or advisable way to communicate. But in those cases when you want to induce supportiveness and reduce the potential for defensiveness, conditional, flexible language works best.

Present Yourself as Equal Rather Than Superior

You can antagonize others by letting them know that you view yourself as better or brighter than they are. You may be gifted and extraordinarily intelligent, but it's not necessary to announce or publicize it. And although some people have the responsibility and authority to manage others, "pulling rank" does not usually produce a supportive climate. With phrases such as "Let's work on this together" or "We each have a valid perspective," you can avoid erecting walls of resentment and defensiveness. "We" language can be preferable to "you" language; it builds a sense of camaraderie and shared experience, and by using it you avoid setting yourself apart from listeners.

Also, avoid using "high-falutin'" (or unnecessarily complicated) words just to impress others or to project some image. Sometimes referred to as "bafflegab," this kind of language can come in the form of words, phrases, or verbal shorthand that no one understands but you. Persons with particular expertise may use abbreviated terms or acronyms (words derived from the first letters of several words in a phrase). The military is notorious for its use of language that doesn't easily translate outside of military circles. "Be sure to

On the Web

If you encounter someone whose language is such "bafflegab" that a common dictionary won't help you decipher meanings, try the Extelligence Creative Word Dictionary. This site offers seldom-used words and their definitions, so that you won't be stumped again by someone who is "ultracrepidarian" (acting or speaking outside one's experience, knowledge, or ability). The address is

www.extelligence.co.uk

(Once at the site, try the link **/words/**).

complete the Fit Reps on those Non-Coms ASAP before returning to the BOQ."
Translation: "Be sure to complete the Fitness Reports on those Non-Commis-
sioned Officers as soon as possible before returning to the Bachelor Officers'
Quarters." If both speaker and listener are military personnel, then such a sentence may be a perfectly acceptable way to communicate. The problem comes
when you use lingo no one understands, perhaps to create drama, exclude
someone from the conversation, or posture yourself. It's better to use informal
language appropriate to the situation and your listeners than to attempt to talk
over the heads of everyone in the room.

You can also create defensiveness by using language that is too simplistic
for your listeners. Granted, when you communicate with someone from
another culture or even from another U.S. cultural group, you may need to
alter your message to get your meaning across. But this means that your verbal communication should be explicit, not condescending. For example, some
people use oversimplified words when communicating with elderly persons.
It's inappropriate to assume that aging diminishes one's capacity to understand. Try to use language to present yourself on equal ground with your listeners and establish a supportive, open climate for communication.

Avoid Gunny-Sacking

In one of his hit songs, Garth Brooks sings, "We buried the hatchet; we left the
handle sticking out." Brooks makes mild reference here to a process known as
gunny-sacking, which can be like a handle sticking out within easy reach;
when grasped, it serves to remind you of a past conflict or wound. Gunny-sacking involves dredging up someone's past mistakes or problems and linking them
to a current situation. The language comes from the imagery of reaching down
into a bag (a gunny sack) to pull out something from the past. For example,
suppose your best male friend has just been dumped by his "one true love," but
you—being the good friend that you are—remind him that the last three
women he dated were also his "one true love," at least at the time. Your friend
wants empathy, but you respond by highlighting his tendency to turn "Miss
Right" into "Miss Right Now." Such an approach will likely make him feel criticized and engender defensive reactions in him. This kind of scenario rarely
deepens a relationship.

However, in some situations, it may be wise to point out a pattern of
destructive behavior that you observe in someone, especially if the person is
someone you value highly and with whom you want to maintain a healthy,
supportive relationship. Occasionally, people repeat behaviors that are not to
their benefit, but they are unaware that a pattern is being established. A caring friend, romantic partner, or family member might use the supportive communication techniques described in this chapter to describe past instances and
reveal the pattern to the person. Once the negative patterns are revealed and
explored, he or she may work to overcome them so that the destructive behavior isn't repeated.

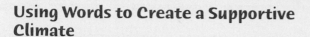

RECAP

Using Words to Create a Supportive Climate

- Describe your own feelings instead of evaluating the points of view or behavior of others.
- Keep the focus on problem solving, not control of others.
- Be genuine rather than manipulative in your approach.
- Show that you understand others' points of view instead of ignoring their feelings.
- Use conditional language and demonstrate flexibility rather than rigidity in your communication with others.
- Present yourself as an equal rather than as a superior. Make it clear that you do not have all the answers; avoid acting like a know-it-all. Don't attempt to talk over the heads of listeners or condescend to them, because either approach can breed defensiveness.
- Avoid gunny-sacking, or reminding someone of past mistakes or issues, unless you believe the person remains blind to his or her destructive patterns.

QUICK REVIEW

PRINCIPLES FOR A LIFETIME: Enhancing Your Skills

Verbal

Principle Two: Effectively use and interpret verbal messages.

- Realize that communication problems may not have to do with the words used, but with the meanings that people attach to the words.
- Recognize the difference between denotative and connotative language.
- Use concrete terms whenever appropriate, because abstract language is harder to understand than concrete language.
- Understand that meanings of words are affected by the culture within which the language is used.
- Pay attention to the words communicators choose to use and attempt to interpret those words in the spirit and context in which they were intended.
- Avoid biased language when speaking about race, ethnicity, nationality, religion, gender, sexual orientation, age, class, and ability.
- Use words to engender supportiveness, rather than defensiveness.

SUMMARY

In this chapter, we explored the importance of effective verbal communication with others. The words we choose have great power to communicate who we are and to influence the relationships we establish. People use words as symbols for thoughts, and they create meanings for those symbols. We interpret their meanings in terms of the culture and context to which they belong. Communication is complex because people develop both denotative (literal) meanings and connotative (subjective) meanings for words and because meanings range from concrete to abstract.

The power of words stems from their ability to create images and to help us label and understand our experience. Words influence our thoughts and actions, as they both shape culture and are shaped by culture. Language also has the power to make and break relationships.

Biased language that is insensitive and exclusive of others creates noise that interferes with the meaning of a message; it also can create the impression that the user of such language is biased and can impede the development of satisfying relationships. The most common forms of biased language relate to race, ethnicity, nationality, religion, gender, sexual orientation, age, class, and ability.

The words you use can enhance or detract from the quality of relationships you establish with others. In contrast to defensive communication, supportive communication is descriptive rather than evaluative, problem oriented rather than control oriented, genuine rather than contrived or manipulative, empathic rather than neutral, flexible rather than rigid, equal rather than superior, and focused on current behaviors, not on past mistakes.

DISCUSSION AND REVIEW

1. Why should we focus on language?
2. Explain the nature of words as symbols to which people attach meanings. How can meanings vary?
3. Describe what is meant by denotative and connotative meanings for words.
4. Describe what is meant by concrete and abstract meanings for words.
5. What does it mean to say that language is culture bound and context bound? How does one's cul-

ture shape language? How does one's language shape culture?
6. Identify four ways that words have power.
7. Provide some examples of biased language related to race, ethnicity, nationality, and religion. Then generate unbiased terms as alternatives.
8. Provide some examples of biased language related to gender, sexual orientation, age, class, and ability. Then generate unbiased terms as alternatives.
9. What is the role of verbal communication in the establishment of supportive relationships? Identify some ways that one can create a supportive communication climate with others.

PUTTING PRINCIPLES INTO PRACTICE

1. Below we review the differences between denotative and connotative meanings of words and provide examples.

Level	Definition	Examples
Denotative	Literal, restrictive definition of a word	*Teacher*: the person primarily responsible for providing your education
Connotative	Personal, subjective reaction to a word	*Teacher*: the warm, supportive person who fostered a climate in which you could learn OR the cold taskmaster who drilled lessons into you and made you feel inferior

For each of the following terms, provide a denotative, or dictionary-type, definition; then generate connotative meanings of your own.

work

parent

love

commitment

professionalism

loyalty

2. We know that words have the power to influence our thoughts and actions. In a small group, have each member reveal a nickname given by either a family member or friends. Discuss whether group members attribute positive or negative meanings to the nicknames and whether each person's development was affected by his or her nickname.

3. This activity illustrates how people reveal their biases through their use of language. Generate a list of stereotypical language that is often associated with each of the words below. For example, for the word *Democrat*, you might think of positive and negative terms like "liberal," "tax and spend," "big government," "dove," and "populist."

conservatives

foreigners

homeless persons

the military

churchgoers

politicians

4. With a group of classmates, generate and write down a list of trigger words—terms that set off emotional reactions. Consider words that evoke positive emotions, such as happiness and surprise. Then explore words that prompt anger, fear, sadness, and disgust. Discuss how certain words came to trigger your emotions; look for common experiences among group members.

5. In this chapter you've learned that the words you use can enhance or detract from the quality of relationships you establish with others. Conduct role plays with classmates to demonstrate ways to establish supportive communication climates with others: (1) being descriptive rather than evaluative, (2) being problem oriented rather than control oriented, (3) communicating in a genuine rather than a contrived or manipulative manner, (4) showing empathy rather than neutrality, (5) being flexible rather than rigid, (6) representing yourself as equal rather than superior to others, and (7) concentrating on the present, rather than gunny-sacking and dredging up the past. First act out the wrong way to behave or an example of ineffective communication that leads to defensiveness. Then repeat the role play, using the same or different players, altering the conversation so that a supportive climate is established.

Chapter 1.3   *Practice Test*

MULTIPLE CHOICE.   Choose the *best* answer to each of the following questions.

1. The type of meaning for a word found in the dictionary is
   a. connotative.
   b. denotative.
   c. abstract.
   d. concrete.

2. Amanda spent her entire lunch with Savannah talking about the business interview she had the day before. Amanda is using the power of words primarily to
   a. shape and reflect culture.
   b. make and break relationships.
   c. create and label experience.
   d. impact thoughts and actions.

3. Jimmy Swaggart said, "Evolution is a bankrupt speculative philosophy, not a scientific fact. Only a spiritually bankrupt society could ever believe it. . . . Only atheists could accept this Satanic theory." This statement is an example of
   a. bypassing.
   b. polarization.
   c. allness.
   d. exclusive language.

4. Using general terms, such as *she* or *he*, to refer to all people is an example of
   a. defensive language.
   b. generic language.
   c. trivial language.
   d. supportive language.

5. Language that reveals an assumption that only a man and a woman can be involved in an intimate relationship is
   a. homophobic.
   b. heterosexist.

   c. homosexist.
   d. heterophobic.

6. Doug says to his employee, "Either we are going to build this front porch my way or we are not going to build it at all!" This is an example of
   a. defensive communication.
   b. supportive communication.
   c. empathic communication.
   d. problem-solving communication.

7. The Sapir–Whorf Hypothesis would ***not*** support the idea that
   a. you can only think of things for which you have words.
   b. you can think of something for which there is no word.
   c. our thoughts are based on the language we use.
   d. our language may affect our perceptions of the world around us.

8. Sexist language
   a. is the same thing as generic language.
   b. perpetuates sex-biased perceptions.
   c. is the same thing as inclusive language.
   d. is not related to perceptions of men's and women's status.

9. Which of the following terms is the most abstract?
   a. sandwich
   b. hamburger
   c. lunch
   d. food

10. To comfort his upset friend Hunter, Austin says, "I am so sorry that you lost your job this week. I can imagine that you are feeling very upset about it. Is there anything I can do to help you to feel better?" Austin's statement is an example of

a. empathic communication.

b. neutral communication.

c. bypassing communication.

d. concrete communication.

11. In referring to members of other ethnic groups, it's best to

a. rely on traditional ethnic labels.

b. use ethnic-neutral labels.

c. use the current ethnic labels preferred by a group's members.

d. use whichever term you are most comfortable with.

12. Australian communication scholar Dale Spender has argued that

a. there is no connection between our language use and our perception of the world.

b. our language reflects the natural ordering and classification of the world.

c. our language reflects the natural meanings of the world.

d. our language creates an order and classification of the world.

13. Alan and Cliff were discussing breakfast cereals. Cliff said, "Alan, I might be wrong, but I think Cocoa Puffs are better than Cap'n Crunch." Cliff was using what kind of language?

a. rigid

b. conditional

c. defensive

d. detached

14. Trigger words

a. convey a negative evaluation of another person.

b. are used to control others.

c. express sincere feelings.

d. arouse both positive and negative emotions in us.

15. When two people in a relationship use nicknames, such as "my little pookie" or "snuggle-buns," they are using language to

a. shape a culture of two people.

b. make or break a relationship.

c. create experience.

d. create action.

16. A language is a system of _____ structured by _____ and _____ common to a _____ of people.

a. words, experience, syntax, community

b. words, grammar, rules, culture

c. symbols, experience, rules, community

d. symbols, grammar, syntax, community

17. Meaning exists

a. in the words themselves.

b. in the way the communicators use the words.

c. in the culture and context of the interaction.

d. only in the mind of the receiver.

18. Homosexuals' reclaiming the term *queer* and making it a term of pride is an example of language's power to

a. create and label experience.

b. impact thoughts and actions.

c. shape and reflect culture.

d. make and break relationships.

19. Bailey and Victoria are having an argument. Bailey says to Victoria, "I see you crossing your arms and rolling your eyes. When I try to talk to you, you turn your head away from me and sigh loudly. You do this all of the time, and then wonder why people don't like you. That's why Makayla doesn't like you anymore, and you know it. That's why you keep ending up alone." Bailey has violated which of Gibbs's recommendations?

a. Be descriptive rather than evaluative.

b. Solve problems rather than control others.

c. Empathize rather than remain detached from others.

d. Avoid gunny-sacking.

20. Mason does not understand computers and has asked Kylie to help him. Kylie explains to Mason, "The problem with your Internet connection is

that either your DHCP server is not assigning an IP address or the WEP key for your Wi-Fi is wrong." Kylie is violating which of Gibb's recommendations?

a. Be descriptive rather than evaluative.

b. Solve problems rather than control others.

c. Present yourself as equal rather than superior.

d. Be flexible rather than rigid toward others.

TRUE/FALSE.   Indicate whether the following statements are *true* or *false*.

1. T or F   Words have the power to create or destroy relationships.

2. T or F   Culture influences the meaning of words.

3. T or F   A word is abstract if we can experience it with one of our senses.

4. T or F   We are often unaware of the bias that exists in our use of language.

5. T or F   The words you use to label your feelings impact your moods and emotions.

6. T or F   It is acceptable to avoid sexist language by using generic language in its place.

7. T or F   Ironically, when people use demeaning labels to describe individuals with disabilities, those individuals with disabilities are perceived as trustworthy, competent, persuasive, and sociable.

8. T or F   The use of generic language reflects a cultural trend in the United States to think of people as neuter, rather than as male or female.

9. T or F   Bypassing refers to two people speaking at the same time and not hearing what the other says.

10. T or F   Language use is a purposeful act.

FILL IN THE BLANK.   Complete the following statements.

1. _____ is the sense you make out of a symbol.

2. The dictionary definition of a word is its _____ meaning.

3. Feeling what another person is feeling is _____.

4. Language that creates a climate of hostility and mistrust is _____ communication.

5. A _____ is any word, sound, or visual device that represents something else.

6. Your subjective or personal interpretation of a word is its _____ meaning.

7. _____ meanings are reserved for referents that cannot be experienced with one of your senses.

8. A common system of symbols organized around rules and patterns is called _____.

9. _____ communication creates a climate of trust, caring, and acceptance.

10. _____ meanings are derived from being able to experience a referent with one of your senses.

Understanding Nonverbal Messages

CHAPTER OUTLINE

Why Focus on Nonverbal Communication?

The Nature of Nonverbal Communication

Codes of Nonverbal Communication

How to Interpret Nonverbal Cues More Accurately

Summary

CHAPTER OBJECTIVES

After studying this chapter, you should be able to

1. Provide four reasons for studying nonverbal communication.

2. Describe the five ways in which nonverbal communication functions with verbal communication.

3. Discuss six elements that reveal the nature of nonverbal communication.

4. Be able to identify and explain the seven groupings of nonverbal communication codes.

5. Summarize major research findings regarding codes of nonverbal communication.

6. Explain Mehrabian's three-part framework for interpreting nonverbal cues.

We respond to gestures with an extreme alertness and, one might say, in accordance with an elaborate and secret code that is written nowhere, known by none, and understood by all.

Edward Sapir

Edouard Vuillard, Girls Walking, c. 1891–92. Oil on canvas, 81.2 × 65 cm. Erich Lessing/Art Resource, NY. © 2007 Artists Rights Society (ARS), New York/ADAGP, Paris.

"Don't give me that confused look—you know what I'm talking about."
"I knew that was you at my door; I know your knock."
"Hey, is this really you? You sound just like your sister on the phone."
"If I tied your hands together, I bet you couldn't talk."
"Back off from me; I need my space."

What do these statements have in common? They all have to do with a form of human communication that occurs without words—what we term *nonverbal communication*. **Nonverbal communication is communication other than written or spoken language that creates meaning for someone.** The one exception to this definition is that to hearing persons, sign language appears to be nonverbal communication. However, to persons who are deaf, sign language is verbal communication, with certain movements, signs, and facial expressions conveying words, phrases, and emphasis.

We know you're becoming familiar with our five-sided model of communication principles for a lifetime, but let's do a quick recap (see Figure 1.4.1). In Chapter 1.2 we explored ways to become more aware of yourself and your perceptions of things and people with whom you come into contact. An important step in this process of coming to know and understand yourself better is an honest, insightful examination of how you talk. In Chapter 1.3 we challenged you to consider the power of words, to take inventory of your use of language, and to think about ways to improve your verbal communication so that you extend yourself to others and respond to them in an appropriate, effective manner. Now we get to what most people consider an even greater challenge—understanding and evaluating your nonverbal communication and

**FIGURE 1.4.1
Communication
Principles for a
Lifetime**

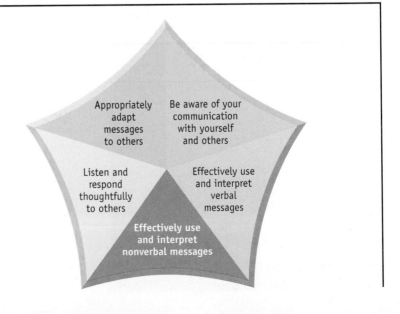

improving your ability to interpret the nonverbal behavior of others. Nonverbal communication is of great importance; a person who can read others' nonverbal communication with sensitivity and skill makes a memorable impression on other people. Because of the power of nonverbal communication to complement verbal communication, to further reveal the self—particularly in those situations when talking is inappropriate, impossible, or inadequate—and to affect how you connect with others as you initiate and build relationships, we've chosen to make this the third of our five key principles for a lifetime.

We have two primary goals in this chapter. The first is to help you become more aware of your own nonverbal behavior—to help you understand how and why you behave as you do. Because much nonverbal communication behavior is subconscious, most people have limited awareness or understanding of it. Once you become more aware of this important form of communication, you will increase your ability to use nonverbal skills to interact more effectively with others. The second goal is to enhance your nonverbal receiving skills, or your ability to more accurately detect and interpret the nonverbal communication of others.

Why Focus on Nonverbal Communication?

Have you ever watched someone interact with someone else and thought, "That person just doesn't have a clue"? We've all seen or met people who appear not to pick up on the communication clues of others. For example, have you ever tried to end a conversation because you were late or needed to be somewhere else, and the person you were talking to just wouldn't let you out of the conversation? The person didn't seem to notice you looking at your watch, angling your body away, taking a few steps back, and making minimal vocal responses to what was being said. Now, we all have times when we can't "catch a clue," even if we consider ourselves to be fairly sensitive, perceptive people. Certain people, places, moods, or topics of conversation may impede our ability to give and receive nonverbal communication effectively. But we don't want to be clueless. We want to be able to exhibit effective nonverbal communication and to read and interpret the clues others give us more sensitively and accurately.

However, there's something very important to keep in mind as we proceed: No one can become a perfect interpreter of the nonverbal communication of others. It's unwise and inappropriate to assume that you can become an infallible judge of others' nonverbal cues, because human beings are unique, complicated, and ever-changing creatures. Although we encourage you to deepen your understanding of nonverbal communication, sharpen your powers of observation, and develop greater skill in interpreting the meanings behind others' nonverbal actions, we also suggest that you remain keenly aware of the idiosyncratic and complex nature of nonverbal communication. We hope that you catch more clues as a result of studying this topic,

Which communicates the emotions more effectively: body movements; the volume, pitch, and intensity of the voice; or the meaning of the actual words spoken?

but avoid making the mistake of believing that your interpretations of nonverbal messages are always correct. To begin to explore this topic, let's look at four reasons for studying nonverbal communication.

Nonverbal Messages Communicate Feelings and Attitudes

What do you look like when you're happy and excited about something? When you're mad? When you're really worried about something? When you're surprised or disappointed? Videotapes or pictures of yourself in different moods can be quite revealing, because your face, body, and voice communicate volumes about what's going on inside of you.

Nonverbal communication is a primary tool for conveying our feelings and attitudes and for detecting the emotional states of others. In the study of nonverbal communication, Albert Mehrabian is an expert. He concluded from his research that the most significant source of emotional information is the face, which can channel as much as 55% of our meaning. Vocal cues such as volume, pitch, and intensity convey another 38% of our emotional meaning. In all, we communicate approximately 93% of the emotional meaning of our messages nonverbally; as little as 7% of the emotional meaning is communicated through explicit verbal channels.[1] Although these percentages do not apply to every communication situation, Mehrabian's research illustrates the potential power of nonverbal cues to communicate emotion and attitude.

Nonverbal Messages Are More Believable Than Verbal Ones

"Hey—are you mad or something?" asks Jonas.
(Big sigh.) "Oh, no. I'm not mad," responds Danita (in a subdued tone of voice and without making eye contact).
"You sure? Because you're acting funny, like you're ticked off." (One more try and then Jonas will likely give up.)
"I SAID I'M NOT MAD, OKAY? WILL YOU LEAVE IT ALONE PLEASE?"

Despite Danita's claim to the contrary, the real story is—she's mad. "Actions speak louder than words." This cliché became a cliché because nonverbal communication is more believable than verbal communication. Verbal communication is a conscious activity; it involves the translation of thoughts and impulses into symbols. Some nonverbal communication is conscious, but a

Technology *and* Communication

Conveying Emotions Online

*W*ithout the usual nonverbal mechanisms that allow us to reveal our emotions to others in face-to-face communication, how do we let others at a distance know what we're feeling? E-mail has all but replaced the fine art of letter writing, but people who used to or still write letters typically insert parenthetical phrases or symbols to convey the nonverbal message behind the verbal. The most common one is the happy face, or "smiley," which, when typed, is made by combining a colon, dash, and right parenthesis mark, as in :-).

If you use e-mail, perhaps you've learned a few other nonverbal methods for communicating emotion. One is to put certain words in all caps, a technique known as "shouting," which typically reveals emphasis, frustration, or even anger. You may have also seen the clever use of punctuation and other keyboard symbols to form a visual image. These sideways images, termed "emoticons," are forms of nonverbal communication that help convey the meaning or emotion behind a message. Here are some emoticons located from various sources.[2]

:-(	Depressed or upset by a remark
:-l	Indifferent
:-|	Straight face
:-o	Surprise
;-)	Winking at a suggestive or flirtatious remark
:-/	Skeptical
:-P	Sticking your tongue out
:-D	Laughing
:-@	Screaming
8-)	Wearing sunglasses
::-)	Wearing regular glasses
(-:	Left-handed

great deal of it is generated subconsciously as we act and react to stimuli in our environment. It's easier to control your words than to control a quiver in your voice when you're angry, the heat and flush in your face when you talk to someone you're attracted to, or shaky knees when you're nervous.

When a person's verbal and nonverbal communication contradict, as in Danita's case, which should an astute observer believe? The nonverbal actions carry the truer message most of the time. When we can't catch a clue, it's most likely because we're wrapped up in ourselves or because we attend more to a person's verbal messages than to her or his nonverbal messages.

Nonverbal Messages Are Critical to Successful Relationships

One researcher suggests that as much as 65% of the way we convey meaning in our messages is through nonverbal channels.[3] Of course, the meaning others interpret from your behavior may not be the one you intended. But we begin making judgments about people just a fraction of a second after meeting them, based on nonverbal information. You may decide whether a date is going to be pleasant or dull during the first 30 seconds of meeting your date, before your date has had time to utter more than "Hello."[4]

As another example, consider the handshake—a simple ritualistic greeting between two people, used in many cultures. Have you ever considered the power of a handshake to communicate? If you get a weak, half-handed, limp handshake from someone, what are you likely to conclude about that person? Research has focused on judgments we make about someone's personality based on a simple greeting ritual. William Chaplin and his colleagues determined characteristics of handshakes that contribute to what they term a handshake index.[5] These researchers examined such attributes as strength, vigor, completeness of grip, and duration. The high index or most positive handshake was strong (but not so strong as to cut off the blood supply), vigorous (meaning it conveyed an appropriate amount of energy), adequate in duration (not too brief or too long), and complete in its grip (meaning that the people gripped each others' hands fully, with palms touching). Next the researchers studied subjects' judgments of persons with a high handshake index versus those with a low handshake index. These researchers found that the higher a person's handshake index, the more extroverted, open to experience, and less shy that person was believed to be. In addition to these traits, women with high handshake indexes were also perceived to be highly agreeable, in comparison to women with weak or poor handshakes. Subjects in the study also formed more favorable first impressions of those persons with high handshake indexes than those with low indexes. Thus, even a simple symbolic, culturally rooted gesture can have a definite and long-lasting impact on how others perceive you.

Nonverbal cues are important not only in the early stages of relationships, but also as we maintain, deepen, and sometimes terminate those relationships. In fact, the more intimate the relationship, the more we use and understand the nonverbal cues of our partners. Long-married couples spend less time verbalizing their feelings and emotions to each other than they did when they were first dating; each learns to interpret the other's subtle nonverbal cues. If a spouse is silent during dinner, the other spouse may deduce that the day was a tough one and decide to give the person a lot of space. In fact, all of us are more likely to use nonverbal cues to convey negative messages than to announce our explicit dislike of something or someone.[6] We also use nonverbal cues to signal changes in the level of satisfaction with a relationship. When we want to cool things off, we may start using a less vibrant tone of voice and cut back on eye contact and physical contact with our partner.

Functions of Nonverbal Messages

Nonverbal messages can serve multiple functions. First, nonverbal cues can *substitute* for verbal messages. An extended thumb signals that a hitchhiker would like a ride, a water skier wants more speed, or a pilot is ready for takeoff. When someone asks, "Where's the elevator?" we can point instead of voicing a response. In these instances, we substitute nonverbal cues for verbal messages.

Nonverbal cues delivered simultaneously with verbal messages *complement*, clarify, or extend the meaning of the verbal, conveying more information and allowing for a more accurate interpretation. When someone waves, makes eye

contact, and says "hello," the gesture and eye contact serve as nonverbal complements to the verbal greeting. Complementary cues also help color our expressed emotions and attitudes. The length of a hug while you tell your daughter you're proud of her provides additional information about the intensity of your pride. A long, heavy sigh may reveal how tired or bored you are.

Sometimes, however, our nonverbal cues *contradict* rather than complement our verbal cues. Remember Danita, who said she wasn't mad even though she was acting and sounding mad? In an instance like this, the nonverbal cues contradict the verbal ones. The nonverbal message is almost always the one we should believe.

We also use nonverbal cues to *repeat* our words. "I'm new on campus; where's the Center for the Arts?" asks a student. "Go to the right of that two-story, red brick building, and it's just on the other side" says a security guard, who then points to the building. The guard's pointing gesture repeats the verbal instruction and clarifies the message.

We also use nonverbal cues to *regulate* our participation in conversation. In most informal meetings, it's not appropriate or necessary to signal your desire to speak by raising your hand. Yet somehow you're able to signal to others when you'd like to speak and when you'd rather not. You use eye contact, raised eyebrows, an open mouth, an audible intake of breath, a change in posture or seating position, or a single raised index finger to signal that you would like to make a point. If your colleagues don't see these signals, especially the eye contact, they may assume you're not interested in engaging in conversation.[7]

Finally, we use nonverbal behavior to *accent* or reinforce a verbal message. "We simply must do something about this problem," bellows the mayor, "or else we will all bear the blame." When the mayor says the word *must,* she pounds the podium and increases her volume for emphasis. When she says "all bear the blame," she uses a circling gesture with her arms to convey a shared responsibility among those in the room. These vocalizations and gestures serve to accent or add intensity to the verbal message.

RECAP

Why Focus on Nonverbal Communication?

- Nonverbal communication is our primary means of communicating feelings and attitudes toward others.
- Nonverbal messages are usually more believable than verbal messages.
- Nonverbal communication is critical in the initiation, development, and termination of relationships.
- Nonverbal messages can substitute for, complement, contradict, repeat, regulate, and accent verbal messages.

QUICK REVIEW

The Nature of Nonverbal Communication

While the benefits of studying and improving one's facility with nonverbal communication are clear, deciphering unspoken messages is a tricky activity. Dictionaries help us interpret words, but no handy reference book exists to help decode nonverbal cues. Below are some of the challenges inherent in the interpretation of nonverbal communication.

The Culture-Bound Nature of Nonverbal Communication

Some evidence suggests that humans from every culture smile when they are happy and frown when they are unhappy.[8] They also all tend to raise or flash their eyebrows when meeting or greeting others, and young children in many cultures wave to signal they want their parents, raise their arms to be picked up, and suck their thumbs for comfort.[9] This evidence suggests that there is some underlying commonality in human emotion. Yet each culture tends to develop unique rules for displaying and interpreting the expression of emotion.

It's important to realize that nonverbal behavior is culture bound. No common cross-cultural dictionary of nonverbal meaning exists. You will make critical errors in communicating nonverbally, as well as in attempting to interpret the nonverbal behavior of others, if you don't situate nonverbal actions within a cultural context. As intercultural communication scholars Richard Porter and Larry Samovar explain, one culture's friendly or polite action may be another culture's obscene gesture.[10] For example, during his second inaugural parade, Pres-

Most nonverbal communication is culture bound. But one of the most universal nonverbal cues among human beings is the smile.

ident George W. Bush displayed the two-finger, "hook 'em horns" gesture to salute members of the University of Texas marching band as they passed by his stand. According to the Associated Press, a Norwegian newspaper expressed outrage over the gesture, since it is considered an insult or a sign of the devil in Norse culture. In sign language used by and for deaf persons, the gesture translates into "bull_____." In Mediterranean countries, the gesture implies that a man is the victim of an unfaithful wife. In Russia, it is considered a symbol for newly rich, arrogant, and poorly educated Russians; in many European countries it serves to ward off the "evil eye"; and in some African nations, it's used to put a hex or curse on another person.[11] Concerns about potential international gaffes led Southern Methodist University to publish a pocket-size guide for its students studying abroad. Tips include sticking out your tongue as a way of saying hello in Tibet; making certain to take your hands out of your pockets when talking with someone in Belgium; and avoiding touching someone's head in Indonesia, where such an action would be considered a serious insult.[12]

The Rule-Governed Nature of Nonverbal Communication

You operate according to many rules in your nonverbal communication. You may be unaware that you function according to these rules, but when your rules are violated, you definitely know it. For example, have you ever been in a conversation with someone who seemed as though he or she couldn't talk to you without touching you? Maybe it's just a series of simple touches on the forearm or shoulder, but it's not what you expect in casual conversation. For some reason, the other person's rule about appropriate touch is likely to be different from yours. Or perhaps you've been annoyed when people talk at the movie theater, as if they were sitting at home in their own living rooms instead of out in public. Maybe you have a rule that says people lower their voices and whisper at movie theaters, if they must talk at all; other people may not conform to that same rule.

One of the most prolific nonverbal communication researchers is Judee Burgoon, who developed a fascinating model for how nonverbal communication functions.[13] **The expectancy violations model suggests that we develop expectations for appropriate nonverbal behavior in ourselves and others, based on our cultural backgrounds, personal experiences, and knowledge of those with whom we interact.** When those expectations (or rules) are violated, we experience heightened arousal (we become more interested or engaged in what's happening), and the nature of our interpersonal relationship with the other person becomes a critical factor as we attempt to interpret and respond to the situation. Because the expectancy violations model was first developed with regard to personal space, let's consider an example that deals with this form of nonverbal communication.

One *Seinfeld* episode depicted a person nicknamed the "close talker," because he got too close for most people's comfort when he talked to them. Most people within a given culture adhere to a widely agreed-on rule or expectation as to appropriate conversational distances. But there are those people who don't seem to catch the cultural clue—those who get too close to our face in casual conversation. Burgoon's model says that we register such a nonverbal violation and react in order to adjust to the circumstances. If the violating person is what Burgoon terms a "rewarding" communicator, meaning that the person has high credibility, status, and attractiveness (physically or in personality), we may view the behavior as less of a rule violation and simply adjust our expectations. We may even reciprocate the behavior. However, if the violator is not a rewarding communicator, we will use reactive nonverbal behaviors in an effort to compensate for or correct the situation. So if an attractive, credible, and high-status person stands too close to you while talking, you may adapt to the situation and not think negatively of the person. If the person has less attractiveness, credibility, and status, you may back away from the person or move to the side so as to increase the conversational distance, break eye contact, and so forth.

Our tendency in a rules violation situation is to attempt to adapt or correct the violation by nonverbal means before resorting to verbal communication. You're more likely to back away from a "close talker" than to say to her or him, "Please back up; you're violating my personal space." We all violate nonverbal rules from time to time; it is at those moments when we become acutely aware that rules or expectations of appropriateness have a powerful influence on nonverbal communication.

The Ambiguous Nature of Nonverbal Communication

Most words are given meaning by people within a culture who speak the same language. But the exact meaning of a nonverbal message is known only to the person displaying it; the person may not intend for the behavior to have any meaning at all. Some people have difficulty expressing their emotions nonverbally. They may have frozen facial expressions or monotone voices. They may be teasing you, but their deadpan expressions lead you to believe that their negative comments are heartfelt. Often it's a challenge to draw meaningful conclusions about other people's behavior, even if we know them quite well. One strategy that helps us interpret others' nonverbal cues is called **perception checking, the skill of asking other observers or the person being observed whether your interpretation of his or her nonverbal behavior is accurate**. Observe in detail the nonverbal cues, make your own interpretation, and then do one of two things (or both): (1) Ask the people you're observing how they feel or what's going on and (2) run your interpretation by another observer, to get a second opinion or more input before you draw a conclusion. Remember our earlier warning about not assuming that your interpretation is necessarily the right one; perception checking can enhance the likelihood of your interpretation's being more accurate.

The Continuous Nature of Nonverbal Communication

Words are discrete entities; they have a beginning and an end. You can point to the first word in this sentence and underline the last one. Our nonverbal behaviors are not as easily dissected. Like the sweep of a second hand on a watch, nonverbal behaviors are continuous. Because gestures, facial expressions, and eye contact can flow from one situation to the next with seamless ease, interpreting nonverbal cues is challenging.

The Nonlinguistic Nature of Nonverbal Communication

Even though some writers in the 1960s and 70s tried to make readers think otherwise, there is no "language of the body." Julius Fast, author of the 1970 book *Body Language*, believed that nonverbal communication was a language with pattern and grammar, just like verbal communication.[14] He suggested that if you were savvy and observant enough, you could quickly and easily interpret certain nonverbal behaviors to mean certain things—in any case, at any time. For example, Fast contended that if a woman sat cross-legged and pumped her foot up and down while talking to a man, that was a clear-cut sign of her romantic interest in him. If someone didn't make eye contact, she or he was automatically dishonest and untrustworthy. If people crossed their arms in front of them, that indicated hostility.

The problem with this approach is that it didn't take into account the complexities of individual, contextual, and cultural differences. Pumping the foot might be an indication of nervousness, not attraction. Some people are shy; others come from a culture in which making direct eye contact is considered rude. It's important to remember that nonverbal communication doesn't conform to the patterns of a language.

The Multichanneled Nature of Nonverbal Communication

Have you ever tried to watch two or more TV programs at once? Some television sets let you see as many as eight programs simultaneously so that you can keep up with three ball games, two soap operas, the latest news, and your favorite sitcom. Like programs on a multichannel TV, nonverbal cues register on our senses from a variety of sources simultaneously. Just as you can really pay close attention to only one program at a time on your multichannel television, you actually attend to only one nonverbal cue at a time, although you can switch your attention very rapidly. Before you try to interpret the meaning of a single nonverbal behavior, look for clusters of corroborating nonverbal cues, in conjunction with verbal behavior, to get the most complete picture possible.

RECAP

The Nature of Nonverbal Communication

- *Nonverbal communication is culture bound.*   Nonverbal behaviors vary widely across cultural and co-cultural groups. Interpret nonverbal cues within a cultural context.
- *Nonverbal communication is rule governed.*   We develop rules or expectations for appropriate nonverbal behavior in ourselves and others.
- *Nonverbal communication is ambiguous.*   Nonverbal behavior is difficult to interpret accurately because the meanings for different actions vary from person to person.
- *Nonverbal communication is continuous.*   Unlike the stop-start nature of verbal communication, nonverbal messages flow from one situation to the next.
- *Nonverbal communication is nonlinguistic.*   Nonverbal communication does not have the regularities of vocabulary, grammar, and pattern that language has.
- *Nonverbal communication is multichanneled.*   Nonverbal cues register on our senses from a variety of sources simultaneously, but we can actually attend to only one nonverbal cue at a time.

Codes of Nonverbal Communication

Because human nonverbal behavior is so diverse and vast, the need arises for classifications. Many individuals have long been fascinated with nonverbal communication, but those who have made perhaps the greatest contributions to our understanding are Paul Ekman and Wallace Friesen, sometimes referred to as the "great classifiers" of nonverbal behavior.[15] The primary categories or codes of nonverbal information researchers have studied include appearance; body movement, gestures, and posture; eye contact; facial expressions; touch; vocalics; and use of the physical environment, space, and territory. Although we concentrate on these codes as they are exhibited in mainstream Western culture, recognize that these behaviors are evidenced differently in other cultures. We introduce and explain each code, then provide a few research findings to illustrate how we can apply knowledge of nonverbal communication to further our understanding of human behavior.

Appearance

Many cultures around the world place a high value on appearance—body size and shape, skin color and texture, hairstyle, and clothing. We realize that we're writing from an American perspective, but it seems as though Americans place an undue emphasis on looks. For example, our views of and preferences for government leaders, especially presidents, are affected by their height.[16] College students give higher evaluation scores to professors whom they deem physically attractive.[17] We put such pressure on ourselves and others to be physically attractive that our self-esteem may decline when we realize we cannot match up with some perceived "ideal."[18] Americans elevate onto a pedestal persons who are perceived to be highly physically attractive, whether or not they actually deserve this kind of accolade. We also attach all sorts of desirable qualities to highly attractive people. Research shows that we tend to think physically attractive people are more credible, happy, popular, socially skilled, prosperous, employable, persuasive, honest, poised, strong, kind, outgoing, and sexually warm.[19]

Clothing functions primarily to keep us warm and within society's bounds of decency. Another important function is to convey a sense of one's culture. **Clothing such as baseball caps, baggy pants, and distinctive T-shirts, as well as other appearance aspects, (jewelry, tattoos, piercings, makeup, cologne, eyeglasses, and so on), termed artifacts,** are displays of culture. This is particularly detectable when you travel abroad or entertain foreign visitors in your home country. The brightly colored gowns and matching headpieces worn by some African women, the beautiful saris (draped dresses) many Indian women wear, and veils over the faces of Muslim women are but a few examples of how clothing reveals one's culture.

Although we don't believe that "clothes make the man," clothing and artifacts do affect how we feel about ourselves and how we are perceived by others.[20] Studies have attempted to identify a "power" look. Advertisers are constantly giving us prescriptions for ways to be attractive and stylish, but the fact is that there is no formula for dressing for success.[21] Styles and expectations about appearances change. We have only to look at the clothing norms of the 1950s, 60s, or 70s to note how they are different from those of today. Other interesting applications of what we know about appearance include the

When your clothing functions as an artifact rather than simply a way to cover your body, it conveys some sense of your culture.

development of "casual Friday" in the corporate world, the connection between black uniforms and aggression in sports, and the growing trend in public schools to require school uniforms.[22]

Body Movement, Gestures, and Posture

Have you ever traveled in a country where you couldn't speak the language? Or have you tried to have a conversation locally with a person who didn't speak English or who was deaf and didn't read lips? What do you do in these situations? Chances are, you risk looking extremely foolish by using overexaggerated gestures or slowly and deliberately shouting words the listener cannot understand. These responses are nonverbal attempts to compensate for a lack of verbal understanding. Even when we do speak the same language as others, we often use gestures to help us make our point.

Kinesics is a general term for human movements, gestures, and posture. Technically, movements of the face and eyes are included in this category, but because one's face and eyes can produce such a wealth of information, we discuss them as separate codes. Researchers have long recognized that our kinesics provide valuable information to others. Have you ever seen someone and said "I just really like the way he carries himself"? We know that a person can't literally carry himself or herself, but what we refer to in this description is a person's posture, stance, and walk. Posture is greatly affected by self-esteem and emotional state, such that when you're feeling upbeat and good about yourself, you're likely to carry yourself more upright and possibly exhibit a "spring in your step." Conversely, if you're having a bad day, your posture might be more slumped over or stooped, because some days it's just hard to hold your head and shoulders up.

Gestures are also a subset of kinesics and, as we've said earlier in this chapter, they are culture bound, context bound, and rule governed. Nancy Armstrong and Melissa Wagner are the authors of a book entitled *Field Guide to Gestures*, in which they describe and interpret a wide variety of gestures, particularly as used in U.S. culture.[23] They organize gestures into such categories as Arrival and Departure, Approval and Disapproval, Mating, and Offensive and Profane. Among the gestures in the Arrival and Departure category are the Bow, the Blown Kiss, the Fist-Chest Pound, and the Live Long and Prosper gesture (which needs no interpretation for *Star Trek* fans).

Various scholars and researchers have proposed models for analyzing and coding kinesics, just as we do for spoken or written language.[24] In one of their most comprehensive contributions to nonverbal research, Ekman and Friesen classified movement and gestures according to their function. They identified five kinesic categories: emblems, illustrators, affect displays, regulators, and adaptors.[25]

Emblems **Nonverbal cues that have specific, widely understood meanings in a given culture and may actually substitute for a word or phrase are called emblems.** When you're busy typing a report that is due tomorrow and your roommate barges in to talk about weekend plans, you turn from your computer and hold up an open palm to indicate your desire for uninterrupted quiet. A librarian who wants people to stop talking in the stacks puts an index finger up to pursed lips. But remember that emblems emerge or are negotiated within cultures. Something as seemingly universal as a pointing gesture can be used in a culturally specific way to mean something different than you expect.

Illustrators **We frequently accompany a verbal message with nonverbal illustrators, or behaviors that either contradict, accent, or complement the message.**[26] Yawning while proclaiming that you're not tired is an example of a nonverbal illustrator that contradicts the verbal message. Slamming a book closed while announcing "I don't want to read this any more" is a nonverbal accent to a verbal message. Frequent complementary illustrators are used when one person gives another directions to a location. You probably even use them when you talk on the phone, although probably not as many as you use in face-to-face conversation.[27]

Affect Displays **Nonverbal cues that communicate emotion are called affect displays.** As early as 1872, when Charles Darwin systematically studied the expression of emotion in both humans and animals, scientists realized that nonverbal cues are the primary ways humans communicate emotion.[28] Facial expressions, posture, and gestures reveal our emotions.[29] Your face tends to express which *kind* of emotion you are feeling, while your body reveals the intensity or how *much* of the emotion you are feeling. If you're happy, for example, your face may telegraph your joy to others. The movement of your hands, the openness of your posture, and the speed with which you move tell others just how happy you are. Likewise, if you're depressed, your face reveals your sadness or dejection, unless you're very practiced at masking your emotions. Your slumped shoulders and lowered head indicate the intensity of your despair.

Regulators **Regulators are nonverbal behaviors that help control the interaction or flow of communication between people.** When we're eager to respond to a message, we're likely to make eye contact, raise our eye-

Ethics and Communication

Lie Detectors

We have good information now as to how most people behave when they are being untruthful. Unless we have ice in our veins, most of us register some kind of higher activation in our bodies when we attempt to deceive, such as increased heart rate and elevated skin temperature. Lie detector machines track just such physiological changes as indications of deception. Other instruments track patterns in the voice, such as vocal emphasis and rising intonation. Research has shown that most people's voices have a tendency to get higher in pitch when they try to deceive. What lie detector professionals look for is a change in a person's normal behavior, any change from the baseline that is typically taken at the beginning of a lie detector session. Do you think that modern lie detectors are sophisticated enough that the results of lie detector tests should be allowed as evidence in court trials? Is it unethical to "wire up" a suspect in order to track bodily and vocal changes that might indicate deception? Do you believe that someone can actually "beat" a lie detector?

brows, open our mouths, take in a breath, and lean forward slightly. When we do not want to be part of the conversation, we do the opposite: We tend to avert our eyes, close our mouths, cross our arms, and lean back in our seats or away from the verbal action.

Adaptors   As teachers, we find it interesting to watch a group of students take an exam. Students who are nervous about the exam or who have general test anxiety exhibit their nervousness in many different ways. They shift frequently in their seats, tap their pencils or pens on the desktop (often unconsciously), or run their hands through their hair over and over again. Then there's the thigh shaker. Some students can make their legs quiver up and down at a high speed, and they don't usually realize they're doing it. All of these behaviors are examples of **adaptors—nonverbal behaviors that help us to satisfy a personal need or adapt to the immediate situation**.

What are some of the more interesting applications of the research on kinesics? Consider flirting. Even if you're married or in some other form of committed relationship, you probably find it interesting to think about how people flirt or show attraction and interest in one another. Research has explored verbal and nonverbal indications of attraction.[30] One study found 52 gestures and nonverbal behaviors that women use to signal their interest in men. Among the top nonverbal flirting cues were smiling, surveying a crowded room with the eyes, and moving closer to the object of one's affection.[31] However, other studies have found that men tend to view flirting as more sexual than women do, and men often misinterpret women's friendly behaviors as signs of sexual attraction and interest.[32] One study found that the likelihood for this kind of misinterpretation greatly increased as alcohol consumption increased.[33]

Another body of research along these lines has examined **quasi-courtship behavior**, **those nonverbal actions we consciously and**

unconsciously exhibit when we are attracted to someone.[34] The first stage of quasi-courtship behavior is *courtship readiness*. When we are attracted to someone, we may alter our normal pattern of eye contact, suck in our stomach, tense our muscles, and stand up straight. The second stage includes *preening* behaviors, which include combing our hair, applying makeup, straightening our tie, pulling up our socks, and double-checking our appearance in the mirror. Research shows that women tend to preen more than men.[35] In stage three, we demonstrate *positional cues*, using our posture and body orientation to make sure we are seen and noticed by another person, as well as to position ourselves to prevent invasion by a third party. We intensify these cues in the fourth stage, termed *appeals to invitation*, using close proximity, exposed skin, open body positions, and direct eye contact to signal our availability and interest.

RECAP

Categories of Movements and Gestures

Category	Definition	Example
Emblems	Behaviors that have specific, generally understood meanings	A hitchhiker's raised thumb
Illustrators	Cues that accompany verbal messages and provide meaning	A speaker pounding on the podium to emphasize a point
Affect Displays	Expressions of emotion	Hugging to express love
Regulators	Cues that control and manage the flow of communication	Making eye contact when you wish to speak
Adaptors	Behaviors that help you adjust to your environment	Chewing your fingernails, indicating nervousness

Eye Contact

Do you agree that the eyes are the "windows to the soul"? What can people tell about you by looking into your eyes? Are you comfortable making eye contact with most people or only with people you know well? Eye contact is extremely important in U.S. culture, as well as in many other cultures around the world. Americans, in particular, make all kinds of judgments about others—particularly about their trustworthiness and sincerity—on the basis of whether they make or avoid eye contact. It's an interesting exercise to inventory your own eye behavior, thinking about when you're apt to look at someone and when you're apt to avert your gaze.

On the Web

Are you a "people watcher"? Most of us who study communication become more avid people watchers, particularly in the realm of nonverbal communication, because human beings are truly fascinating creatures. The human face is capable of producing an enormous number of expressions, most of which arise through a combination of movements of various areas of the face. The more aware you become of your own capacity for facial expression, the better able you will be to convey your emotions and thoughts to others. In addition, the more perceptive and sensitive a receiver and interpreter of others' facial expressions you become, the better a communicator you will become as you listen, respond, and adapt to other people.

To help you develop these skills, we direct your attention to a Web site entirely devoted to the study of the human face:

www.face-and-emotion.com/dataface

On this site, scholars who study the face for its communicative abilities explore its permanent and transient features and offer research citations and information about people who study this topic.

You are most likely to look at a conversational partner when you are physically distant from her or him, are discussing impersonal topics, have nothing else to look at, are interested in your partner's reactions, are romantically interested in your partner, wish to dominate or influence your partner, come from a culture that emphasizes visual contact in interaction, are an extrovert, are listening rather than talking, or are female. You are less likely to look at your partner when you are physically close; are discussing intimate topics; have other objects, people, or backgrounds to look at; are not interested in your partner's reactions; are talking rather than listening; are not interested in or dislike your partner; come from a culture that does not value visual contact during interaction; are an introvert; are embarrassed, ashamed, sorrowful, sad, submissive, or trying to hide something; or are male.[36]

Research shows that eye contact plays a significant role in judgments of a public speaker's credibility.[37] In the first televised presidential debate, John F. Kennedy appeared comfortable and confident as he made eye contact with television cameras. It seemed as though he was making eye contact directly with the American public. In contrast, Richard Nixon darted his eyes nervously from side to side at times and generally made less eye contact with the camera and the viewing audience. This created a perception that Nixon was shifty, untrustworthy, and lacking credibility. American presentational speaking teachers emphasize eye contact as a key nonverbal element of speech delivery.

Studies on eye behavior continue to contribute to our understanding of deception and how people behave when they lie or mislead others.[38] Eye behaviors most often associated with deception include rapid blinking, diminished eye contact, and rapid eye movement. One fascinating study examined videotaped footage of the Senate Confirmation Hearings in which now–Supreme Court Justice Clarence Thomas and Anita Hill offered strikingly different accounts of events in their professional relationship, with Hill claiming that Thomas had sexually harassed her.[39] The researchers concluded, from evaluating a range of deception cues (including eye behavior), that Thomas exhibited a pattern of deception in his testimony to the Senate committee, while Hill did not.

Facial Expressions

Whether or not you like actor/comedian Jim Carrey, you've got to admit that the guy's face seems made of rubber. He seems to be able to display a broader range of emotions and reactions on his face than the average person, even if many of these facial contortions are more exaggerated than those the average person would use. Ekman and Friesen suggest that the human face is capable of producing 250,000 different facial expressions.[40] Jim Carrey can probably make all of them.

The face is the exhibit gallery for our emotional displays. Suppose you buy a new expensive gadget and show it to your romantic partner or a friend. Or as an interviewer reads your resumé you sit in silence across the desk. In both of these situations, you scan the other person's face, eagerly awaiting some reaction. To interpret someone's facial expressions accurately, you need to focus on what the other person may be thinking or feeling. It helps if you know the person well, can see her or his whole face, have plenty of time to observe, and understand the situation that prompted the reaction.[41]

How accurately do we interpret emotions expressed on the face? Researchers who have attempted to measure subjects' skill in identifying the emotional expressions of others have found it a tricky business.[42] According to Ekman and Friesen, the human face universally exhibits six primary emotions: happiness, sadness, surprise, fear, anger, and disgust or contempt. But these researchers note that, even though our faces provide a great deal of information about emotions, we quickly learn to control our facial expressions.[43] One fascinating study examined children's facial expressions when they received either wonderful, new toys or broken, disappointing toys.[44] When they received the disappointing toys, the children showed a flash of disappointment on their faces, but then very quickly they masked their disappointment and changed their facial expressions to reveal a more positive, socially appropriate reaction. Even very young children learn to control the way an emotion registers on their face. Another study found that abused children, sensitive to violence at home, are hypersensitive to anger in facial expressions. They are more likely to interpret sad or fearful facial expressions as angry.[45]

As adults, we come to realize that there are times when it is inappropriate and unwise to reveal our emotions fully, such as crying in front of superiors when we've been passed over for promotion or becoming visibly angry when a project doesn't come our way. But there are times when this learned masking of emotion—the development of a "poker face"—can endanger your relationships. Consider aloof, distant parents who can't separate themselves from

CONGRATULATIONS, ALICE. YOU'RE ONE OF MY TWO CANDIDATES FOR A PROMOTION TO MANAGEMENT.

THE OTHER CANDIDATE HAS NO QUALIFICATIONS EXCEPT FOR HIS MANAGER-SOUNDING VOICE.

AND HE DOESN'T MAKE THAT FACE.

their work to enjoy the company of their own children, or romantic partners who complain that they can't tell how their partners feel about them because emotional displays have been squelched. The best approach is a balance of control and spontaneity. You want to stay real and human, to be able to reveal to others what you feel, but there are times when doing so can be inappropriate or damaging.

Touch

Touch is the most powerful form of nonverbal communication; it is also the most misunderstood and carries the potential for the most problems if ill used. Consider some moments involving accidental touch. Standing elbow to elbow in an elevator or sitting next to a large individual in a crowded airplane, you may find yourself in physical contact with total strangers. As you stiffen your body and avert your eyes, a baffling sense of shame and discomfort floods over you. Why do we react this way to accidental touching? Normally, we touch to express intimacy. When intimacy is not our intended message, we instinctively react to modify the impression our touch has created.

Countless **studies on human touch, termed haptics in research,** have shown that intimate human contact is vital to our personal development and well-being.[46] Infants and children need physical contact to confirm that they are valued and loved. Advocates of breast-feeding argue that this form of intimate touching strengthens the bond between mother and child.[47]

Think about your role models and the lessons you learned about touch while growing up. If you grew up in a two-parent family, did your parents display affection in front of the children? If not, you may have grown up believing that affectionate touching should not be done in front of others. As an adult, you may be uncomfortable with public displays of affection. If you grew up with parents or family members who were affectionate with each other and their children, then, as an adult, **your touch ethic—what you consider appropriate touching—**is influenced by that experience. We don't mean to insinuate that a touch ethic that accepts public affection is somehow more psychologically healthy than one that relegates touching to private moments. But what if you date or partner with someone whose experiences while growing up led to a very different touch ethic than yours? You may be headed for some conflict, but ideally some compromise as well.

The amount of touch we need, initiate, tolerate, and receive depends on many factors. As we've indicated, the amount and kind of touching you receive in your family is the biggest influence. Your cultural background has a significant effect as well. Certain cultures are high-contact—meaning that touching is quite commonplace—such as some European and Middle Eastern cultures in which men kiss each other on the cheek as a greeting. Other cultures are low-contact, like some Asian cultures in which demonstrations of affection are rare and considered inappropriate.[48]

Research on haptics has explored such topics as the role of touch in receiving sexual consent and how touch may be involved in behavior deemed sexually harassing.[49] Other research continues to focus on gender differences and touch. For years, studies showed that women touched members of both sexes more often and received more touches than men, leading to the conclusion that touch was more appropriate behavior for females than for males. Recent studies suggest that sex differences in the frequency of touch have diminished, but men and women still tend to differ in the meanings they assign to touch.[50]

The Voice

"We have nothing to fear but fear itself."
"Ask not what your country can do for you—ask what you can do for your country."
"I have a dream . . . I have a dream today."
"I am not a crook."
"Mr. Gorbachev, tear down this wall."

If you read these statements and recognize them as having been made by American leaders, you are likely to read them using the same pauses and changes in pitch, volume, and emphasis as did the famous person. John F. Kennedy greatly emphasized the word *not*, as in "Ask NOT what your country. . . ." Martin Luther King Jr. used rising pitch and increased volume as he uttered the word *dream* over and over again in his speech. These leaders learned to use the tremendous capacity and versatility of the voice to create memorable moments, even if those moments occurred in unpleasant circumstances.

Like your face, your voice is a major vehicle for communicating your thoughts and emotions. **The pitch, rate, and volume at which you speak and your use of silence—elements termed paralanguage or vocalics—** all provide important clues. Imagine that your spouse, romantic partner, or best friend modeled a new outfit, asking you what you think. If you really hated the person's new outfit, would you say enthusiastically, "That looks GREAT!"— which could either be an untruth designed to prevent hurt feelings or an expression of sarcasm? Or would you say, "That looks nice" in a halfhearted way? Or would you go into some long, careful explanation of why you thought the outfit was okay, but just not your favorite thing? Your ability to convey these different reactions is accomplished by the human voice.

The voice reveals our thoughts, emotions, and the nature of our relationships with others, but it also provides information about our self-confidence and knowledge, and influences how we are perceived by others.[51] Most of us would conclude, as has research, that a speaker who mumbles, speaks very slowly and softly, continually mispronounces words, and uses "uh" and "um" is less credible and persuasive than one who speaks clearly, rapidly, fluently, and with appropriate volume.[52]

In addition to providing information about thoughts, emotions, self-confidence, and knowledge, vocal cues serve a regulatory function in conversation, signaling when we want to talk and when we don't.[53] When we're finished talking, we tend to lower the volume and pitch of our final words. When we want to talk, we may start by interjecting sounds such as "I . . . I . . . I . . ." or "Ah . . . Um . . ." to interrupt the speaker and grab the verbal ball. We also may use more cues like "Sure," "I understand," "Uh-huh," or "Okay" to signal that we understand another's message and now we want to talk or end the conversation. These **vocal cues that signal when we want to talk and when we don't, termed back-channel cues,** are particularly useful in telephone conversations when no other nonverbal cues can help signal that we would like to get off the phone.

Sometimes it's not what we say or even how we say it that communicates our feelings. Pausing and being silent communicate volumes.[55] You may be at a loss for words or need time to think about what you want to contribute to a conversation, so pausing or being silent may be better than fumbling about for the right way to express yourself. When someone tells a lie, he or she may need a few moments to think up what to say. Nonverbal researchers have studied **response latency, or the amount of time it takes someone to formulate a response to a statement or question in conversation,** to better understand vocal cues that may indicate deception.[56] You may be silent because you want to distance yourself from those around you or indicate that you don't want to engage in conversation. Silence can be a sign of respect, but it can also be an indication of anger (as when you give someone "the silent treatment") or discomfort (as in "an awkward silence"). At other times you may feel so comfortable with someone that words aren't necessary; psychologist Sidney Baker calls these moments "positive silence."[57]

Diversity and Communication

Cultural Meanings of Silence

*I*n his essay "Cultural Uses and Interpretations of Silence," communication scholar Charles Braithwaite explores the functions of silence "beyond one's own speech community" in an effort to discover cross-cultural generalizations.[54] He examined descriptions of the use of silence within many cultural groups and found two common themes:

1. When people don't know each other very well or circumstances between them create a degree of uncertainty, silence may increase, but it is seen as expected and appropriate. This tendency emerged within cultural groups as diverse as some Indian tribes, Japanese Americans in Hawaii, Japanese, and Americans in rural Appalachia.

2. Recognized status differences are associated with silence. When a difference in power level or status is detected, lower status persons are expected to be silent and monitor when it is appropriate to engage in conversation. This tendency was particularly distinct within parent–child relationships, evidenced in such diverse peoples as the Anang of Southwestern Nigeria, the Wolof of Senegal, some urban African American women, the residents of the LaHave Islands (off the coast of Nova Scotia), some Indian tribes, and some American blue-collar workers.

Physical Environment, Space, and Territory

Close your eyes and picture your bedroom as it is right now—whether it's a dorm room that you share with someone, the room you've lived in for many years in your parents' house, or a bedroom shared with a spouse or partner. Try to get a clear, detailed mental image of how that room looks right now. Then think about this: If one of your professors were to walk into your bedroom right now, what would she or he think about you? What impressions about you would he or she form, given the physical setup of that room? Does the room reveal your need for privacy? Are there hints as to who owns the space, meaning do you have any territorial clues in the room? Is the closet door in that room open or closed?

These questions all have to do with your interaction with the physical environment and the space around you. You may be unused to looking at the environment as a form of nonverbal communication, but the mini-world you create for yourself reveals a good deal about you. Also, your preferred amount of space, the level of ownership you attach to that space, and your behavior as you delineate and protect that space are fascinating nonverbal elements that researchers continue to study.

The Physical Environment   What's so great about a corner office with wall-to-wall windows? It's one of many indications in U.S. culture of high status. In a working world increasingly structured into cubicles, an employee's desk location serves as a symbol of importance.[58] As one scholar put it, "People cannot be understood outside of their environmental context."[59] In Chapter 1.3 we discussed several principles governing the use of verbal language, one being that language is context bound—people derive the meaning of words in context. Likewise, nonverbal actions are only meaningfully interpreted when context is taken into account.[60] The environment is important to the study of nonverbal behavior in two ways: (1) The choices you make about the environment in which you live and operate reveal a good deal about who you are, and (2) your nonverbal behavior is altered by the various environments in which you communicate.

First, the physical environments in which we function can be seen as extensions of our personalities. You may not be able to manipulate all elements of your environment, like the physical limitations of room size, but to whatever extent you are allowed, you will make your "signature" on your physical environs. Humans like to structure and adorn the settings in which they work, study, and reside to make them unique and personal. Rarely will you find an office, even a cubicle, that contains absolutely no personal artifacts.

Second, your behavior and perceptions are altered because of the physical environments in which you find yourself.[61] Your body may be more rigid, gestures more restrained, clothing more formal, and speech limited and whispered when you're in a church. (Obviously, this depends on the church.) In contrast, at a concert by a favorite musician, you move freely, wear comfortable clothing, and scream and applaud wildly.

The knowledge that humans react according to their interface with a physical environment has been put to some interesting uses. For example, designers of fast-food restaurants often use vibrant colors, uncomfortable seating, and brightly lit eating areas to discourage patrons from lingering. The point in the fast-food business is high volume, which means high turnover. So these environments are constructed so that you will be attracted to come in, eat, and leave quickly to make room for another customer. In contrast, some restaurants offer an intimate and warm environment, one that makes customers want to linger and enjoy a long meal (with a pricey tab).[62]

Space   Imagine that you are sitting alone at a long, rectangular table in your campus library. As you sit dutifully with your head in a textbook, you are startled when a complete stranger sits directly across from you at the table. Since there are several empty chairs at the other end of the table, you may feel uncomfortable that this unknown individual has invaded *your* area.

Every culture has well-established ways of regulating spatial relations. Normally, we don't think much about the rules or norms we follow regarding space until those rules are violated. Violations can be alarming, possibly even threatening. How physically close we are willing to get to others relates to how well we know them, to considerations of power and status, and to our cultural background.

One of the pioneers in helping us understand personal space was Edward T. Hall. In his study of **proxemics, the distances that people allow**

FIGURE 1.4.2
Edward T. Hall's Four Zones of Space

From *The Hidden Dimension* by Edward T. Hall, copyright 1966, 1982 by Edward T. Hall. Used by permission of Doubleday, a division of Random House, Inc.

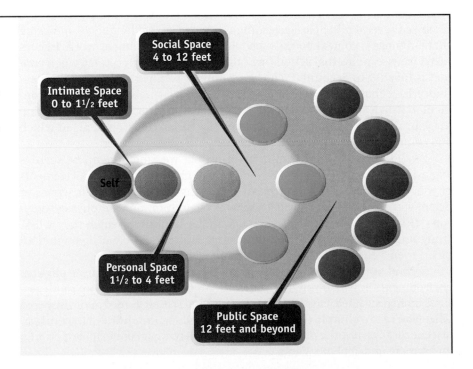

between themselves and objects or other people, Hall identified four spatial zones that we unconsciously define for ourselves, as shown in Figure 1.4.2.[63] Two people who are between 0 and 1½ feet apart are occupying an *intimate space,* in which the most personal communication occurs. This space is open only to those with whom we are well acquainted, unless we're forced to stand in an elevator or some other crowded space.

The second zone, ranging from 1½ to 4 feet from another person, is called *personal space.* Most of our conversations with family and friends occur in this zone. If someone we don't know well enters this space on purpose, we may feel uncomfortable. Zone three, *social space,* ranges from 4 to 12 feet from another person. Most formal group interactions, as well as many of our professional relationships, take place in this zone. *Public space,* the fourth zone, begins at 12 feet from another person. Interpersonal communication does not usually occur in this zone; many presentational speakers position themselves at least 12 feet away from their audiences.

The specific space that you and others choose depends on several variables, most specifically your cultural background. But the more you like people, the closer you will stand to them. Higher-status and larger persons are afforded more space than lower-status and smaller persons.[64] We also tend to stand closer to others in a large room than we do in a small room. In general, women tend to stand closer to others than men do.[65]

RECAP

Edward T. Hall's Classification of Spatial Zones

Category	Definition	Distance between Individuals
Zone One	Intimate Space	0–1½ feet
Zone Two	Personal Space	1½–4 feet
Zone Three	Social Space	4–12 feet
Zone Four	Public Space	12 feet and beyond

Territory **The study of how people use space and objects to communicate occupancy or ownership of space is termed territoriality.**[66] You assumed ownership of that table in the library and the right to determine who sat with you. You may have reacted negatively not only because your sense of personal space was invaded, but also because the intrusive stranger broke a cultural rule governing territoriality.

You announce your ownership of space with **territorial markers— things and actions that signify an area has been claimed.** When you arrive at class, for example, you may put your book bag on a chair while you get up and sharpen a pencil or run across the hall to the "facilities." That book bag signifies temporary ownership of your seat. If you returned to find that someone had moved your stuff and was sitting in your seat, you would probably become indignant. The most common form of territorial marker is a lock. We lock our doors and windows, cars, offices, briefcases, luggage, televisions (using V-chips), and computers so as to keep out intruders.

We also use markers to indicate where our space stops and someone else's starts. "Good fences make good neighbors," wrote the poet Robert Frost. When someone sits too close, we may try to erect a physical barrier, such as a stack of books or a napkin holder, or we might use our body as a shield by turning away. If we can't erect a physical barrier, we may erect a symbolic barrier to convey ownership, through the use of such things as partitions, objects, lighting, or elevation.[67] If an intruder doesn't get the hint that "this land is our land," we may ultimately resort to words to announce that the space is occupied.

One interesting line of research explores verbal and nonverbal behaviors in the workplace that contribute to a "hostile climate" of sexual harassment.[68] In relation to the environment, space, and territoriality, a workplace might contain art (posters, flyers on bulletin boards) that depicts sexual images, a boss might come too far into the personal space of an employee, or a coworker might commit a territorial breach by "snooping" in someone's office for evidence of personal relationships, like photos.

RECAP

Codes of Nonverbal Communication

Appearance	Influences perceptions of credibility and attractiveness
Body Movement, Gestures, and Posture	Communicate information, status, warmth, credibility, interest in others, attitudes, and liking
Eye Contact	Conveys trustworthiness, sincerity, honesty, and interest
Facial Expressions	Reveal thoughts and express emotions and attitudes
Touch	Communicates intimacy, affection, and rejection
Voice	Communicates emotion and clarifies the meaning of messages through pitch, rate, and volume
Environment	Communicates information about the person who functions in that environment; provides context that alters behavior
Space	Provides information about status, power, and intimacy
Territory	Provides cues as to use, ownership, and occupancy of space

QUICK
REVIEW

How to Interpret Nonverbal Cues More Accurately

How do we make sense out of all of the nonverbal cues we receive from others? Time and patience improve your receiving ability. If you earnestly want to accurately interpret and sensitively respond to someone's nonverbal communication, you must be willing to spend time and effort to develop this skill. You have already learned a good deal about nonverbal communication from reading this chapter, studying this topic in class, and living as many years as you have lived. But enhancing your interpretive skills requires, first, an awareness of the importance of nonverbal elements in the communication process. Many people make interpretive mistakes because they overemphasize the words people say. Verbal communication is important, but remember that the greater portion of someone's total message is conveyed nonverbally. A second requirement is the willingness and emotional maturity to make your own behavior secondary to that of someone else. In other words, if you're so wrapped up in yourself that you can only think about and deal with how *you're* feeling, what *you're* thinking, and what *you* want at a given moment, you can't possibly hope to take in others' nonverbal cues, interpret them accurately, and respond appropriately. As we discussed in Chapter 1.2, an awareness of oneself as a communicator expands with each interaction with another person.

It's also important to remember to take into account the cultural backgrounds of those with whom you communicate. Be careful not to automatically attach your own cultural frame of reference when you decipher nonverbal cues. As we've stated, the context within which nonverbal cues are communicated plays an important role. It's wise to be aware of your surroundings and other situational factors when interpreting the meaning of nonverbal actions. Be prepared to fail. We all struggle to make sense out of others' actions; no one has this skill down pat. Use your interpretive failures to learn lessons you can apply to the next encounter.

Beyond these suggestions, we recommend that you keep in mind a three-part framework developed by Albert Mehrabian to help you improve your nonverbal interpretive skills. Mehrabian found that we synthesize and interpret nonverbal cues along three primary dimensions: immediacy, arousal, and dominance.[69]

What nonverbal cues tell you that these three men are friends who genuinely like each other? Are there any cues that contradict that impression?

Immediacy

Why do we like some people and dislike others? Sometimes we can't put a finger on the precise reason. Mehrabian contends that **immediacy—nonverbal behavior, such as eye contact, foward lean, touch, and open body orientation, that communicates liking and engenders feelings of pleasure—**is a probable explanation. The principle underlying immediacy is simple: We like and respond positively to people who tend to display immediacy cues and avoid or respond negatively to those who don't. Among the immediacy cues that show liking and interest are the following:[70]

- Proximity: close, forward lean
- Body orientation: face-to-face or side-by-side position
- Eye contact: eye contact and mutual eye contact
- Facial expression: smiling
- Gestures: head nods, movement
- Posture: open and relaxed, arms oriented toward others
- Touch: culture- and context-appropriate touch
- Voice: higher pitch, upward pitch

So how do you apply this information to help you improve your nonverbal receiving skills? Let's say that you go to a party and become attracted to someone there. You're introduced to the person and engage in a get-to-know-you kind of conversation. Your best bet is to attend to the person's nonverbal cues to determine if the person likes you. Although you can't know for sure that someone's nonverbal behavior translates into liking, immediacy cues can provide some information. Watch for a direct body orientation, as opposed to turning away from you and orienting toward the rest of the room. Watch for eye contact, smiling and other pleasant facial expressions, a rising intonation in the voice, and a forward lean toward you, rather than a backward lean, which can signal disinterest.

Arousal

Arousal is a feeling of interest and excitement communicated by such nonverbal cues as vocal expression, facial expressions, and gestures. When the term *arousal* is used in nonverbal research, it doesn't necessarily mean sexual arousal. According to nonverbal scholar Peter Andersen, the term relates to "the degree to which a person is stimulated or activated."[71] Arousal prepares the body for action, with such physiological indications as increased heart rate, blood pressure, and brain temperature. Arousal, in this sense, can occur when you drive fast or experience athletic exhilaration. Externally, the face, voice, and movement are primary indicators of arousal. If you detect arousal cues in someone, such as increased eye contact, closer conversational distances, increased touch, animated vocalics, more direct body orientation, and more smiling and active facial expressions, you can conclude with some degree of certainty that the other person is responsive to and interested in you or what you have to say. If the person acts passive or bored, as evidenced by few (or no) arousal cues, you can safely conclude that he or she is uninterested.

The next time you're at a party, become a people-watcher for a moment. Check out which people look interested in the persons they're talking to and which ones look bored or like they'd rather be somewhere else, anywhere else. You can tell how people feel about each other—not with absolute accuracy, but with a high degree of certainty—just by looking for things like body orientation (whether they are facing each other directly or not), synchronized movement (meaning that when one shifts in position, the other shifts, as in a rhythmic response), smiling, laughter, and other arousal cues.[72]

Dominance

The third dimension of Mehrabian's framework communicates the balance of power in a relationship. **Dominance is a feeling of power, status, and control communicated by such nonverbal cues as relaxed posture, greater personal space, and protected personal space.** Dominance cues communicate status, position, and importance. When interacting with a person of lower status, a higher-status person tends to have a relaxed body posture, less direct body orientation to the lower-status person, a downward head tilt, and less smiling, head nodding, and facial animation.[73] When you talk to professors, they may lean back in the chair, put their feet on the desk, and fold their hands behind their head during the conversation. But unless your professors are colleagues or friends, you will maintain a relatively formal posture during your interaction in their offices.

The use of space is another dominance cue. High-status individuals usually have more space around them; they have bigger offices and more "barriers" (human and nonhuman) protecting them. A receptionist in an office is usually easily accessible, but to reach the CEO of the company you probably have to navigate through several corridors and past several secretaries and administrative assistants who are "guarding" the door.

Other power cues are communicated by clothing, furniture, and locations. You may wear jeans and a T-shirt to class; the president of the university probably wears a business suit. You study at a table in the library; the college dean has a large private desk. Your dorm may be surrounded by other dorms; the president's residence may be a large house surrounded by a lush, landscaped garden in a prestigious neighborhood. You struggle to find a parking place within a half-a-globe of your classroom buildings; high-ranking campus administrators usually have reserved parking spots (sometimes with their names on them).

When you attempt to interpret someone's nonverbal communication, realize that there is a good deal of room for error. Humans are complex, and they don't always send clear signals. But the more you learn about nonverbal communication, the more you become aware of your own communication and the communication of others, the greater your chances of accurately perceiving and interpreting someone's nonverbal message.

RECAP

Dimensions for Interpreting Nonverbal Behavior

Dimension	Definition	Nonverbal Cues
Immediacy	Cues that communicate liking and pleasure	Eye contact, touch, forward lean, direct body orientation, physical closeness, smiling
Arousal	Cues that communicate active interest and emotional involvement	Eye contact, varied vocal cues, touch, animated facial expressions, direct body orientation, movement, physical closeness
Dominance	Cues that communicate status	Larger and protected space, eye contact, initiated touch, relaxed posture, status symbols

QUICK REVIEW

PRINCIPLES FOR A LIFETIME: Enhancing Your Skills

Nonverbal

Principle Three: Effectively use and interpret nonverbal messages.

- Realize the importance of physical appearance and attractiveness in U.S. culture.
- Use culturally appropriate body movement, including posture and gestures, to convey messages.
- Work on making appropriate eye contact with others, given that eye contact is the key nonverbal behavior linked with credibility and trustworthiness.
- Become more aware of your facial expressions and the facial expressions of others, since this nonverbal channel is a primary one for conveying emotions.
- Use touch appropriately, given the cultural context within which you communicate.
- Become more aware of the potential you have for vocal expression and of how others use their vocal capacities to communicate emotions and ideas.
- Survey yourself to become aware of your own rules regarding space and territoriality, so that you may better understand and enact proxemic nonverbal behaviors in your interactions with others.
- Recognize that body movement, eye contact, facial expressions, touch, vocal behaviors, and use of space and territory can all communicate liking, interest, and dominance.

SUMMARY

Successful communicators effectively use and interpret nonverbal messages. Nonverbal communication is central to our ability to function competently in relationships, because we convey our feelings and attitudes and detect the emotional states of others primarily through nonverbal channels. In most cases when verbal and nonverbal messages contradict, we should believe the nonverbal because it tends to carry the truer meaning of the message. (Again, leave open the option that you may be wrong.) Nonverbal cues are important not only in the early stages of relationships, but also as we maintain and deepen and sometimes terminate those relationships. Nonverbal messages function with verbal messages, in that they can substitute for, complement, contradict, repeat, regulate, and accent our words.

Accurately interpreting nonverbal cues is a challenge because of the nature of nonverbal communication. First, nonverbal communication is culture bound, meaning that we must account for the cultural context within which behavior occurs before making an interpretation of that behavior. Second, nonverbal communication is rule governed, in that we form rules or expectations as to appropriate behavior. Third, nonverbal communication is ambiguous; the exact meanings of nonverbal messages are truly known only to the person displaying them. Fourth, nonverbal communication is continuous; it flows in a steady stream without a definite starting and stopping point. Fifth, unlike verbal communication, nonverbal communication is not a language with a set pattern and rules of usage. Its nonlinguistic nature makes for more complicated interpretation. Finally, nonverbal communication is multichanneled, meaning that cues register on our senses from a variety of sources simultaneously.

Nonverbal cues have been categorized into separate codes. Personal appearance is a powerful communicator, especially in U.S. culture, where people make all sorts of judgments based on someone's looks. Kinesics, which include body movement, posture, and gestures, communicate both content and relational information when we use them as emblems, illustrators, affect displays, regulators, and adaptors. Eye contact is an important code for conveying liking and regulating interaction. Facial expressions and vocal cues provide a wealth of information about our thoughts, emotions, and attitudes. Touch is the most powerful nonverbal cue; it communicates the level of intimacy in a relationship, as well as liking and status. Finally, the way we react to and manipulate environments, as well as our use of space and territory, communicates a variety of messages related to power and status.

It is a challenge to assess our own nonverbal communication and to read and interpret others' nonverbal messages, but a general framework of three dimensions developed by Mehrabian can assist us in the process. Immediacy cues provide information about liking; arousal cues tip others off as to our interest and level of engagement with them; and position, power, and status are often communicated through dominance cues. Humans are complex, so the interpretation of nonverbal cues is never simple. However, the more we learn about this form of behavior and become aware of our own and others' nonverbal communication, the more sensitively and effectively we will interact with others.

DISCUSSION AND REVIEW

1. Why focus on nonverbal messages? Why are nonverbal cues important?

2. Identify six elements that describe the nature of nonverbal communication. Then think about people who seem to be "clueless," meaning that they do not readily attend to or accurately interpret others' nonverbal behavior. What makes some people savvy readers of nonverbal cues while others remain clueless?

3. How is nonverbal communication affected by culture? Provide examples of ways that a lack of cultural understanding can cause problems.

4. Why do you think that people in the United States place such importance on appearance and attractiveness? Is this emphasis helpful, harmful, or a bit of both?

5. Explain how eye contact, facial expressions, and various vocal cues reveal our thoughts, emotions, and attitudes.

6. What is your "touch ethic"? What experiences growing up contributed to your standards for appropriate and inappropriate touch?

7. How you manipulate the environments within your control and use space and territory reveal a great deal about you. What would someone learn about you if she or he observed you in your home environment? What kind of interpretations would the observer make from watching you use and control space?

8. Explain Mehrabian's three-part system for interpreting nonverbal cues more accurately.

PUTTING PRINCIPLES INTO PRACTICE

1. Take a field trip with some classmates to a fast-food restaurant. Assign some members the task of observing nonverbal cues in the environment, noting colors, furniture and other fixtures, lighting, and temperature. Others should take note of the employees' appearance, paying special attention to clothing and signs of status and individuality. Finally, have some members watch for gestures that act as emblems, such as signals indicating how many burgers a customer wants. Coworkers often develop nonverbal "shorthand" that facilitates efficient communication; note any such behaviors.

2. Generate examples of how nonverbal behaviors in the categories of kinesics, facial expressions, eye contact, and proxemics are affected by deception. For example, how is eye contact affected? Do the best liars avert their gaze, or do they learn to lie while looking right in someone's eyes?

3. Generate examples of body movements that reveal the following six emotions. Then generate alternative meanings for the movement. For example, we've said that crossed arms might reveal either anger or that someone is closed off or not open to discussing something. We've provided an example.

Emotion	Body Movements	Alternative Meanings
Embarrassment	Covering the face with one's hands	Could also indicate deception
Happiness		
Anger		
Surprise		
Fear		
Disgust		
Sadness		

4. We've explored the nonverbal codes of space and territory, and you should now have a better understanding of the range of human reactions to space invasions. Read each of these situations, decide if a proxemic or territorial violation has occurred, and then generate two tactics you would use in response to each situation. Try not to think of things a person *might* do, but of what you actually would do in the situation.

   a. You are at a bar or club, sitting alone, possibly waiting to order or for a friend to join you. A stranger sits down beside you and starts a conversation.

   b. You are a business executive. You enter your office after lunch and find your secretary sitting at your desk.

   c. You are taking racquetball lessons and it is your turn on the glass (observable) court. A group of people gather to watch your lesson.

   d. You are interviewing for a part-time job. The interviewer moves from behind the desk toward you and touches you on the knee.

   e. You want to wear your favorite sweater but can't find it. You discover it wadded up in the bottom of the laundry hamper, reeking of smoke, and you realize that your roommate or a family member wore it without your permission.

5. Conduct a series of role plays that illustrate Mehrabian's system for interpreting nonverbal behavior. Have someone in your group play the role of a student who is sitting in a small auditorium waiting for a lecture to begin. Another person should play the role of a student who arrives for the lecture at the last moment. This second student must shuffle past already seated students to the last empty seat in the auditorium, next to the first student. Role play the nonverbal cues the two students would use with each other that would communicate immediacy, arousal, and dominance, and explain how such cues might be interpreted.

Chapter 1.4   *Practice Test*

MULTIPLE CHOICE.   Choose the *best* answer to each of the following questions.

1. Giovanni just moved into his new dorm room at school. He spends the day hanging pictures and putting his favorite souvenirs and objects on his bookshelves. Giovanni is relying on what code of nonverbal communication to personalize his new room?

   a. proxemics

   b. territorial markers

   c. haptics

   d. artifacts

2. If someone of high credibility, status, and attractiveness uses unexpected nonverbal behavior, we tend to

   a. adjust our expectation of what is appropriate behavior.

   b. change our behavior to meet the expectation.

   c. think less of the person.

   d. attempt to correct the rule violation.

3. Trinity is really angry with her girlfriend, so she refuses to sit near her while they are watching television. To communicate her anger, Trinity is relying on

   a. eye contact.

   b. haptics.

   c. vocalics.

   d. proxemics.

4. During a shopping trip, Logan bought T-shirts with his favorite sports team's emblem on the front, a new pair of jeans, and a pair of sunglasses. Logan was shopping for

   a. adaptors.

   b. territorial markers.

   c. emblems.

   d. artifacts.

5. According to Albert Mehrabian, the most significant nonverbal source of emotional information is

   a. vocal cues.

   b. the face.

   c. personal space.

   d. emblems.

6. Which of the following is *not* a vocalic behavior?

   a. raising your volume while speaking

   b. lowering your pitch at the end of a sentence

   c. refusing to make eye contact

   d. placing stress on a certain word in a sentence

7. Current research into the way men and women use touch during interactions reveals that

   a. men tend to touch others more than women do.

   b. women tend to touch others more than men do.

   c. men and women tend to interpret touching behavior in similar ways.

   d. men and women tend to interpret touching behavior in different ways.

8. A person of high dominance, when talking to a person lower in status, will

   a. have a more formal posture.

   b. face the other person directly.

   c. smile less.

   d. have more facial animation.

9. When your nonverbal message contradicts your verbal message, other people will tend to

   a. believe the nonverbal message.

   b. believe the verbal message.

   c. believe both the nonverbal and the verbal message.

   d. believe neither the nonverbal nor the verbal message.

10. The study of body motion and nonverbal behaviors related to body position is called
    a. kinesics.
    b. emblems.
    c. haptics.
    d. territoriality.

11. While listening to Alexis explain how her day went, Joshua repeatedly used the phrase "uh-huh." Joshua's behavior is an example of
    a. response latencies.
    b. affect displays.
    c. back-channel cues.
    d. haptics.

12. Maria's family watched closely as she opened the letter from her university's medical school. Her face broke out into a big smile before she even read the letter to her family, and they all knew she had been accepted. In this example, Maria's smile is a type of
    a. adaptor.
    b. regulator.
    c. illustrator.
    d. affect display.

13. According to Edward T. Hall, your personal space zone, where most of your conversations with others take place, is anywhere from
    a. 0 to $1\frac{1}{2}$ feet.
    b. $1\frac{1}{2}$ to 4 feet.
    c. 4 to 12 feet.
    d. 12 feet on.

14. Immediacy, in nonverbal communication, refers to
    a. the physical distance between two people in conversation.
    b. the recency of the topic under discussion.
    c. how fast two people are talking to each other.
    d. feelings of liking between two people in conversation.

15. Gerald was telling Linda all about the movie he saw last night. Linda was running late for a meeting and kept looking at her watch, hoping that Gerald would see she needed to bring the conversation to a close. In this example, looking at the watch would be a(n)
    a. adaptor.
    b. regulator.
    c. emblem.
    d. illustrator.

16. Stan is talking to Jenny about his trip to the mountains. Jenny wants Stan to keep talking, so she responds by smiling, nodding her head, and saying "uh-huh." The function of nonverbal communication, as it relates to verbal communication, best illustrated in this situation is
    a. accenting.
    b. contradicting.
    c. regulating.
    d. repeating.

17. Kaylee and Maddison are working out at the campus recreation center. Maddison sees a couple of good-looking men walking their way. Kaylee and Maddison stand up straight, suck in their stomachs, tense up their muscles, and try not to look at the guys as they approach. Kaylee and Maddison's behaviors illustrate
    a. affect displays.
    b. positional cues.
    c. back-channeling cues.
    d. courtship readiness.

18. You're flirting with someone at the park and notice that the person appears to be interested in you and excited to be talking to you. The reason you know this is that the person's vocalics are animated, posture is very straight and leaning forward, eye contact is increased, and facial expressions are very active. Which dimension for interpreting nonverbal communication are you using?
    a. arousal
    b. immediacy
    c. dominance
    d. emotion

19. Using the phrase "body language" to refer to nonverbal communication is misleading because language rules, including grammar and syntax, do not usually regulate nonverbal cues. Which challenges inherent in interpreting nonverbal communication does this explanation reflect?

    a. the multi-channeled nature of nonverbal communication

    b. the nonlinguistic nature of nonverbal communication

    c. the ambiguous nature of nonverbal communication

    d. the continuous nature of nonverbal communication

20. In order to improve the accuracy with which you interpret nonverbal cues, you should

    a. find a book that catalogs the various nonverbal behaviors and explains their meanings.

    b. pay more attention to verbal cues since we often rely too much on nonverbal cues.

    c. use your cultural frame of reference to interpret the cues.

    d. be prepared to fail and use those failings to increase your accuracy next time.

TRUE/FALSE.   Indicate whether the following statements are *true* or *false*.

1. T or F   Culture influences the interpretation of nonverbal behaviors.

2. T or F   The touch ethic you have as an adult was most likely formed during your early family experiences.

3. T or F   Verbal messages are usually more believable than nonverbal messages.

4. T or F   Nonverbal messages can substitute for our verbal messages.

5. T or F   Nonverbal messages are not important in the initiation of relationships.

6. T or F   A shocking 93% of a message's total meaning is communicated nonverbally.

7. T or F   Nonverbal messages are fairly consistent from culture to culture, with a few exceptions.

8. T or F   The pictures you hang on your wall, the mementos on your shelves, and other things you use to decorate your space are referred to as artifacts.

9. T or F   Arousal cues communicate liking, pleasure, and attraction.

10. T or F   Using a high upward pitch, nodding your head, leaning forward, and maintaining an open posture are all examples of cues that communicate immediacy.

FILL IN THE BLANK.   Complete the following statements.

1. Creating meaning for someone with behavior other than written or spoken language is _____ communication.

2. The vocal nonverbal cues that accompany your speech are called _____.

3. _____ _____ is clarifying your interpretation of someone's nonverbal behavior with another person.

4. Any element of appearance (e.g., clothing, jewelry, makeup) is considered a(n) _____.

5. The study of how near or far we stand from someone while speaking to him or her is called _____.

6. The nonverbal cues you give someone you are attracted to are called _____ behaviors.

7. _____ is the study of human touch.

8. The guidelines you use to define appropriate and inappropriate touch make up your touch _____.

9. _____ _____ is the amount of time it takes someone to answer a question.

10. The study of human movement, gesture, and posture is called _____.

CHAPTER 15

Listening and Responding

CHAPTER OBJECTIVES

After studying this chapter, you should be able to

1. Explain the principle of listening and responding thoughtfully to others.

2. Identify the elements of the listening process.

3. Identify and describe barriers that keep people from listening well.

4. Describe four listening styles.

5. Identify and use strategies that can improve your listening skills.

6. Identify and use appropriate responding skills.

© Phoebe Beasley, Training Ground #2, collage. Omni-Photo Communications, Inc.

Listening, not imitation, may be the sincerest form of flattery.

Joyce Brothers

It shows up on every list of what effective communicators do: They listen. You spend more time listening to others than doing almost anything else you do. Americans spend up to 90% of a typical day communicating with people, and they spend 45% of that communication time listening to others.[1] As shown in Figure 1.5.1, if you're typical, you spend the *least* amount of your communication time writing, yet you receive more training in writing than in any other communication skill. One of the hallmarks of an effective leader is being a good listener.[2] To be sensitive is to be aware of others and to be concerned about others. Increasing your skill in listening to others is one of the most productive ways to increase your communication sensitivity.

Most people have not had formal training in listening or responding. In this chapter we focus on the principle of increasing your sensitivity to others by listening. Becoming sensitive to others includes more than just understanding and interpreting their words, thoughts, and ideas—sensitivity also involves understanding the emotions underlying the words and unspoken messages of others.

As shown in our now familiar model of the communication principles for a lifetime in Figure 1.5.2, effective communicators do more than absorb a message; they provide an appropriate response to the speaker. We'll address both listening and responding to others in this chapter.

Listening and responding to others is an important principle of communication, not only because you spend more time listening than in any other communication activity, but also because of its importance in establishing and maintaining relationships with others. In interpersonal communication situations, the essence of being a good conversationalist is being a good listener.

FIGURE 1.5.1
What You Do with Your Communication Time

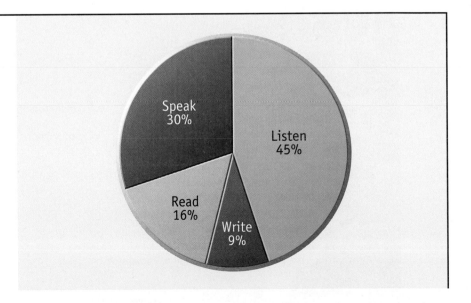

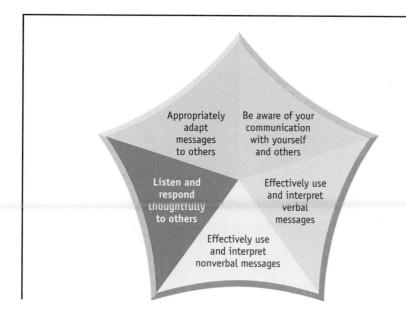

**FIGURE 1.5.2
Communication
Principles for a
Lifetime**

Appropriately adapt messages to others

Be aware of your communication with yourself and others

Listen and respond thoughtfully to others

Effectively use and interpret verbal messages

Effectively use and interpret nonverbal messages

Rather than focusing only on what to say, a person skilled in the art of conversation listens and picks up on interests and themes of others.

Being a good listener is also an essential skill when communicating with others in small groups. Whether you are the appointed or emerging leader of a group or a group or team member, your ability to listen and connect to others will affect your value to other group members. Group members afflicted with bafflegab, those who verbally dominate group meetings, are not usually held in high esteem. Groups need people who can listen and connect conversational threads that often become tangled or dropped in group dialogue.

It may be less clear how being an effective listener can enhance a presentational speaker's ability to connect with an audience. Effective speakers, however, are those who can relate to their listeners; good speakers know how to establish a relationship with the audience by listening to audience members one on one before a talk or lecture. Good speakers are also audience-centered. They consider the needs of their listeners first. They understand what will hold listeners' attention.

How We Listen

Do you know someone who is interpersonally inert? Interpersonally inert people are those who just don't "get it." You can drop hints that it's late and you'd rather they head home instead of playing another hand of cards, but they don't

"I'm sorry, dear. I wasn't listening. Could you repeat what you've said since we've been married?"

pick up on your verbal and nonverbal cues. They may *hear* you, but they certainly aren't listening; they are not making sense out of your symbols. **Hearing is the physiological process of decoding sounds.** You hear when the sound waves reach your eardrum and cause the middle ear bones (the hammer, anvil, and stirrup) to vibrate. Eventually, the sound vibrations are translated into electrical impulses that reach your brain. In order to listen to something, you must first select that sound from competing sounds. **Listening,** defined succinctly, **is the process we use to make sense out of what we hear; it is a complex process of receiving, constructing meaning from, and responding to verbal and nonverbal messages.**[3] Listening involves five activities: (1) selecting, (2) attending, (3) understanding, (4) remembering, and—to confirm that listening has occurred—(5) responding.

Understanding these five elements in the listening process can help you diagnose where you sometimes get off track when listening. Having a framework to better describe the listening process can help you figure out how to get back on track and increase your listening skill.

Selecting

To select a sound is to focus on one sound as you sort through the various noises competing for your attention. Even now, as you are reading this book, there are probably countless sounds within earshot. Stop reading for a moment. What sounds surround you? Do you hear music? Is a TV on? Maybe there is the tick of a clock, a whir of a computer, or a whoosh of a furnace or an air conditioner. To listen—to be sensitive to another person—you must first select the sound or nonverbal behavior that symbolizes meaning.

The interpersonally inert person does not pick up on the clues because he or she is oblivious to the information.

Attending

After selecting a sound, you attend to it. **To attend is to maintain a sustained focus on a particular message.** When you change channels on your TV, you first select the channel and then you attend to the program you've selected. Attention can be brief. You may attend to the program or commercial for a moment and then move on or return to other thoughts or other sounds. Just as you tune in to TV programs that reflect your taste in information while you channel surf, you attend to messages of others that satisfy your needs or whims.

What holds our attention? Typically, conflict, new ideas, humor, or something we can see or that is concrete holds our attention more easily than abstract ideas that don't relate to us. If you're having difficulty sustaining attention to a message, it may be because what you're listening to does not immediately seem to relate to you. So you may need to work a bit harder, either to concentrate on the message or to consider ways in which the message is relevant or important to you.

Understanding

It's been estimated that we hear over one billion words each year, but we understand a mere fraction of that number. **To understand is to assign meaning to messages**—to interpret a message by making sense out of what you hear.

Once we select the sounds we want to listen to, we need to attend to, or focus on, those sounds, for communication to take place.

You can select and attend to sounds and nonverbal cues but not interpret what you see and hear. Hearing and seeing are physiological processes. Understanding occurs when you relate what you hear and see to your experiences or knowledge. Perhaps you have heard the Montessori school philosophy: I hear, I forget; I see, I remember; I experience, I understand. It is when we can relate our experiences to what we hear and see that we achieve understanding.

Remembering

Remembering information is considered part of the listening process because it's the primary way we determine whether a message was understood. **To remember is to recall information that has been communicated.** Some scholars speculate that you store every detail you have ever heard or witnessed; your mind operates like a computer's hard drive, recording each life experience. But you cannot retrieve or remember all of the bits of information. Sometimes, even though you were present, you have no recollection of what occurred in a particular situation. You can't consciously remember everything; your eye is not a camera; your ear is not a microphone; your mind is not a hard drive.

The first communication principle we presented in this book is to become self-aware. When we are not self-aware of our actions, thoughts, or what we are perceiving—when we are mindless—our ability to remember what occurs plummets. We increase our ability to remember what we hear by being not only physically present, but mentally present.

Our brains have both short-term and long-term memory storage. Short-term memory is where you store almost all the information you hear. You look up a phone number in the telephone book, mumble the number to yourself, then dial the number, only to discover that the line is busy. Three minutes later you have to look up the number again because it did not get stored in your long-term memory. Our short-term storage area is limited. Just as airports have only a relatively few short-term parking spaces, but lots of spaces for long-term parking, our brains can accommodate a few things of fleeting significance, but not vast amounts of information. Most of us forget hundreds of bits of insignificant information that pass though our cortical centers each day.

You tend to remember what is important to you, or something you try to remember or have practiced to remember (like the information in this book for your next communication test). You tend to remember dramatic information (such as where you were when you heard about the September 11, 2001, terrorist attacks) or vital information (such as your phone number or your mother's birthday).

Responding

As you learned in Chapter 1.1, communication is a transactive process—not a one-way, linear one. Communication involves responding to others as well as simply articulating messages. **You respond to people to confirm your understanding of their message.** Your lack of response may signal that you didn't understand the message. Your predominant response is often unspoken; direct eye contact and head nods let your partner know you're tuned in. An unmoving, glassy-eyed, frozen stupor may tell your communication partner that you are physically present, yet mentally a thousand miles away. As you'll discover in the next section, most people have a certain style of listening and responding to others.

Listening Styles

Although we've described the typical elements in the listening process, not everyone has the same style or approach to listening. **Your listening style is your preferred way of making sense out of the messages you hear and see.** Some people, for example, prefer to listen to brief chunks of information. Others seem more interested in focusing on the feelings and emotions expressed.

What's your listening style? Knowing your style can help you adapt and adjust your listening style when listening to others. Listening researchers Kitty Watson, Larry Barker, and James Weaver have found that people tend to listen using one or more of four listening styles: people-oriented, action-oriented, content-oriented, or time-oriented.[4]

People-Oriented Listeners

People-oriented listeners tend to prefer listening to people's emotions and feelings. They are quite interested in hearing personal information from others. A people-oriented listener searches for common interests and seeks to empathize with the feelings of others—she or he connects emotionally with the sentiments and passions others express. There is some evidence that people-oriented listeners are less apprehensive when communicating with others in small groups and interpersonal situations.[5]

Action-Oriented Listeners

Action-oriented listeners like information to be well organized, brief, and free of errors. While listening to a rambling story, the action-oriented listener may think, "Get to the point" or "Why should I be listening to this?" Action-oriented listeners want to do something with the information they hear; they want it to serve a purpose or function, and they become impatient with information that doesn't seem to have a "bottom line."

Action-oriented listeners tend to be a bit more skeptical and critical than are people-oriented listeners of the information they hear. Researchers call this skepticism **second-guessing—questioning the assumptions underlying a message.**[6] It's called second-guessing because the listeners don't always assume that what they hear is accurate or relevant; they make a second guess about the accuracy of the information they are listening to. Accuracy of information is especially important to action-oriented listeners, because if they are going to use the information in some way, the information should be valid.

Content-Oriented Listeners

Content-oriented listeners **are more comfortable listening to detailed, complex information** than are those with other listening styles. A content-oriented listener is likely to perceive a message presented without details, facts, and evidence as less important and valuable than a message that includes rich content. Content-oriented listeners, like action-oriented listeners, are likely to second-guess the information they hear.[7] They are constantly checking messages for accuracy, because accurate, detailed information is highly valued. Content-oriented listeners are skilled at listening to arguments and debates, because they prefer to listen to messages with a significant amount of information in them. They are less patient listening to stories, anecdotes, and illustrations that don't convey much information.

Time-Oriented Listeners

Time-oriented listeners **like brief, short messages.** They have much to do and don't want to waste time listening to lengthy talk. A time-oriented listener is likely to look at his or her watch and be conscious of how long it is taking to listen to a message. Whereas the content-oriented listener prefers to hear messages that are chock-full of details, the time-oriented listener would rather hear brief "sound bites" that quickly get to the point. Time-oriented listeners are typically busy people; they gauge their success by what they can accomplish, so they are more sensitive to the length of messages than are people with the other three listening styles.

Adapting to Your Listening Style

How does knowing that most people have preferences for particular types of messages benefit you? There are at least two reasons to give some thought to your listening style and the listening styles of others. First, knowing your own listening style can help you adapt and adjust your listening style to fit the listening situation. If, for example, you are a people-oriented listener and you're listening to a message that has little information about people but lots of technical details, be aware that you will have to work harder to stay tuned in to the message.

Diversity *and* Communication

East and West Listening Styles

North American communication very often centers on the sender. Much emphasis is placed on how senders can formulate better messages, improve credibility, polish their delivery skills, and so forth. In contrast, the emphasis in East Asia has always been on listening and interpretation.

Communication researcher C. Y. Cheng has identified *infinite interpretation* as one of the main principles of Chinese communication.[8] The principle presumes that the emphasis is on the receiver and listening rather than on the sender and speaking. According to T. S. Lebra, "anticipatory communication" is common in Japan: Instead of the speaker's having to tell or ask explicitly for what he or she wants, others guess and accommodate his or her needs, sparing him or her the embarrassment that could arise if the verbally expressed request could not be met.[9] In such cases, the burden of communication falls not on the message sender but on the message receiver. A person who "hears one and understands ten" is regarded as an intelligent communicator. To catch on quickly and to adjust oneself to another's position before his or her position is clearly revealed is regarded as an important communication skill.

One thing that puzzles some foreign students from East Asia is why they are constantly being asked what they want when they are visiting in American homes. In their own countries, the host or hostess is supposed to know what is needed and to act accordingly. The difference, of course, is that in North America it is important to provide individual freedom of choice; in East Asia, it is important to practice anticipatory communication and to accommodate the speaker.

With the emphasis on indirect communication, the receiver's sensitivity and ability to capture the under-the-surface meaning and to understand implicit meaning becomes critical. In North America an effort has been made to improve the effectiveness of message senders through such formal training as debate and public speaking, whereas in East Asia, the effort has been on improving the receiver's sensitivity. One achieves the greatest sensitivity when one empties the mind of preconceptions and makes it as clear as a mirror.[10]

Recently, there has been increased interest in listening in the United States. Both communication scholars and practitioners recognize that listening is necessary not only for the instrumental aspect of communication (comprehension) but, more importantly, for the affective aspect (granting the speaker the satisfaction of being listened to).[11]

Second, it can be useful to be aware of the listening style of others so that you can communicate messages that others are more likely to listen to. If you know your spouse is a content-oriented listener, then communicate a message that is rich in information; that's what your spouse prefers. Tell the content-oriented listener, "Here are three things I have to tell you." Then say those three things. The content preview tells your content-oriented listener that you are about to convey three pieces of information. Content-oriented listeners like to know that the message about to be presented contains useful information. Of course, it may be difficult to determine someone's listening style, especially someone you don't know very well. But it is both easier and worth the time to consider the listening styles of people you *do* know well (such as your family members, your coworkers, your boss). Knowing your listening style and the listening styles of others can help you adapt your communication to enhance the accuracy of your own listening and the appropriateness of information you communicate to others.

RECAP

Listening Styles

People-Oriented Listening Style	Listeners prefer to attend to feelings and emotions and to search for common areas of interest when listening to others.
Action-Oriented Listening Style	Listeners prefer to focus on information that is organized and accurate; they want a speaker to get to the point and emphasize what action should be taken with the information they hear.
Content-Oriented Listening Style	Listeners prefer to hear complex, detailed information and expect facts and evidence to support key ideas.
Time-Oriented Listening Style	Listeners prefer brief messages that are presented efficiently without digressions; they are busy listeners and don't want to spend a lot of time listening to long-winded stories and anecdotes.

Listening Barriers

Although we spend almost half of our communication time listening, some say we don't use that time well. One day after hearing something, most people remember only about half of what was said. It gets worse. Two days later, our memory drops by another 50%. The result: Two days after hearing a lecture or speech, most of us remember about 25% of what we hear.

Our listening deteriorates not only when we listen to speeches or lectures, but when we interact interpersonally. Even in the most intimate relationships (or perhaps we should say *especially* in the most intimate relationships), we tune out what others are saying. One study reported that we sometimes pay more attention to strangers than to our close friends or spouses. Married couples tend to interrupt each other more often than nonmarried couples and are usually less polite to each other than are strangers involved in a simple decision-making task.[12]

What keeps us from listening well? The most critical elements are (1) self barriers—personal habits that work against listening well; (2) information-processing barriers—the way we mentally manage information; and (3) context barriers—the surroundings in which we listen.

Self Barriers

"We have met the enemy and he is us" is the oft-quoted line from the comic strip *Pogo*. Evidence suggests we are our own worst enemy when it comes to listening to others—whether it's listening to enjoy, learn, evaluate, or empathize. We mentally comment on the words we hear and the behavior we observe. Our internal thoughts are like a play-by-play sports commentator describing the action of a sports contest. If our internal narration is focused on the message, then it may be useful. But we often attend to our own internal dialogues and diatribes instead of to others' messages; when we do that, our listening effectiveness plummets.

Self-Focus   That personal play-by-play commentary we may be carrying on in our minds is typically about us. "How long will I have to be here for this lecture?" "Wonder what's for dinner tonight?" "I've got to get that report finished." "She's still talking—will we be out of here in ten minutes?" "Do I have a school meeting tonight or is that tomorrow night?" Focusing on an internal message often keeps us from selecting and attending to the other person's message. If there is a competition between listening to what someone else may be droning on about and focusing on our own needs and agenda, our personal needs often come out on top. Another symptom of self-focus is our tendency to think about what we are going to say while we look like we are listening to someone else.

What can you do to regain your listening focus if you are focused on yourself rather than on the other person's message? Consider these suggestions:

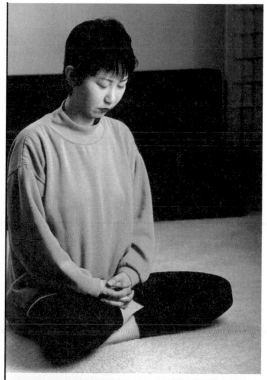

Some people find that yoga or quiet meditation can help them control the internal barriers that prevent them from listening effectively.

- *Become aware of the problem.*   Become consciously competent. Note when you find yourself drifting off, thinking about your agenda, rather than concentrating on the speaker.
- *Concentrate.*   After you become aware that your internal self-focused messages are distracting you from listening well, intensify your efforts to stay on task. If your internal "announcer" is telling you that the message is boring, useless, or stupid, make sure you don't mindlessly tune the message

out. Yes, some messages are boring, useless, and stupid. But the habit of quickly dismissing ideas and messages without making an effort to stay focused on them will keep you from being nominated for the Listening Hall of Fame.

- *Be active rather than passive.*   The key to concentration is finding ways to be involved in the communication process. Taking notes when appropriate and providing nonverbal and even sometimes verbal feedback to the speaker can help keep your focus on the speaker rather than on you. If you don't understand something the speaker says, ask for clarification. Don't just sit there and "take it"; if you find your concentration waning, you'll more than likely "leave it."

Emotional Noise   Emotions are powerful. Your current body posture, facial expression, and even your blood pressure are affected by your emotional state. What we see and hear affects our emotions. **Emotional noise occurs when our emotional arousal interferes with communication effectiveness.** Certain words or phrases can arouse emotions very quickly; and, of course, the same word may arouse different emotions in different people. You respond emotionally because of your cultural background, religious convictions, or political philosophy. Words that reflect negatively on your nationality, ethnic origin, or religion can trigger strong emotional reactions. Cursing and obscene language may also reduce your listening efficiency. If you grew up in a home in which R-rated language was never used, then four-letter words may distract you.

Sometimes it's not just a word but a concept or idea that causes an emotional eruption. Third-trimester abortion and public school prayer, for example, are topics guaranteed to get radio talk show hosts' audiences involved in lively discussion. Whether you love him or hate him, TV talk show host Jerry Springer is a master at pushing emotional hot buttons for his talk show guests; and when emotions become heated, thoughtful listening is rare.

The emotional state of the speaker may also affect your ability to understand and evaluate what you hear. One researcher found that if you are listening to someone who is emotionally distraught, you will be more likely to focus on his or her emotions than on the content of the message.[13] Another researcher advises that when you are communicating with someone who is emotionally excited, you should remain calm and focused, and try simply to communicate your interest in the other person.[14]

What are other strategies to keep your emotions from getting the best of you? It's not always easy, but research suggests there are ways of not letting your emotions run amok. Daniel Goleman offers several research-based strategies in his best-selling book *Emotional Intelligence.*[15] To be emotionally intelligent is to have the ability to understand, manage, and appropriately express emotions. For example, one simple yet powerful strategy to manage emotions when you find you may be ready to lose it is to take a deep breath. Yes, just breathe. Taking a deep, slow breath is a way of regaining control by calming down. It helps make you more conscious of your anger or frustration, much like the old technique of counting to ten.

Another strategy for managing emotions is to use the power of self-talk, a concept we discussed in Chapter 1.2. Tell yourself you won't get angry. Early detection of the emotions bubbling inside you can help you assess and then manage emotions before your nonrational, emotional impulses take control. As we've noted, it's not inappropriate to experience emotions; however, unchecked, intense emotional outbursts do not enhance your ability to listen, comprehend, or empathize with others.

Sometimes, of course, expressing your frustration is appropriate. We're not suggesting you go through life unrealistically serene or that you avoid experiencing emotions. Only the dead never become emotional. We do suggest that you become aware of the effect that emotions have on your listening ability; this is a constructive first step to avoid being ruled by unchecked emotions. The principle of self-awareness gives you *choice* and control. Your listening challenge is to avoid emotional sidetracks and keep your attention focused on the message. When emotionally charged words or actions kick your internal dialogue into high gear, make an effort to quiet it down and steer back to the subject at hand. Becoming con-

Mother Teresa understood the value of open listening without prejudging a person.

sciously aware of our emotions and then talking to ourselves about our feelings is a way of not letting emotions get out of hand.

Criticism   We usually associate the word "criticism" with negative judgments and attitudes. Although critiquing a message can provide positive as well as negative insights, most of us don't like to be criticized. Mother Teresa once said, "If you judge people, you have no time to love them."[16] Being inappropriately critical of the speaker may distract us from focusing on the message.

A person's appearance and speech characteristics can affect your ability to listen to him or her. Many a speaker's droning monotone, lack of eye contact, and distracting mannerisms have contributed to his or her ideas not being well received—even if the ideas are potentially life-changing for the listener. The goal of a sensitive communicator is to be conscious of when the delivery or other distracting features of the message or messenger are interfering with the ability simply to listen. In fact, now that you are studying principles of communication, you may find that this problem looms even larger, because you now pay more attention to nonverbal cues.

It would be unrealistic to suggest that you refrain from criticizing speakers and their messages. It is realistic, however, to monitor your internal critiques of speakers to make sure you are aware of your biases. Good listeners say to themselves, "While this speaker may be distracting, I am simply not going to let appearance or mannerisms keep my attention from the message." For example, Stephen Hawking is a prize-winning physicist at Cambridge University in England; because of a disability, he is able to speak only with the aid of computer-synthesized sounds. He is unquestionably brilliant. If you let his speaking delivery overpower you, you'd miss his marvelous message. Avoid using your mental energy to criticize a speaker unnecessarily; the longer your mental critique, the less you'll remember.

Information-Processing Barriers

In addition to self barriers that contribute to our loss of focus on messages, sometimes the way in which we use the information that comes to our eyes, minds, and hearts creates listening problems. The way in which we process the information we hear may keep us from being good listeners. Four information-processing listening barriers are (1) our information-processing rate, (2) information overload, (3) receiver apprehension, and (4) shifting attention.

Processing Rate   One of the barriers to listening that has long been documented is the difference between our ability to process information and the rate at which information comes to us. The barrier boils down to this: You can think faster than people speak. Most people speak 125 words per minute, give or take a few words. You have the tremendous ability, however, to process four to ten times that amount of information. Some people can listen to 600 to 800 words a minute and still make sense out of what the speaker is saying; another estimate puts the processing rate up to 1200 words per minute. Yet another estimate claims that we think not just in words but also in images and sounds: We can process 2000 bits of information a minute for short periods of time. This difference between average speaking rate and your capacity to make sense out of words as they register in your cortical centers can cause trouble. You have extra time on your hands to tune in to your own thoughts, rather than focus on the speaker.[17]

You can use your information-processing rate to your advantage if you use the extra time to summarize mentally what a speaker is saying. By periodically sprinkling in mental summaries during a conversation, you can dramatically increase your listening ability and make the speech-rate/thought-rate difference work to your advantage.

Information Overload   Information abounds. We are constantly bombarded with sights and sound bites, and experts suggest that the amount of information competing for our attention is going to increase in the future. Incoming messages and information on computers, fax machines, e-mail, mobile phones, beepers, and other devices can interrupt conversations and distract us from listening to others.

The amount of information coming at us on any given day also wears us out. The one word to describe many a poor listener is "weary." We spend 45% of our communication time listening, and the pace at which the information zips toward us exhausts us. The billion words that we hear contribute to our fatigue.

Again we recommend self-awareness. Be on the alert for drifting attention due to information overload. And when the encroaching information dulls your attentiveness, either take a break or consider conducting some *communication triage* (determining what's urgent and what's not urgent) so you can focus on the information that is most important.

Receiver Apprehension Just as some people are fearful of presenting a speech or speaking up during a meeting, research suggests that some people are fearful of receiving information. **Receiver apprehension is fear of misunderstanding or misinterpreting the messages spoken by others or of not being able to adjust psychologically to messages expressed by others.**[18] Some people may just be fearful of receiving new information and being able to understand it. Or it may just be a characteristic or pattern in the way some people respond psychologically to information; they may not be able to make sense out of some of what they hear, which causes them to be anxious or fearful of listening to others.[19] If you are fearful of receiving information, you'll remember less information.

What are the implications for you of research on receiver apprehension? If you know that you are fearful of listening to new information, you'll have to work harder to understand the information presented. Using a tape recorder to record a lecture may help you feel more comfortable and less anxious about trying to remember every point. Becoming actively involved in the listening experience by taking notes or mentally repeating information to yourself may also help.

Shifting Attention Can you multitask? Some people can easily do two things at once; some people can't. Emerging research evidence suggests that men are more likely to have difficulty attending to multiple messages: When they are focused on a message, they may have more difficulty than women in carrying on a conversation with another person.[20] Men have a tendency to lock on to a message, while women seem more adept at shifting between two or more simultaneous messages. When many men watch a TV program, they seem lost in thought—oblivious to other voices around them. Women, on the other hand, are more likely to be carrying on a conversation with one person and also focusing on a message they may hear nearby. No, this difference doesn't mean that women are more likely to eavesdrop intentionally but that some women have greater potential to listen to two things at once. What are the implications? It may be especially important for women to stop and focus on the messages of others, rather than on either internal or external competing messages. And men may need to be sensitive to others who may want to speak to them, rather than becoming fixated on their own internal message or on a single external message such as a program on TV.

Context Barriers

In addition to listening barriers related to how you process information and self barriers that occur when your emotions and thoughts crowd out a message, listening barriers can arise from the communication context or situation. Specifically, time, place, and outside noise can distract you from selecting, attending, understanding, remembering, and responding to messages.

Barriers of Time and Place   The time of day can interfere with your listening acuity. Are you a morning person or an evening person? Morning people are cheerfully and chirpily at their mental peak before lunch. Evening people prefer to tackle major projects after dark; they are at their worst when they arise in the morning. Use the skill development activity on pages 171–172 to plot your ideal work time, the period when you are at your sharpest.

If you know you are sharper in the morning, whenever possible schedule your key listening times then. Evening listeners should try to shift heavy listening to the evening hours. Of course, that's not always practical. If you can't change the time of listening, you can increase your awareness of when you will need to listen with greater concentration.

Don't assume that because you are ready to talk, the other person is ready to listen. If your message is particularly sensitive or important, you may want to ask your listening partner, "Is this a good time to talk?" Even if he or she says yes, look for eye contact and a responsive facial expression to make sure the positive response is genuine.

External Noise   Noise is anything that interferes with your ability to listen to a message. Although you may think of noise as sounds you hear, noise can be processed by any one of your five senses. Not just sounds but also sights, the feeling of something touching you, even tastes and smells can affect your listening ability.

For most people, the best listening environment is one that offers as few distractions as possible. When you want to talk to someone, pick a quiet time and place, especially if you know you will be discussing a potentially difficult topic. Even in your own home it may be a challenge to find a quiet time to talk. (Perhaps a good title for a text on listening would be *How to Turn Off the TV.*) Listening takes all the powers of concentration that you can muster. A good listener seeks a quiet time and place to maximize listening comprehension. Closing a door or window, turning off the television or radio, asking noisy or offensive talkers to converse more quietly or not at all, or simply moving to a less distracting location are steps that you may need to pursue to manage the noise barrier.

Managing Listening Barriers

Listening Barriers	What to Do
Self Barriers	
Self-Focus	• Consciously become aware of the self-focus and shift attention back to the speaker.
	• Concentrate: Find ways of becoming actively involved in the message, such as taking meaningful notes.
Emotional Noise	• Act calm to remain calm.
	• Use self-talk to stay focused on the message.
	• Take a deep breath if you start to lose control.
Criticism	• Focus on the message, not on the messenger.
Information-Processing Barriers	
Processing Rate	• Use the difference between speech rate and thought rate to mentally summarize the message.
Information Overload	• Realize when you or your partner is tired or distracted and not ready to listen.
	• Assess what is urgent and not urgent when listening.
Receiver Apprehension	• If you are fearful or anxious about listening to new information, use a backup strategy, such as recording the message, to help you capture the message; review the tape later. Seek ways to become actively involved when listening, such as taking notes or making mental summaries of the information you hear.
Shifting Attention	• Men are more likely to focus on a single message; women typically shift their attention between two or more messages. If you know you have a tendency to shift your attention between two or more messages, make a conscious effort to remain focused on one message.
Context Barriers	
Barriers of Time and Place	• Note when your best and worst listening times are; if possible, reschedule difficult listening situations for when you're at your best.
External Noise	• When possible, modify the listening environment by eliminating distracting noise.

QUICK REVIEW

Improving Your Listening Skills

At the heart of listening is developing sensitivity to focus on the messages of others, rather than on your own thoughts. Improving your listening involves a set of skills that can increase your sensitivity toward others. At first glance, these skills may look deceptively simple—as simple as the advice given to most elementary students about crossing the street: (1) stop, (2) look, and (3) listen. Despite the appearance of simplicity, these three words summarize decades of research and insight about how to avoid being labeled "interpersonally inert." Let's consider each separately.

Stop: Turn Off Competing Messages

Many of the barriers to improved listening skill arise because we focus on ourselves and our own messages, rather than focusing on others. As we noted earlier, while you are "listening," you may also be "talking" to yourself—providing a commentary about the messages you hear. These internal, self-generated messages may distract you from giving your undivided attention to what others are saying. In order to select and attend to the messages of others, we need to become aware of our internal dialogue and stop our own running commentary about issues and ideas that are self-focused rather than other-focused.[21]

Members of some religious groups take a vow to be silent and not talk to anyone else. They literally stop talking. Does this make them better listeners? One research team wanted to know the impact of various types of listening training, including being silent for 12 hours.[22] One group heard a lecture about how to be better listeners—probably like the lectures you hear in this course; the group then took a test to assess their overall listening skill. A second group promised not to talk to anyone for 12 hours—they literally gave others the "silent treatment." Then they, too, took a test to assess their listening ability. A third group both heard a listening lecture and were silent for 12 hours; then they also took the listening test. The results: There were no differences in listening test scores among the groups—all groups seemed to listen equally well, according to test results. But those who kept silent for 12 hours reported that

they thought they were more attentive to others, more conscious of being good listeners. The researchers concluded that literally stopping to listen more and talk less can increase awareness of listening. Their research supports the maxim that "You have been given two ears and one mouth so that you will listen more and talk less." We're not suggesting you not talk, but we are suggesting that you increase your awareness of how your own thoughts and talk can interfere with being a good listener. Stop—do your best to eliminate mental messages that keep you from listening well.

Try a process called social decentering. **Social decentering involves stepping away from your own thoughts and attempting to experience the thoughts of another.** In essence, you're asking yourself this question: "If I were the other person, what would I be thinking?" To decenter is to practice the first principle of communication—self-awareness—and to be aware that your own thoughts are keeping you from focusing on another's message, so that you can focus on the other person.[23] Of course, we are not suggesting that your own ideas and internal dialogue should be forever repressed; that would be both impossible and inappropriate. We are suggesting, however, that to connect to another, you must place the focus on the other person rather than on yourself.

To decenter requires conscious effort. Decentering is a mental or cognitive process that involves trying to guess what someone else may be thinking. In attempting to decenter, consider this question, "If I were my communication partner, what would I be thinking?"

The essence of the "stop" step is to become aware (our first communication principle for a lifetime that we discussed in Chapter 1.2) of whether you are listening or not listening to someone. You are either on task (focusing on another) or off task (oblivious to another and focusing on your own thoughts and emotions). The goal, of course, is to be on task—listening to others.

Look: Listen with Your Eyes

As you learned in Chapter 1.4, nonverbal messages are powerful, especially in communicating feelings, attitudes, and emotions.[24] A person's facial expression, presence or lack of eye contact, posture, and use of gestures speak volumes, even when no word is uttered. When words are spoken, the added meaning that comes from vocal cues provides yet another dimension to the emotion and nature of the relationship.

Sensitive listeners are aware of nonverbal as well as verbal messages; they listen with their eyes as well as their ears. A person's body movement and posture, for example, communicate the intensity of his or her feelings, while facial expression and vocal cues provide clues as to the specific emotion being expressed. A competent listener notices these cues, and an incompetent listener attempts to decode a message based only on what is said rather than "listening between the lines." When there is a contradiction between the verbal and nonverbal message, we will almost always believe the unspoken message; nonverbal cues are more difficult to fake.

Besides looking at someone to discern his or her emotions and relational cues, it is important to establish eye contact, which signals that you are focusing your attention on your partner. Even though mutual eye contact typically lasts only one to seven seconds, when we carry on an interpersonal conversation, it is important to establish and reestablish eye contact to signal that you are on task and listening. We usually have more eye contact with someone when we are listening than when talking.[25] Looking over your partner's head, peeking at your watch, or gazing into space will likely tell him or her you're not tuned in. Even though there are cultural variations in the advice to establish eye contact (for example, some children in African American homes have been taught to avoid eye contact with high-status people), generally, for most North Americans, eye contact signals that the communication channel is open and the communication is welcome.

In addition to eye contact, other nonverbal cues signal whether you are on task and responsive to the messages of others. If you look like you are listening, you will be more likely to listen. Remaining focused, not fidgeting with your hands and feet, and even leaning forward slightly are other nonverbal cues that communicate to someone that you are listening. Appropriate head nods and verbal responses also signal that you are attending to your partner's message.[26]

Listen: Understand Both Details and Major Ideas

How do you improve your listening skill? Now that you've stopped your own internal dialogue and looked for nonverbal cues, it's time to listen. Here are six additional strategies for improving your listening skill.

Identify Your Listening Goal   You listen to other people for a variety of reasons. Knowing your listening goal can increase your self-awareness of the listening process and increase your skill. If you're listening to Aunt Deonna talk about her recent trip to Northern Minnesota for her annual bear hunt, you need not worry about taking extensive notes and trying to remember all of the details of her expedition. But when your sociology professor tells a story to illustrate a sociological theory, you should be more attuned to the point he is making; his theory may be on a test. There are also times when you need to be on your guard to evaluate the message of a politician or salesperson. There are four primary listening goals: to enjoy, to learn, to evaluate, and to empathize.

- *Listening to enjoy.*   Sometimes we listen just because it's fun. You might listen to music, watch TV, go to a movie, or visit with a friend. Because you know you won't be tested on Jay Leno's *Tonight Show* monologue, you can relax and just enjoy his humor; you don't have to worry about passing a test to remember each punch line.
- *Listening to learn.*   Nothing snaps a class to attention more quickly than a professor's proclamation that "This next point will be covered on the

Diversity and Communication

Who Are Better Listeners, Men or Women?

There is evidence that men and women can be equally good listeners, but research suggests that they sometimes (although not always) have different approaches to listening. The following chart summarizes research conclusions about how men and women listen.[27]

	Women	Men
Differences in Attending to Information	• Tend to search for the relationships among separate pieces of information • Tend to identify individual facts and other isolated pieces of information	• Tend to look for a new structure or organizational pattern when listening • Tend to listen for the "big picture" and seek the major points being communicated
Differences in Listening Goals	• More likely to listen to new information to gain new understanding and new insights • Tend to use information to develop relationships with their listening partners	• More likely to listen to new information to solve a problem • Tend to listen to reach a conclusion; are less concerned about relationship cues and more concerned about using the information gained
Differences in Attending to Nonverbal Cues	• Tend to emphasize meaning communicated through nonverbal cues • Typically have more eye contact with the other person when listening	• Tend to emphasize the meaning of the words and information exchanged • Typically have less eye contact with the other person when listening

So what does all this information mean? How is knowing differences in the way men and women listen useful to us? Although not all men and women fit into these categories of listening behavior, we think there are several good reasons to be mindful of gender-based differences in listening.[28] First, it's useful to be aware of different tendencies in listening so that we can be less critical and more accepting of others, should differences in communication arise. Conflicts may arise simply because you and your listening partner are focusing on different parts of the message expressed.

Second, by being aware of whether you fit the general profile of male or female listener, you can determine whether you need to adapt your listening style. If, for example, you know you have a tendency to be less interested in relational information and that you listen to get to the "bottom line" or solve a problem, being aware that your listening partner is not as focused on those objectives when listening can be helpful.

Third, the best listener may be one who is the most flexible and doesn't always default to his or her typical pattern or preferred listening approach, but rather combines listening approaches.[29] Make an effort to listen for both individual facts and the overall ideas. Listening for both relational and emotional meaning as well as for explicit content can also enhance listening skill. Be more aware of the way you tend to listen to others, and expand your listening repertoire to increase your ability to be other-oriented.

Finally, although we've noted differences in the way men and women listen, we end our discussion of men's and women's listening styles by repeating our caution: Don't assume that all men or all women have typical male or female listening styles. Listening expert Stephanie Sargent suggests that studies of listening style differences between men and women may simply be measuring listening stereotypes.[30] Because it's often assumed that men and women listen differently, researchers may be documenting listening stereotypes or self-expectations. What may be occurring is a self-fulfilling prophecy—men and women assume they *are* listening the way they think they *should* listen.[31] But although there are some discernible patterns in male and female listening styles, the differences may not be as consistently pronounced as was once thought. Our conclusion: Differences in the way men and women listen may indeed exist, but these differences are only a few of a host of factors that may explain why men and women sometimes have difficulty reaching a common understanding.

test." Another key reason we listen is to learn. But you don't have to be a college student to listen to learn. Phone calls and conversations with family and friends contain information that we want to remember. In interpersonal situations, you listen for such everyday information as who will pick up the kids after school and what to buy at the grocery store for tonight's dinner. If you are aware that your listening goal is to learn and remember information, you can increase your powers of concentration and pay more attention to understanding and remembering the message.

- *Listening to evaluate.*   When you listen to evaluate, you try to determine whether the information you hear is valid, reliable, believable, or useful. One problem you may have when you listen to evaluate is that you may become so preoccupied with your criticism that you may not completely understand the message. Often the very process of evaluating and making judgments and decisions about information interferes with the capacity to understand and recall. To compensate for this tendency, first make sure that you understand what a person is saying before making a judgment about the value of the information. When listening to evaluate, you use critical-listening skills such as separating facts from inferences, identifying fallacies in reasoning, and analyzing evidence. We discuss these important skills throughout this book.

- *Listening to empathize.*   The word *empathy,* which we introduced in Chapter 1.3 and will discuss in more detail later in this chapter, comes from a Greek word for "passion" and the German word *Einfühlung,* meaning "to feel with." To empathize with someone is to try to feel what he or she is feeling, rather than just to think about or acknowledge the feelings. In effect, you act as a sounding board for the other person. Empathic listening serves an important therapeutic function. Just having an empathic listener may help someone out. No, we are not empowering you to be a therapist, but we are suggesting that simply listening and feeling with someone can help your communication partner sort things out. Empathic listeners don't judge or offer advice. They listen because being listened to is soothing and can often restore a person's perspective. Being aware that your listening goal is to empathize, rather than to remember or to evaluate what you are listening to, is the first step to being a skilled empathic listener.

If you were listening to someone give you directions to Centennial Hall, one of the oldest buildings on campus, you would listen differently than if your sister were telling you about her fears that her marriage was on the rocks. In the case of your sister, your job is to listen patiently and provide emotional support. In trying to get to Centennial Hall, you would be focusing on the specific details and making either mental or written notes.

Mentally Summarize the Details of the Message   This suggestion may seem to contradict the suggestion to avoid focusing *only* on facts, but it is important to have a grasp of the details your partner presents. Yet to listen is to do more than focus on facts. Studies suggest that poor listeners are more likely to focus on *only* facts and data, rather than the overall point of the message.[32] To listen is to connect the details of the message with the major points. You can process words more quickly than a person speaks, so you can use the extra time to your advantage by periodically summarizing the names, dates, and facts embedded in the message. If the speaker is disorganized and rambling, use your tremendous mental ability to reorganize the speaker's information into categories, or try to place events in chronological order. If you miss the details, you will likely miss the main point.

Link Message Details with the Major Idea of the Message   Facts and data make the most sense when we can use them to support an idea or point. Mentally weave your summaries of the details into a focused major point or series of major ideas. So as you summarize, link the facts you have organized in your mind with key ideas and principles. Use facts to enhance your critical thinking as you analyze, synthesize, evaluate, and finally summarize the key points or ideas your partner makes.

One of the pleasures of developing good listening skills is the ability to listen for pure enjoyment.

Practice by Listening to Difficult or Challenging Material   You learn any skill with practice. Listening experts suggest that our listening skills deteriorate if we listen only to easy and entertaining material. Make an effort to listen to news or documentary programs. As you listen to material in a lecture that may seem chock full of content, make a conscious effort to stay focused, concentrate, and summarize facts and major ideas.

Work to Overcome Listening Barriers   If you can avoid the listening barriers we presented earlier, you will be well on your way to improving your listening skill. Make it a deliberate goal not to be self-focused, let emotional noise distract you, or criticize a message before you've understood it. Watch out for information overload. And, when possible, take steps to minimize external noise and provide an environment more conducive to listening.

Listen Actively   Our suggestion that you listen actively is a distillation of the other recommendations we've offered. Active listeners are engaged listeners who listen with both their minds, and their hearts. They are engaged physically and mentally in the listening process.[33] They are aware of what they are doing; they stop thinking about things that might take them off the track.[34] They also have good eye contact with the speaker and communicate their interest with an intent facial expression and slight forward lean. By contrast, passive listeners are not involved listeners; they are detached and may fake attention with a frozen, nonexpressive facial expression. One listening research team noted that a passive listener receives information by being talked to rather than as an equal partner in the speaking-listening exchange.[35]

This same team described active listeners as people who

- give full attention to others.
- focus on what is being said.
- expend considerable energy participating in the listening process.
- have an alert posture.
- maintain much direct eye contact.

It seems the best listeners are mentally alert, physically focused on the other person, and actively involved in seeking understanding. In short, they stop, they look, and they listen.

RECAP

How to Listen Well

What to Do	How to Do It
Identify your listening goal.	Decide whether you are listening to enjoy, to learn, to evaluate, or to empathize. Your listening goal should determine the strategies you use to achieve it.
Mentally summarize the details of the message.	Every few minutes, take time to create your own mental recap of the key information presented. In just a few seconds, you can summarize much information.
Link message details with the major ideas of the message.	Consciously relate the bits of information you hear to the key points the speaker is developing, rather than focusing only on facts and details or only on major points.
Practice by listening to difficult or challenging material.	Periodically make an effort to listen to material that is complex and richer in detail and information than you typically listen to; while listening to this more complex material, make a conscious effort to stop, look, and listen.
Work to overcome listening barriers.	Identify the key obstacles that keep you from listening at peak effectiveness (self barrier, information-processing barrier, or context barrier); make conscious efforts to overcome their underlying causes.
Listen actively.	Be engaged in the listening process by maintaining good eye contact with the speaker and an alert posture (slight forward lean; sitting up rather than slouching).

QUICK
REVIEW

Responding Skills

To respond is to provide feedback to another about his or her behavior or communication. Your response can be verbal or nonverbal, intentional or unintentional.

Your thoughtful response serves several purposes. First, it tells a speaker how well you have understood his or her message. Second, your response lets a speaker know how the message affects you. It indicates whether you agree or disagree. Third, it provides feedback about statements or assumptions that you find vague, confusing, or wrong. It helps an individual keep the communication on target and purposeful. Finally, your response signals to the speaker that you are still "with" him or her—that you are still ready to receive messages. To respond appropriately and effectively, consider the following strategies.

Be Descriptive

"I see that from a different point of view" sounds better than "You're wrong, I'm right." Effective feedback describes rather than evaluates what you hear. Although one listening goal is to evaluate and make critical judgments of messages, evaluate once you're sure you understand the speaker. We're not suggesting it's easy to listen from a nonevaluative perspective, or that you should refrain from ever evaluating messages and providing praise or negative comments. Remember: Feedback that first acts like a mirror to help the speaker understand what he or she has said is more useful than a barrage of critical comments. Describing your own reactions to what your partner has said rather than pronouncing a quick judgment on his or her message is also more likely to keep communication flowing. If your partner thinks your prime purpose in listening is to take pot-shots at the message or the messenger, the communication climate will cool quickly.

Be Timely

Feedback is usually most effective at the earliest opportunity after the behavior or message is presented, especially if the purpose is to teach. Waiting to provide a response after much time has elapsed invites confusion.

By permission of Jerry Van Amarongen and Creators Syndicate, Inc.

Boyd likes to bring empathy to the task at hand.

Now let us contradict our advice. Sometimes, especially if a person is already sensitive and upset about something, delaying feedback can be wise. Use your critical-thinking skills to analyze when feedback will do the most good. Rather than automatically offering immediate correction, use the just-in-time (JIT) approach. Provide feedback just before the person might make another mistake, just in time for the feedback to have the most benefit.

Be Brief

Less information can be more. Cutting down on the amount of your feedback can highlight the importance of what you do share. Don't overwhelm your listener with details that obscure the key point of your feedback. Brief is usually best.

QUICK REVIEW

Be Useful

Perhaps you've heard this advice: "Never try to teach a pig to sing. It wastes your time, it doesn't sound pretty, and it annoys the pig." When you provide feedback to someone, be certain that it is useful and relevant. Ask yourself, "If I were this person, how would I respond to this information? Is it information I can act on?" Immersing your partner in information that is irrelevant or that may be damaging to the relationship may make you feel better but may not enhance the quality of your relationship or improve understanding.

Responding with Empathy

EXPLORE

Empathy, as we noted earlier in the chapter, is the process of feeling what another person is feeling. To empathize is more than just to acknowledge that another person feels a particular emotion—being empathic is making an effort to feel the emotion yourself. Responding with empathy is especially important if you are listening to provide support and encouragement to someone. Being empathic is not a single skill but several related skills that help you predict how others will respond.[36]

Central to being empathic is being emotionally intelligent. As we noted earlier in this chapter, emotional intelligence is the ability to understand and express emotion, interpret emotions in yourself and others, and regulate or manage emotions.[37] Daniel Goleman suggests that people who are emotionally intelligent—sensitive to others, empathic, and other oriented—have better relationships with others. Goleman summarizes the importance of emotions in developing empathy by quoting Antoine De Saint-Exupery: "It is with the heart that one sees rightly; what is essential is invisible to the eye."[38]

At the heart of empathic listening is the ability not only to know when to speak but also to know when to be silent. Henri Nouwen eloquently expressed both the challenge and the rewards of empathic listening:

> To listen is very hard, because it asks of us so much interior stability that we no longer need to prove ourselves by speeches, arguments, statements, or declarations. True listeners no longer have an inner need to make their presence known. They are free to receive, to welcome, to accept.
>
> Listening is much more than allowing another to talk while waiting for a chance to respond. Listening is paying full attention to others and welcoming them into our very beings. The beauty of listening is that those who are listened to start feeling accepted, start taking their words more seriously and discovering their true selves. Listening is a form of spiritual hospitality by which you invite strangers to become friends, to get to know their inner selves more fully, and even to dare to be silent with you.[39]

Some people are simply better at being empathic than others. Just as you inherit physical qualities from your parents, there is also evidence that you inherit communication traits as well.[40] This does not mean that if you are not naturally empathic, you can never develop empathic skills; it does mean you may have to work a bit harder to enhance these skills. To assess your empathic skill, take the "Test Your Empathy Ability" quiz at the end of this chapter.

Here are four strategies to help you respond empathically when you listen.

Understand Your Partner's Feelings

If your goal is to empathize, or "feel with," your partner, you might begin by imagining how you would feel under the same circumstances. If your roommate comes home from a hassle-filled day at work or school, try to imagine what you might be thinking or feeling if you had had a stressful day. If a friend calls to tell you his mother died, consider how you would feel if the situation were reversed. Even if you've not yet experienced the loss of your mother, you can identify with what it would be like to suffer such a loss. Of course, your reaction to life events is unlikely to be exactly like someone else's response. Empathy is not telepathically trying to become your communication partner.[41] But you do attempt to decenter—to consider what someone may be thinking— by first projecting how you might feel and then asking appropriate questions and offering paraphrases to confirm the accuracy of your assumptions. Considering how others might feel has been called the Platinum Rule—even more valuable than the Golden Rule ("Do unto others as you would have others do unto you"). The Platinum Rule invites you to treat others as *they* would like to be treated—not just as *you* would like to be treated.

Ask Appropriate Questions

As you listen for information and attempt to understand how another person is feeling, you may need to ask questions to help clarify your conclusions. Most of your questions will serve one of four purposes: (1) to obtain additional

Ethics *and* Communication

Honest Listening

*I*s it ethical to just pretend to listen to someone? Imagine this situation: You've had a stress-filled day. As you come in your front door and sink down into your favorite chair, all you want to do is relax. Perhaps you'll just fix a little dinner, watch TV, and unwind. Then the phone rings. It's your good friend, and she too has had a difficult, stressful day and needs a listener. Since you're on the phone, you could probably get away with just adding a few "uh-huhs" and "mm-hmms" and your friend would think you were listening to everything she is saying. While appearing to listen you could even read your e-mail and do other daily tasks, and your friend would never know it. Your friend is not likely to take offense at your inattentiveness because she'll not be aware that you're just going through the motions of listening. Consider these questions: Is it ethical to fake paying attention to someone? By faking your attention you are not harming your friend. In fact, the case could be made that you're helping her out by giving her an audience.

Should you be honest and disclose that you're tired and would rather listen when you can be more attentive? How might your friend react to your honesty? How would you respond empathically to her reaction?

information ("How long have you been living in Buckner?"); (2) to check how the person feels ("Are you frustrated because you didn't get your project finished?"); (3) to ask for clarification ("What do you mean when you say you wanted to telecommute?"); or (4) to verify that you have reached an accurate conclusion about your partner's intent or feeling ("So are you saying you'd rather work at home than at the office?").

Another way to sort out details and get to the emotional heart of a dialogue is to ask questions to help you (and your partner) identify the sequence of events. "What happened first?" and "Then what did he do?" can help both you and your partner clarify a confusing event.

Your ability to ask appropriate questions will demonstrate your supportiveness of your partner and signal that you are interested in what he or she is sharing. Of course, if you are trying to understand another's feelings, you can just ask how he or she is feeling in a straightforward way—don't ask questions just for the sake of asking questions. Also, monitor how you ask your questions. Your own verbal and nonverbal responses will contribute to the emotional climate of your interaction.

Technology and *Communication*

Can Computers Listen Empathically?

*I*s it possible for a computer to listen and respond sensitively to others? Although there is software that permits you to speak words that your personal computer will then print, computers do not yet have the sophistication to listen and respond with the same sensitivity as people. But computer programmers are working on it. Stanford University professors Clifford Nass and Byron Reeves have been working since 1986 to devise software that will enable PCs to interact with people in human ways.[42] They have summarized research regarding how people respond to other people and have been trying to translate these research conclusions into strategies that can be used by a computer to interact with others in real-time dialogues. Professors Nass and Reeves have identified four major personality types—dominant, submissive, friendly, and unfriendly—and have programmed computers to respond to the computer user. The researchers are trying to match more than personality. As Professor Nass explains, "Personality is one aspect. Gender, politeness, cooperation, and even humor are other factors. We decide what the agent [computer user] is going to do, then develop a backstory—each character's likes and life history. This guides the scripting, voice type, animation, and interaction style."[43] The researchers are also working on integrating computer-generated speech into the program. Although computers may not yet listen with the sensitivity and empathy of your best friend, researchers are working on software that can emulate human interaction and responses. So for now, realize that the opportunity to listen to others is something that can't be delegated to a virtual friend.

Paraphrase Message Content

After you have listened and asked questions, check whether your interpretations are accurate by paraphrasing the content you have heard. **Paraphrasing is restating in your own words what you think a person is saying.** Paraphrasing is different from repeating something exactly as it was spoken; that would be parroting, not paraphrasing. Your paraphrase can summarize the essential events, uncover a detail that was quickly glossed over, or highlight a key point. Typical lead-ins to a paraphrase include statements such as

> "So here is what seems to have happened . . ."
> "Here's what I understand you to mean . . ."
> "So the point you seem to be making is . . ."
> "You seem to be saying . . ."
> "Are you saying . . ."

Here's an example of a conversation punctuated by appropriate paraphrases to enhance the message receiver's understanding:

Alice: I'm swamped. My boss asked me to take on two extra projects this week. And I already have the Henrikson merger and the Affolter project. I promised I'd arrange to have the lawnmower fixed and pay the bills, but I don't see how I can take the dog to the vet, pick up the kids after school, *and* get Keshia to the orthodontist at 7 a.m. I'm up to my neck in work.

Matt: It sounds like you're feeling overwhelmed with responsibilities. Would you like me to take care of the stuff around the house so you can focus on office assignments?

Alice: Well, some of them, yes. Could you take on a couple of things I said I'd do?

Matt: Okay. I'll take care of the kids and run the errands.

We are not suggesting that you paraphrase when it's not needed or appropriate, only when you need to confirm your understanding of a murky message or to help the speaker sort out a jumbled or confusing situation. When a listener paraphrases the content and feelings of a speaker's message, the speaker is not only more likely to know that the message is understood but also more likely to trust and value the listener.

Paraphrase Emotions

The bottom line in empathic responding is to make certain that you understand your communication partner's emotional state.

"So you feel . . ."
"So now you feel . . ."
"Emotionally, you are feeling . . ."

These are typical lead-in phrases when paraphrasing feelings.

We have discussed empathic responses and the active listening process using a tidy, step-by-step textbook approach. Realize that in practice, the process won't be so neat and tidy. You may have to back up and clarify content, ask more questions, and rethink how you would feel before you summarize how your partner feels. Or you may be able to summarize feelings without asking questions or summarizing the content of the message. A sensitive communicator tries not to let his or her technique show. Overusing paraphrasing skills can slow down a conversation and make the other person uncomfortable or irritated. But if used with wisdom, paraphrasing can help both you and your partner clarify message accuracy.

Reflecting on the content or feeling through paraphrasing can be especially useful in the following situations:

Before you take an important action
Before you argue or criticize
When your partner has strong feelings

When your partner just wants to talk

When your partner is speaking "in code"—using unclear jargon or unclear abbreviations

When your partner wants to understand your feelings and thoughts

When you are talking to yourself (you can question and check your own emotional temperature)

When you encounter new ideas[44]

When you ask questions and paraphrase content and feelings, keep the following additional guidelines in mind:

Use your own words—don't just repeat exactly what the other person says.

Don't add to the information presented when paraphrasing.

Be brief.

Be specific.

Be accurate.

On the Web

Several Web sites provide a wealth of information about how to improve your listening skills. There are also many Internet resources to bolster your responding and paraphrasing skills. The following Web addresses give you tips, tools, and techniques to help you listen and respond better:

http://conflict911.com/resources/Communication/ Listening is a site from Project911.com that provides resources and assistance in improving communication and listening skills.

www.listen.org is the Web site of the International Listening Association. It offers a panoply of resources, quotations, and information about improving listening skills.

http://web.cba.neu.edu/~ewertheim/interper/ commun.htm#top provides numerous practical tips and techniques to enhance listening and responding skills.

Don't use paraphrasing skills if you aren't able to be open and accepting; if you try to color your paraphrased comments to achieve your own agenda, you aren't being ethical.

Don't be discouraged if your initial attempts to use these skills seem awkward and uncomfortable. Any new set of skills takes time to learn and use well. The instructions and samples you have seen here should serve as a guide, rather than as hard-and-fast prescriptions to follow every time. Being an empathic listener can be rewarding in both your personal and your professional lives.[45] And here's some encouraging news about listening and responding skills: These skills can be improved. People who have received listening training show overall improvement in their ability to listen to others.[46] Reading this chapter, listening to your instructor give you tips to enhance your skills, and participating in skill-building activities is well worth your time.

The poem below, "Listen," by an unknown author, summarizes the essential ideas of how to listen and respond with empathy.

Listen

When I ask you to listen to me and you start giving advice, you have not done what I asked.

When I ask you to listen to me and you begin to tell me why I shouldn't feel that way, you are trampling on my feelings.

When I ask you to listen to me and you feel you have to do something to solve my problems, you have failed me, strange as that may seem.

Listen! All I asked was that you listen. Not talk or do—just hear me.

Advice is cheap: 50 cents will get you both Dear Abby and Billy Graham in the same newspaper.

And I can do for myself; I'm not helpless. Maybe discouraged and faltering, but not helpless.

When you do something for me that I can and need to do for myself, you contribute to my fear and weakness.

But when you accept as a simple fact that I do feel what I feel, no matter how irrational, then I quit trying to convince you and can get about the business of understanding what's behind this irrational feeling.

And when that's clear, the answers are obvious and I don't need advice.

Irrational feelings make sense when we understand what's behind them.

Perhaps that's why prayer works, sometimes, for some people, because God is mute, and doesn't give advice or try to fix things,

God just listens and lets you work it out for yourself.

So, please listen and just hear me, and, if you want to talk, wait a minute for your turn; and I'll listen to you.

—Anonymous

RECAP

How to Respond with Empathy

Strategy	Action
Understand Your Partner's Feelings	Ask yourself how you would feel if you had experienced a similar situation or recall how you *did* feel under similar circumstances. Or recall how your *partner* felt under similar circumstances.
Ask Questions	Seek additional information to better understand your partner's message.
Reflect Content by Paraphrasing	Summarize for your partner the essence of the information, as you understand it.
Reflect Feelings by Paraphrasing	When appropriate, try to summarize what you think your partner may be feeling.

QUICK REVIEW

PRINCIPLES FOR A LIFETIME: Enhancing Your Skills

Listen and Respond

Principle Four: Listen and respond thoughtfully to others.

- Stop: Work to turn off competing mental messages that distract your listening focus.
- To overcome self barriers to listening effectively, consciously become aware of your drifting attention. Then, to get back in sync, use self-talk skills and emotion management skills (such as deep breathing) to remain calm and focused on the message, not the messenger.
- To overcome information-processing listening barriers, make mental summaries of the message you hear, recognize when you are tired and not at your listening best, take effective notes, and remain focused.
- To overcome context listening barriers, become aware of your best and worst times of the day for listening; consciously intensify your concentration if you know you're not at your listening best, and assertively take action, such as closing a door or a window, to reduce external noise when listening.
- Look: Listen with your eyes to discern nonverbal information that provides important information about emotions, attitudes, and relationship cues.
- Listen: Work to link facts and details with major ideas you hear.
- Respond: Use effective responding skills by providing feedback that is descriptive, timely, brief, and useful while remaining an active listener.
- Be empathic: Try to imagine how you would feel in a situation like the one your communication partner is in. To confirm your interpretation of his or her message, ask appropriate clarifying questions, then paraphrase both the content and the emotions expressed.
- Paraphrase by briefly summarizing the message in your own words while trying to accurately capture the essence of what your listening partner said; don't add to the information presented when paraphrasing.

SUMMARY

An important principle of communication is to listen and respond thoughtfully to others. Listening is the process of receiving, constructing meaning from, and responding to verbal and nonverbal messages. It includes the processes of selecting, attending, understanding, remembering, and responding to others.

Each person develops a preferred listening style. The four listening styles are people-oriented, action-oriented, content-oriented, and time-oriented. Knowing your listening style can help you adapt your listening approach for maximum listening effectiveness.

Most people struggle with the skill of listening. Barriers to effective listening include focusing on our personal agenda, being distracted by emotional noise, criticizing the speaker, daydreaming, shifting attention, and being distracted by information overload and external noise.

To become a better listener, consider three simple steps: Stop, look, and listen. To stop means to be mindful of the message and avoid focusing on your own distracting inner "talk," which may keep you from focusing on the messages of others. To look is to listen with your eyes—to focus on nonverbal information that provides a wealth of cues about emotional meaning. To listen involves the skill of capturing the details of a message while also connecting those details to a major idea.

The other half of listening is responding to others accurately and appropriately. To respond thoughtfully means to stop and consider the needs of the other person. Check the accuracy of your listening skill by reflecting your understanding of what your partner has said. Responding skills are especially important if your listening goal is to empathize with and support others. Responding skills include understanding the feelings of others, asking appropriate questions, and paraphrasing the message's content and the speaker's feelings. Responding effectively does not mean being a parrot and repeating a message exactly as it was spoken. Paraphrasing means summarizing the gist of the message. The most effective responses to others are carefully timed, provide usable information, avoid cluttering details, and are descriptive rather than evaluative.

DISCUSSION AND REVIEW

1. What is the difference between listening and hearing?
2. What are some of the key barriers that keep people from listening effectively?
3. What are similarities and differences between listening to gain information, to evaluate, to enjoy, and to empathize?
4. Identify and describe the four listening styles.
5. List the essential skills to improve your listening, and discuss strategies that will help you improve your listening skills.
6. What are suggestions for improving your ability to empathize with others?
7. What are suggestions for effectively paraphrasing or reflecting messages back to others?
8. How can you respond appropriately and thoughtfully to others?

PUTTING PRINCIPLES INTO PRACTICE

1. *Test Your Empathy Ability*

   Take this short test to assess your empathy. Respond to each statement about how you typically communicate with others by indicating the degree to which the statement is true. Use a 5-point scale: 1 = Always false; 2 = Usually false; 3 = Sometimes false and sometimes true; 4 = Usually true; 5 = Always true.

   _____ 1. I try to understand others' experiences from their perspectives.

   _____ 2. I follow the Golden Rule ("Do unto others as you would have them do unto you") when communicating with others.

   _____ 3. I can "tune in" to emotions others are experiencing when we communicate.

   _____ 4. When trying to understand how others feel, I imagine how I would feel in their situation.

_____ 5. I am able to tell what others are feeling without being told.

_____ 6. Others experience the same feelings I do in any given situation.

_____ 7. When others are having problems, I can imagine how they feel.

_____ 8. I find it hard to understand the emotions others experience.

_____ 9. I try to see others as they want me to.

_____ 10. I never seem to know what others are thinking when we communicate.

To determine your score, first reverse the responses for the even-numbered items (if you wrote 1, make it 5; if you wrote 2, make it 4; if you wrote 3, leave it as 3; if you wrote 4, make it 2; if you wrote 5, make it 1). Next add the numbers given to the ten statements. Scores range from 10 to 50. The higher your score, the more you are able to empathize.

Source: _Bridging Differences: Effective Intergroup Communication_ by WIlliam Gudykunst. Copyright 1998 by Sage Publications Inc Books. Reproduced with permission of Sage Publications Inc Books in the format Textbook via Copyright Clearance Center.

2. _Assessing Receiver Apprehension_

Take the following test to assess your level of receiver apprehension. Respond to each of the statements by indicating how much it describes you, using a 5-point scale: 5 = Strongly agree; 4 = Agree; 3 = Uncertain or sometimes; 2 = Disagree; 1 = Strongly disagree.

_____ 1. When I am listening, I feel nervous about missing information.

_____ 2. I worry about being able to keep up with the material presented in lecture classes.

_____ 3. Sometimes I miss information in class because I am writing notes.

_____ 4. I feel tense and anxious when listening to important information.

_____ 5. I am concerned that I won't be able to remember information I've heard in lectures or discussions.

_____ 6. Although I try to concentrate, my thoughts sometimes become confused when I'm listening.

_____ 7. I worry that my listening skill isn't very good.

_____ 8. I regularly can't remember things that I have just been told.

_____ 9. I feel anxious and nervous when I am listening in class.

_____ 10. I prefer reading class material rather than listening to it, so I don't have to be stressed about catching all the information the first time.

Scores range from 30 to 10. The higher your score, the more you're likely to experience some anxiety when you listen to others and the harder you'll have to work at developing strategies to improve your listening comprehension.

Source: "An Investigation of Receiver Apprehension and Social Context Dimensions of Communication Apprehension", L. Wheeless, _The Speech Teacher 24_ (1975), pp. 261–268. Reprinted by permission of Taylor & Francis Ltd, http://www.informaworld.com.

3. On pages 147–153 we noted several barriers to listening. Rank order these barriers, with 1 being the most problematic for you. After you have identified your top three or four barriers, identify at least one specific strategy for overcoming each barrier.

4. _Charting Your Listening Cycle_

Are you a morning person or an evening person? Use the chart shown below to plot your listening energy cycle. Draw a line starting at 6:00 a.m., showing the highs and lows of your potential listening effectiveness. For example, if you are usually still asleep at 6:00 a.m., your line will be at 0 and start upward when you awake. If you are a morning person, your line will peak in the morning. Or perhaps your line will indicate that you listen best in the evening.

After you have charted your typical daily listening cycle, compare listening cycles with your classmates. Identify listening strategies that can help you capitalize on your listening "up" periods. Also, based on information you learned from this chapter and your own experiences, identify ways to enhance your listening when you traditionally have low listening energy.

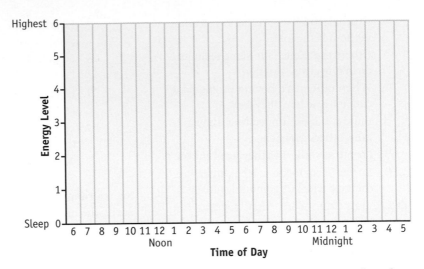

5. The following items relate to your listening style. Circle the response to each statement. Please be candid.

Listening Styles Inventory[47]

Item	Almost Always	Often	Sometimes	Seldom	Almost Never
1. I want to listen to what others have to say when they are talking.	5	4	3	2	1
2. I do not listen at my capacity when others are talking.	1	2	3	4	5
3. By listening, I can guess a speaker's intent or purpose without being told.	5	4	3	2	1
4. I have a purpose for listening when others are talking.	5	4	3	2	1
5. I keep control of my biases and attitudes when listening to others speak so that these factors won't affect my interpretation of the message.	5	4	3	2	1
6. I analyze my listening errors so as not to make them again.	5	4	3	2	1
7. I listen to the complete message before making judgments about what the speaker has said.	5	4	3	2	1
8. I cannot tell when a speaker's biases or attitudes are affecting his or her message.	1	2	3	4	5
9. I ask questions when I don't fully understand a speaker's message.	5	4	3	2	1
10. I am aware of whether a speaker's meaning for words and concepts is the same as mine.	5	4	3	2	1

Grand total _____ = _____ + _____ + _____ + _____ + _____

Now consult the Interpretation Scale on the next page.

Listening Styles Inventory Interpretation Scale

Place an X on the part of the scale below that corresponds to your grand total score. Your listening style is described below.

Active. The active listener gives full attention to listening when others are talking and focuses on what is being said. This person expends a lot of energy participating in the speaking-listening exchange, which is usually evidenced by an alert posture or stance and much direct eye contact.

Involved. The involved listener gives most of his or her attention to the speaker's words and intentions. This person reflects on the message to a degree and participates in the speaking-listening exchange. The involved listener practices some direct eye contact and may have alert posture or stance, although this may be intermittent.

Passive. The passive listener receives information as though being talked to rather than as an equal partner in the speaking-listening exchange. While the passive listener assumes that the responsibility for the success of the communication is the speaker's, he or she is usually attentive, although attention may be faked at times. The passive listener seldom expends any noticeable energy in receiving and interpreting messages.

Detached. The detached listener withdraws from the speaking-listening exchange and becomes the object of the speaker's message rather than its receiver. The detached listener is usually inattentive, disinterested, and may be restless, bored, or easily distracted. This person's noticeable lack of enthusiasm may be marked by slumped or very relaxed posture and avoidance of direct eye contact.

Note: (1) The listening inventory gives you a general idea of your preferred listening style, based on how you view yourself. The scores indicating styles are approximations and should be regarded as such. (2) You may change your listening style, depending on the given situation or your interests, intentions, or objectives.

Chapter 1.5   *Practice Test*

MULTIPLE CHOICE.   Choose the *best* answer to each of the following questions.

1. If you sit in class on Monday and listen to a lecture, how much of that lecture will you remember on Tuesday?

   a. about 25%

   b. about 50%

   c. about 75%

   d. almost all of it

2. Hearing refers to the _____ process of decoding sounds.

   a. psychological

   b. physiological

   c. affective

   d. behavioral

3. You are having a conversation with a roommate, who says something you completely disagree with. Which of the following is something you *don't* want to do when making a response?

   a. Say "I see that differently than you."

   b. Wait until the end of the conversation before letting him know that you disagree.

   c. State your objection clearly and briefly.

   d. Suggest ways to resolve your difficulty with his message.

4. All of the following behaviors indicate that you are listening carefully to a message *except*

   a. closing your eyes to focus on what is being said.

   b. nodding your head at important points.

   c. leaning forward.

   d. keeping your hands from fidgeting.

5. A presidential candidate comes to town to deliver a speech. You attend the event to decide how to cast your vote. Which of the following should be your listening goal?

   a. listening for enjoyment

   b. listening to learn

   c. listening to evaluate

   d. listening to empathize

6. The stages of the listening process, in order, are

   a. selecting and attending, understanding, interpreting.

   b. attending, selecting, understanding, rehearsing, responding.

   c. selecting, attending, understanding, remembering, responding.

   d. selecting, attending, interpreting, remembering, responding.

7. Fernando is visiting with Aalyiah in the student union. During the whole conversation, Aalyiah is looking at other students as they walk by, occasionally saying "uh-huh" or "right," and mainly thinking about her breakup with Caleb last night, but not really attending to what Fernando is saying. Aalyiah is experiencing which barrier to listening?

   a. place and time

   b. self-focus

   c. information overload

   d. external noise

8. Which of the following is *not* an activity involved in listening?

   a. selecting

   b. attending

   c. criticizing

   d. responding

9. Brayden is sitting in a lecture, and his attention keeps shifting from the professor speaking to his thoughts about whom he will be taking to his fraternity's party. Brayden is having a problem with which part of listening?

   a. selecting

   b. attending

   c. aligning

   d. emotional noise

10. While you are giving your friend a detailed account of your weekend, the people you saw, the parties you went to, and what you did, your friend appears to be getting antsy and keeps looking at the clock. Your friend likely has what type of listening style?
    a. people-oriented
    b. action-oriented
    c. content-oriented
    d. time-oriented

11. Peyton is telling Kamryn about his ideas for improving their service organization's recruiting efforts. Kamryn is responding skeptically and questioning the assumptions Peyton is making. This is likely due to
    a. an action-oriented listening style.
    b. criticism as a barrier to listening.
    c. difficulty with the remembering stage of the listening process.
    d. receiver apprehension.

12. Mike interviewed for a job, but the interviewer just couldn't get past Mike's pierced lip and nose and Mike didn't get the job. More than likely, the interviewer was suffering from
    a. emotional noise.
    b. information overload.
    c. self-criticism.
    d. self-focus.

13. The empathic process of shifting attention away from your own thoughts to the thoughts of the other person is called
    a. a people-centered listening style.
    b. self-focus.
    c. active listening.
    d. decentering.

14. Almost all speakers can
    a. speak faster than they can listen.
    b. listen faster than they can speak.
    c. speak and listen at about the same rate.
    d. speak fast, but only if they don't listen.

15. Christy is doing her best to pay attention in class, but the lecturer is unbelievably boring. So, instead of writing down notes, Christy spends most of class thinking about the test she has coming up next period. In this example, Christy is suffering from
    a. emotional noise.
    b. information overload.
    c. self-criticism.
    d. self-focus.

16. According to your text, after spending 12 hours in silence, research participants
    a. scored significantly higher on listening tests than individuals who were taught listening skills.
    b. spoke more softly than normal, which caused others to listen more attentively and remember more.
    c. were more aware of their listening.
    d. were more likely to experience self-focus as a barrier to listening.

17. Which of the following probably *won't* help you manage your emotions while listening to someone?
    a. telling yourself not to get angry
    b. thinking about the way your emotions affect your listening
    c. taking a deep breath
    d. trying to keep your frustrations to yourself

18. The last step of the listening model discussed in the text is
    a. remembering.
    b. understanding.
    c. responding.
    d. forgetting.

19. Recent research seems to suggest that
    a. men can shift listening between messages better than women.
    b. men are more likely than women to focus their listening on one message.
    c. men and women can shift listening between messages equally well.
    d. men and women both tend to focus their listening on one message.

20. While listening to Savannah talk about her new job, Connor notices that she has animated facial expressions and open posture, is smiling a lot, is making direct eye contact, and is speaking with a raised pitch and tempo. When Savannah is done speaking, Connor says to her, "So you're feeling pretty good about this job. I'm clear that you're really excited." Connor's statement reflects which guideline of responding effectively?

    a. Be timely.

    b. Be useful.

    c. Paraphrase content.

    d. Paraphrase emotion.

TRUE/FALSE.   Indicate whether the following statements are *true* or *false*.

1. T or F   The average person spends more time listening than in any other communication activity.

2. T or F   The more similar you are to another, the easier it is to understand him or her.

3. T or F   Men tend to listen to solve problems.

4. T or F   The point of empathic listening is to actively help solve the speaker's problems.

5. T or F   Your appearance and your style of speaking have little, if any, effect on the ability of others to listen to you.

6. T or F   With respect to giving feedback, the guideline "Be timely" means that you should wait to give feedback until it will benefit the speaker the most.

7. T or F   Emotional noise can be caused by the emotional state of both the speaker and the listener.

8. T or F   There is evidence that people-oriented listeners have less apprehension than others when communicating in small groups and interpersonal situations.

9. T or F   Content-oriented listeners are mainly concerned with the purpose and function of what they hear.

10. T or F   Decentering involves attempting to experience the thoughts and feelings of another instead of your own.

FILL IN THE BLANK.   Complete the following statements.

1. _____ is the process of sorting through competing sounds.

2. A competent listener engages in _____ to confirm his or her understanding of the message.

3. The purely physiological process of decoding sounds is _____.

4. _____ is the process of focusing on a particular message.

5. Focusing on the thoughts of another, as opposed to your own thoughts, is _____.

6. The stage of the listening model that results in assigning meaning to a message is _____.

7. _____ _____ is your preferred way of making sense out of the messages you hear.

8. If you are worried about misinterpreting someone else's message, then you are probably suffering from _____ _____.

9. _____ listening requires mental, verbal, and nonverbal responses to another's message.

10. The three steps to effective listening are _____, _____, and _____.

Adapting to Others:
Bridging Culture and Gender Differences

CHAPTER OBJECTIVES

After studying this chapter, you should be able to

1. Define culture.

2. Describe, compare, and contrast high-context and low-context cultures.

3. Describe five cultural values.

4. Identify differences and similarities between male and female communication patterns.

5. Describe the importance of gender within the larger context of culture.

6. Understand how gender relates to content and relational approaches to communication.

7. Illustrate five barriers that inhibit communication between individuals.

8. Describe six strategies that will help bridge differences between people and help them adapt to differences.

There are no ordinary people.

C. S. Lewis

Christian Pierre, Share the World. © SuperStock, Inc.

**FIGURE 1.6.1
Communication
Principles for a
Lifetime**

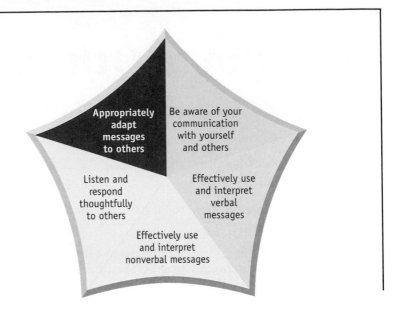

As C.S. Lewis observed, there are no ordinary people—which implies that each of us is unique. And the not-so-startling fact that people *are* different from one another provides the context for discussion of our final communication principle: *Effective communicators appropriately adapt their messages to others.* We introduce this principle last because often people learn how to adapt only after they have learned the other communication principles. Figure 1.6.1 presents our now-familiar model, which includes this final principle of appropriately adapting to others. Being able to adapt to others suggests that you already have a sense of who you are and a consciousness of the presence of others—self-awareness and other-awareness, the components of the first principle we presented. We learn to use verbal and nonverbal messages as infants, though it may take several years to develop sophistication in using language and nonverbal symbols. Hearing and listening also develop early in our lives. Studies in developmental communication suggest that the ability to appropriately adapt our behavior to others evolves after we have become aware that there is a "me," after we have learned to use verbal and nonverbal symbols to communicate, and after we have developed an ability to hear and listen to others. To adapt to others requires a relatively sophisticated understanding of the communication process.

One of life's unprofound principles with profound implications for human communication is this: *We each have different backgrounds and experiences.*[1] As you learned in Chapter 1.2, we each see, hear, and experience the world differently. To some degree, we are each estranged from others.

In a world of ever-increasing tensions and conflict arising from differences in culture, religious beliefs, and political ideologies, being able to understand and appropriately adapt to others is of vital importance. When differences are heightened by attitudes of superiority and beliefs about being divinely ordained to dominate others, violence is the typical result.

The greater our differences in background, experience, religion, and culture, the more difficult it is for us to interpret verbal and nonverbal symbols and to listen accurately to the messages of others, and the more challenging it is to adapt messages to others. When we meet someone for the first time, we often try to determine whether we have people, places, or backgrounds in common. It is usually easier to develop a relationship with someone who is similar to us rather than dissimilar.

The goal of this chapter is to identify culture and gender differences that may inhibit communication with others and to suggest adaptive strategies that can improve the quality and effectiveness of our communication with others. Throughout the first five chapters, we have noted in our discussions (and in the Diversity and Communication boxed feature) that culture and gender differences affect our communication with others. In this chapter we examine in more detail the influence of these differences on our lives and suggest some communication strategies for bridging these differences in our relationships with others.

As we focus on culture and gender differences and how to adapt to them, we will discuss the nature of culture and gender, identify barriers that stem from culture and gender differences, and suggest strategies that can help you better understand, appreciate, and adapt to people who are not just like you. Our premise: In order to live comfortably in the twenty-first century, we must learn ways to appreciate and understand culture and gender differences, rather than ignore them, suffer because of them, or wish they would disappear. But simply understanding that there are differences is not enough to improve communication; it is important to learn how to use effective communication skills to adapt to those differences.

Even though the focus of this chapter is on culture and gender differences, realize that these are only two of many differences that can divide people. Differences in age (sometimes called the generation gap), socioeconomic status, sexual orientation, and even in height, weight, or clothing choices have created tension between people in the past and probably will in the future. The principle of adapting to others is applicable to virtually all communication situations. The ideas and strategies for bridging differences in culture or gender that we suggest at the end of this chapter apply to other differences that create conflict and tension. The challenge is not to let our differences create a chasm so large that we can't find ways to ethically adapt our communication to create shared meaning.

Ethically Adapt Your Communication to Others

The key principle of adapting to others that we propose in this chapter does not mean that you only do or say what others expect or that your primary goal in life is always to please others. You have a responsibility to ethically adapt your messages to others. To be ethical is to be truthful and honest while also observing the rights of others. Ethical communication is communication that is responsible, honest, and fair, that enhances human dignity, and that maintains listener options rather than coerces or forces someone to behave against his or her will. When we encourage you to adapt your messages to others, we are not recommending that you become a spineless jellyfish and say things only to make others happy. It would be unethical to abandon your own ethical principles and only communicate to please others. Such placating behavior is neither wise nor effective; it would also violate the principles of ethical communication.

Effective communicators are *appropriate* communicators—they are sensitive to others' needs while also communicating to enhance the probability that the message expressed will be the message interpreted. To be an appropriate communicator is to express your ideas in ways that fit the time, place, and situation.

Adapting your communication to others also does not mean that you manipulate a conversation so that only *you* can accomplish your goals. Ideally both (or all) parties' goals are met. We do not advocate a form of adapted communication that is false or manipulative. Whether you are in an interpersonal interaction, a group, or a presentational speaking situation, adapting your message to others makes common sense. Even so, being sensitive to others and wisely adapting behaviors to others are often not so common.

Culture and Communication

Overheard from a student before class:

> I've had it with all this cultural diversity and gender stuff. It seems like every textbook in every class is obsessed with it. My music appreciation class is trying to force the music of other cultures down my throat. What's wrong with Bach, Beethoven, and Brahms? In English lit, all we're reading is stuff by people from different countries. And it seems my history prof talks only about obscure people I've never heard of before. I'm tired of all this politically correct nonsense. I mean, we're all Americans, aren't we? We're not going off to live in Africa, China, or India. Why don't they just teach us what we need to know and cut all this diversity garbage?

Have you heard this kind of sentiment expressed before? Perhaps you've encountered this kind of "diversity backlash" among some of your classmates, or you may harbor this attitude yourself. It may seem unsettling to some that school curricula and textbooks are focusing on issues of culture and gender differences. But these changes are not motivated by an irrational desire to be politically correct. They are taking place because the United States is changing. The Diversity and Communication feature documents how diverse the United States is now and will increasingly become in the future. There is evidence that the trend toward greater diversity will continue.[2] With this growing diversity comes a heightened awareness that learning about culture and gender differ-

Diversity and Communication

Diversity Almanac

1. Two-thirds of the immigrants on this planet come to the United States.[3]

2. According to 2000 U.S. Census data, there are more than 35 million people of Hispanic origin in the United States—a 58% gain of 13 million people since 1990.[4]

3. It is estimated that more than 40 million U.S. residents learned something other than English as their first language, including 18 million people for whom Spanish is a first language.[5]

4. Almost one-third of U.S. residents under the age of 35 are members of minority groups, compared with one-fifth of those age 35 or older. According to U.S. Census Bureau population projections, by the year 2025, nearly half of all young adults in this country will come from minority groups.[6]

5. If the current trend continues, by the year 2050 the proportion of the U.S. population of non-Hispanic whites will decrease to 53%, down from a current 72%. Asians will increase to 16%, up from 4.5%; Hispanics will more than double their numbers, to over 25%, up from just over 11.5%;

and African Americans will increase their proportion slightly from the current 12%.[7]

6. It is estimated that between 2000 and 2010, Vermont's Asian population will grow by 80%, Arizona's will increase by 52%, and Delaware's will grow by 56%.[8]

7. Between 1995 and 2005, the combined population of African Americans, Native Americans, Asians, Pacific Islanders, and Hispanics grew 13 times faster than the non-Hispanic white population.[9]

8. One out of every eight U.S. residents speaks a language other than English at home, and one-third of children in urban U.S. public schools speak a first language other than English.[10]

9. For the first time since the 1850s, when California was seized from Mexico, a majority of the babies born in California in 2004 were Hispanic.[11]

10. Non-Hispanic whites constitute a minority of the population in Texas, New Mexico, and California.[12]

11. Sixty percent of the residents of Miami, Florida, are foreign-born.[13]

ences can affect every aspect of our lives in positive ways. You may not plan to travel the world, but the world is traveling to you. Your employers, teachers, religious leaders, best friends, or romantic partners may have grown up with cultural traditions different from your own. School textbooks and courses are *reflecting* the change, not *initiating* it.

One statistician notes that if the world were a village of 1000 people, the village would have 590 Asians, 123 Africans, 96 Europeans, 84 Latin Americans, 55 members of the former Soviet Union, and 53 North Americans.[14] Clearly, a global economy and the ease with which technology permits us to communicate with others around the world increase the likelihood that you will establish relationships with people who are different from you and who have cultural traditions different from your own. You need not travel abroad to encounter cultural differences; the world is here.

Journalist Thomas Friedman argues that **globalization—the integration of economics and technology that is contributing to a worldwide, interconnected business environment**—is changing the way we work and relate to people around the world.[15] The world is now "flat" rather than round,

suggests Friedman, because if you have a computer connected to the Internet or a cell phone, you can connect with anyone else in the world who also has those technologies. Saying that the world is flat is a metaphor Friedman uses to describe the interconnectedness of people throughout the world. Globalization results in a more competitive, level playing field because individuals have increased access to others with whom they can form entrepreneurial partnerships. Hence, globalization increases the probability that you will communicate with someone today who has a cultural background different from your own.

Friedman notes that during what he calls "Globalization 1.0," the period between Columbus's 1492 voyage and approximately 1800, *countries* were involved in globalization. "Globalization 2.0" was between 1800 and 2000, when *companies* were the globalization leaders. Today, to use Friedman's scheme, we are in "Globalization 3.0," and *individuals* are making contact with other individuals.[16] For example, when you call someone to get technical assistance with your computer or advice on fixing your TV, you are more likely to talk to someone who is in India rather than Indiana. Our point is not to debate the advantages or disadvantages of globalization, but only to suggest that one implication of a "flat" world is that you will increasingly communicate with people who have cultural backgrounds different from your own.

Defining Culture

Culture is a learned system of knowledge, behavior, attitudes, beliefs, values, and norms that is shared by a group of people and shaped from one generation to the next.[17] Communication and culture, says anthropologist Edward T. Hall, are inseparable—you can't talk about one without the other.[18] There is ample evidence that documents the influence of culture on how we work and live.[19] In the broadest sense, culture includes how people think, what they do, and how they use things to sustain their lives. Researcher Geert Hofstede says culture is the "mental software" that helps us understand our world.[20] Like the software and operating system in a computer, our culture provides the framework within which we interpret the data and information that enter our life.

Technology and Communication

Adapting to Cultural Differences When Communicating Electronically

*I*t is increasingly likely that you communicate with people who are far away from where you work and live. It's not unusual to have e-mail conversations with people from around the globe. Nor are conference calls or video conferences among people thousands of miles apart rare or surprising. The world is indeed small when it comes to communicating with people from around the globe.

A team of communication researchers points out that when we communicate via e-mail or phone, it takes a bit longer to interpret information about relationships, because often there are fewer nonverbal cues available.[21] In the case of e-mail, we can't see or hear the person we're exchanging messages with. With a telephone call, we can hear a person, but we miss facial expressions and body posture information. Even during a video conference, we're not able to see all of a person's body posture or watch everyone participating 100 percent of the time. The potential for misunderstanding, already present because of cultural differences, a key focus of this chapter, is compounded by the lack of nonverbal information that usually provides vital information about the nature of the relationship we have with others.

When nonverbal messages are diminished because we're not communicating with people face to face, it's important to seek other sources of information about

the nature of the relationship with them. Specifically, what should we do?

- First, you may need to be more direct when responding or expressing how you feel; you may need to describe your emotional responses in writing.
- Second, you may need to ask more questions to clarify meanings.
- Third, it may be necessary to do more paraphrasing to confirm that you understand what others are saying.
- Finally, you simply may need to be more patient with others; relationships may take longer to develop because of the diminished nonverbal cues.

Cultures are not static; they change as new information and new technologies modify them. We no longer believe that bathing is unhealthy or that we should use leeches as the primary medical procedure to make us healthy. Through research, we have replaced both of these cultural assumptions with the values of personal hygiene and modern, sophisticated methods of medical care.

Some groups of individuals can best be described as a **co-culture—a cultural group that exists within a larger culture.** Examples of co-cultures in the United States include the Amish and some communities in Appalachia. A person's gender places her or him in one of the co-cultures that researchers have used to analyze and investigate the influence of communication on our relationships with others. We discuss the impact of gender on our communication in more detail later in the chapter. Gays and lesbians constitute another example of an important co-culture in our society.

Intercultural communication is communication between people who have different cultural traditions. The transactional process of listening and responding to people from different cultural backgrounds can be challenging. As we stressed earlier, the greater the difference in culture between two people, the greater the potential for misunderstanding and mistrust. That's why it is important to understand the nature of culture and how cultural differences influence our communication with others. Such understanding helps us develop strategies to make connections and adapt to others with different "mental software."

When you encounter a culture that has little in common with your own, you may experience culture shock, a sense of confusion, anxiety, stress, and loss.[22] If you are visiting or actually living in the new culture, your uncertainty and stress may take time to subside as you learn the values and message systems that characterize the culture. If you are trying to communicate with someone from a background quite different from yours—even on your home turf—it is important to consider the role of culture as you interact.

Our culture and life experiences determine our **worldview—the general perception shared by a culture or group of people about key beliefs and issues, such as death, God, and the meaning of life, that influences interaction with others.** A culture's worldview, according to intercultural communication scholar Carley Dodd, encompasses "how the culture perceives the role of various forces in explaining why events occur as they do in a social setting."[23] These beliefs shape our thoughts, language, and actions. Your worldview permeates all aspects of how you interact with society; it's like a lens through which you observe the world. If, as we noted in Chapter 1.1, communication is how we make sense out of the world and share that sense with others, our worldview is one of the primary filters that influence how we make sense out of the world. Two frameworks for describing how culture influences our worldview include cultural context and cultural values.

Cultural Contexts

VISUAL
LITERACY

The cultural context of any communication consists of the nonverbal and environmental cues that surround and give additional information about a message. In this sense, *all* nonverbal cues are part of a cultural context. Some cultures give more weight to the surrounding nonverbal context than to the explicit verbal message when interpreting the overall meaning of a message. Other cultures place less emphasis on the nonverbal context and greater emphasis on what someone says.

For example, when you interview for a job, you may be scanning the face of your interviewer and looking for nonverbal messages to provide cues about the impression you are making on the interviewer. These contextual cues (in this case, the nonverbal messages) give meaning to help you interpret the message of your interviewer. Edward T. Hall helped us understand the importance of cultural context when he categorized cultures as either high- or low-context.[24]

High-Context Cultures   In high-context cultures, people derive much information from nonverbal and environmental cues and less information from the words of a message. Communicators rely heavily on the context of more subtle information such as facial expression, vocal cues, and even silence in interpreting messages, hence the term *high-context cultures* to indicate the emphasis placed on the context. Asian, Arab, and Southern European peoples are more likely to draw on the context for message interpretation.

Low-Context Cultures   People in low-context cultures derive much information from the words of a message and less information from nonverbal and environmental cues. Individuals from low-context cultures, such as North Americans, Germans, and Scandinavians, may perceive people from high-context cultures as less attractive, knowledgeable, and trustworthy, because they violate unspoken low-context cultural rules of conduct and communication. Individuals from low-context cultures often are less skilled in interpreting unspoken contextual messages.[25] Figure 1.6.2 describes differences in communication style between high-context and low-context cultures.

Members of high-context cultures are skilled in using nonverbal cues to communicate. Members of low-context cultures rely more on actual words to send and receive messages.

Cultural Values

Ancient Egyptians worshiped cats. The Druids of England believed they could tap into spiritual powers in the shadow of the mysterious rock circle of Stonehenge at the summer solstice. Some would say contemporary Americans place a high value on accumulating material possessions and making pilgrimages to sports arenas on weekends. By paying attention to what a culture values, we can learn important clues about how to respond to communication messages, establish relationships, and avoid making embarrassing errors when interacting with people from a given culture. Identifying **what a given group of people values or appreciates (cultural values)** can give us insight into the behavior of an individual raised within that culture. Although there are considerable differences among the world's cultural values—clearly, not all cultures value the same things—Geert Hofstede has identified five categories for measuring values that are important in almost every culture.[26] Even though his original data were collected more than 30 years ago and only sampled employees (predominantly males) who worked at IBM—a large international company with branch offices in many countries—his original research remains

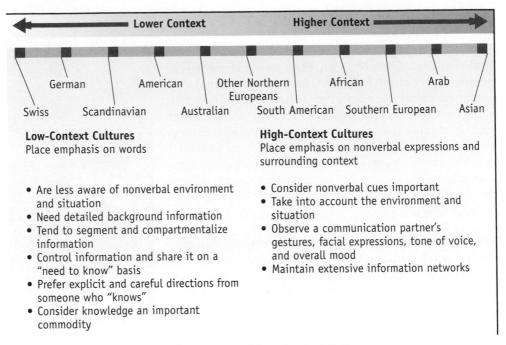

FIGURE 1.6.2   A Scale of High-Context and Low-Context Cultures

one of the most comprehensive studies to help us understand how to describe what people from a culture may value.

According to Hofstede, every culture establishes values relating to (1) individualism versus collectivism, (2) distribution of power (either centralized or shared), (3) avoidance of uncertainty versus tolerance for uncertainty, (4) masculine or feminine cultural perspectives, and (5) long-term and short-term orientations to time. An overview of Hofstede's research conclusions for several countries is included in Table 1.6.1. These generalizations are based on several surveys that he developed and administered to over 100,000 people. We'll consider each of these five categories of values in more detail.

Individualistic and Collectivistic Cultural Values   Which of the following two sayings best characterizes your culture: "All for one and one for all" or "I did it my way"? If you chose the first one, **your culture is more likely to value group or team collaboration—it is what researchers call a collectivistic culture.** Collectivistic cultures champion what people do together and reward group achievement. In contrast, the "I did it my way" phrase emphasizes the importance of the individual over the group. **A culture that celebrates individual achievement and in which individual recognition is important is an individualistic culture.** The United States—with its Academy Awards, its reality TV shows in which contestants vie for the title of "American Idol" or try to be the lone "Survivor," its countless sports con-

TABLE 1.6.1
Countries That Illustrate Five Categories of Cultural Values

Cultural Value	Countries That Scored Higher on This Cultural Value	Countries That Scored Lower on This Cultural Value
Individualism: Societies with higher individualism scores generally value individual accomplishment rather than collective or collaborative achievement.	United States, Australia, Great Britain, Canada, Netherlands, New Zealand, Italy, Belgium, Denmark, Sweden, France	Guatemala, Ecuador, Panama, Venezuela, Colombia, Indonesia, Pakistan, Costa Rica, Peru, Taiwan, South Korea
Power Distribution: Societies with higher power distribution scores generally value greater power differences between people; they are generally more accepting of fewer people having authority and power than are those with lower scores on this cultural dimension.	Malaysia, Guatemala, Panama, Philippines, Mexico, Venezuela, Arab countries, Ecuador, Indonesia, India	Australia, Israel, Denmark, New Zealand, Ireland, Sweden, Norway, Finland, Switzerland, Great Britain, United States
Uncertainty Avoidance: Societies with higher uncertainty avoidance scores generally prefer to avoid uncertainty; they like to know what will happen next. Societies with lower scores are more comfortable with uncertainty.	Greece, Portugal, Guatemala, Uruguay, Belgium, Japan, Peru, France	Singapore, Jamaica, Denmark, Sweden, Hong Kong, Ireland, Great Britain, Malaysia, India, Philippines, United States
Masculinity: Societies with higher masculinity scores value high achievement, men in more assertive roles, and more clearly differentiated sex roles than do societies with lower scores on this cultural dimension.	Japan, Australia, Venezuela, Italy, Switzerland, Mexico, Ireland, Jamaica, Great Britain, United States	Sweden, Norway, Netherlands, Denmark, Costa Rica, Finland, Chile, Portugal, Thailand
Orientation to Time: Societies with higher scores have a longer-term orientation to time; they tend to value perseverance and thrift. Societies with lower scores have a shorter-term orientation to time; they value the past and present, respect for tradition, saving "face," and spending rather than saving money.	China, Hong Kong, Taiwan, Japan, Vietnam, South Korea, Brazil, India, Thailand, Hungary, Singapore, Denmark, Netherlands	Pakistan, Czech Republic, Nigeria, Spain, Philippines, Canada, Zimbabwe, Great Britain, United States, Portugal, New Zealand

Source: Adapted with permission from Geert Hofstede and Gert Jan Hofstede, *Cultures and Organization: Software of the Mind*, Revised and Expanded 2nd Edition (New York: McGraw-Hill, 2005). © Geert Hofstede BV.

tests; its community awards to firefighters for dedicated service, to winners of spelling bees, to chefs for their barbecue recipes—perhaps epitomizes the individualistic culture.

Some researchers believe that the values of individualism and collectivism are the most important values of any culture—they determine the essential nature of every other facet of how people behave.[27] Other researchers, however, caution that cultures are complex and that it is dangerous to label an entire culture as "individualistic" or "collectivistic."[28] We agree—obviously, not everyone in a given culture fits a single label. But in trying to understand the role of culture and its impact on human communication, we believe that Hofstede's concept of cultural values, with special emphasis on individualism and collectivism, helps explain and predict how people may send and interpret communication.[29] Using Hofstede's five cultural values to describe a given culture or geographic region is a bit like flying over a country at 35,000 feet; at that height you can't see the details and note nuances of difference, but you can gain a broad overview of the cultural landscape.

Traditionally, North Americans place a high value on individual achievements. People from Asian cultures are more likely to value collective or group achievement. Hofstede summed up the American value system this way:

> Chief among the virtues claimed … is self-realization. Each person is viewed as having a unique set of talents and potentials. The translation of these potentials into actuality is considered the highest purpose to which one can devote one's life.[30]

In a collectivistic culture, conversely, people strive to accomplish goals for the benefit of the group rather than the individual. Here's a description of the Kenyan culture's emphasis on group or team collaboration:

> … nobody is an isolated individual. Rather, his [or her] uniqueness is a secondary fact. . . . In this new system, group activities are dominant, responsibility is shared and accountability is collective. . . . Because of the emphasis on collectivity, harmony and cooperation among the group tend to be emphasized more than individual function and responsibility.[31]

Individualistic cultures tend to be more loosely knit socially; individuals feel responsibility for taking care of themselves and their immediate families.[32] Individuals in collectivistic cultures expect more loyalty and support from others and demonstrate more loyalty to the community. Because collectivistic cultures place more value on "we" than on "I," teamwork approaches usually succeed better in their workplaces. U.S. businesses have tried to adopt some of Japan's successful team strategies for achieving high productivity. However, while teamwork training has been successful, U.S. workers still need constantly to be reminded to collaborate and work collectively.

Decentralized and Centralized Approaches to Power and Cultural Values
Some cultures are more comfortable with a broad distribution of power. People from such cultures prefer a decentralized approach to power. Leadership is not vested in just one person. Decisions in a culture that values decentralized power distribution are more likely to be made by consensus rather than by decree. Research suggests that people from Australia, Israel, Denmark, New Zealand, and Ireland typically prefer minimized power differences between others; they strive for more equal distribution of authority and control.[33]

Cultures that place a high value on centralized power are more comfortable with a more structured form of government, as well as managerial styles that feature clear lines of authority. Hierarchical bureaucracies are common, and the general assumption is that some people will have more power, control, and influence than others. Research by Hofstede suggests that people from Malaysia, Guatemala, Panama, and the Philippines are all high on the centralized power scale.[34]

Uncertainty and Certainty and Cultural Values   "Why don't they tell me what's going on?" exclaims an exasperated student. "I don't know what my grades are. I don't know what my SAT score is. I'm in a complete fog." Many people like to know "what's going on." They like to avoid uncertainty and to have a general sense of what's going to happen. Too much uncertainty makes them uncomfortable.

Some people tolerate more ambiguity and uncertainty than others. Cultures in which people need certainty to feel secure are more likely to develop and enforce rigid rules for behavior and establish more elaborate codes of conduct. People from cultures with a greater tolerance for uncertainty have more relaxed, informal expectations for others. "It will sort itself out" and "Go with the flow" are phrases that

Members of a *collectivistic* culture may find team sports to be more satisfying than individual sports.

characterize their attitudes.[35] As shown in Table 1.6.1, people from Greece, Portugal, and Guatemala generally do not like uncertainty, while people from Singapore, Jamaica, and Denmark are more comfortable not knowing what will happen next.

Again, we remind you that although there is evidence for the existence of the general cultural value of uncertainty avoidance, not all people in a given culture or country find this cultural value equally important. There is considerable variation within a culture as to how people respond to uncertainty.

Masculine and Feminine Cultural Values   Some cultures emphasize traditional male values—such as getting things done and being more assertive; other cultures place greater emphasis on traditional female values—building relationships and seeking peace and harmony with others. **People from masculine cultures tend to value more traditional roles for men and women, as well as achievement, assertiveness, heroism, and material wealth.** These values are not only about biological differences; they are general approaches to interacting with other people. **Men and women from feminine cultures tend to value such things as caring for the less fortunate, being sensitive toward others, and enhancing the overall quality of life.**[36] Later in this chapter, we will discuss how gender contributes to the

On the Web

You need not travel to a foreign destination to experience another culture; opportunities to experience cultural differences may be as close as talking with your roommate, an instructor, or a good friend. To learn more about the role of culture in communication, check out one of the following Web sites, which offer more information about intercultural communication.

www.awesomelibrary.org is the Web address of Awesome Library. Once you're at this site, type in the words "intercultural communication" in the Search box to access information and resources about intercultural communication skills and principles.

www.takingitglobal.org/home.html is the site for Taking It Global. It provides resources that focus on student travel, including cultural tips and ideas to facilitate better understanding between people from different cultures.

development of a culture, but for now it is enough to realize that whole cultures can be typified by whether they identify with or emphasize masculine or feminine values.

Having said all of the above, we caution you to avoid making sweeping generalizations about every person in any cultural group. Just as there are differences between and among cultures, there are differences within a cultural group. For centuries, most countries have had masculine cultures. Men and their conquests are featured in history books and all aspects of society more than women. But today's cultural anthropologists see some shift in these values. There is some movement toward the middle, with greater equality between masculine and feminine roles.

Long-Term and Short-Term Time Orientation and Cultural Values

A culture's orientation to time falls on a continuum between long-term and short-term.[37] People from a culture with a long-term orientation to time place an emphasis on the future and tend to value perseverance and thrift because these are virtues that pay off over a long period of time. A long-term time orientation also implies a greater willingness to subordinate oneself for a larger purpose, such as the good of society or the group. In contrast, a culture that tends to have a short-term time orientation values spending rather than saving (because of a focus on the immediate rather than the future), tradition (because of the value placed on the past), and preserving "face" of both self and others (making sure that an individual is respected and that his or her dignity is upheld) and has an expectation that results will soon follow the actions and effort expended on a task. Short-term cultures also place a high value on social and status obligations.

As shown in Table 1.6.1, cultures or societies with a long-term time orientation include many Asian cultures such as China, Hong Kong, Taiwan, and Japan. Short-term time orientation cultures include Pakistan, Czech Republic, Nigeria, Spain, and the Philippines. Both Canada and the United States are closer to the short-term time orientation than the long-term time orientation, which suggests an emphasis on valuing quick results from projects and greater pressure toward spending rather than saving, as well as a respect for traditions.[38]

© United Feature Syndicate, Inc.

RECAP

Cultural Values

Individualistic vs. Collectivistic	• Individualistic cultures value individual accomplishments and achievement. • Collectivistic cultures value group and team collaboration.
Decentralized vs. Centralized Power	• Centralized power cultures value having power in the hands of a smaller number of people. • Decentralized power cultures favor more equality and a more even distribution of power in government and organizations.
Uncertainty vs. Certainty	• Cultures that value certainty do not like ambiguity and value feeling secure. • Cultures with a greater tolerance for uncertainty are comfortable with ambiguity and less information.
Masculine vs. Feminine	• Masculine cultures value achievement, assertiveness, heroism, material wealth, and more traditional sex roles. • Feminine cultures value relationships, caring for the less fortunate, overall quality of life, and less traditional distinctions between sex roles.
Long-Term vs. Short-Term Orientation to Time	• Cultures with a long-term orientation to time tend to be future-oriented and value perseverance and thrift. • Cultures with a short-term orientation to time tend to value the past and present, respecting tradition, preserving "face," and fulfilling social obligations.

QUICK REVIEW

Gender and Communication

Perhaps the most obvious form of human diversity is gender—the division of human beings into female and male. As we pointed out in Chapter 1.2, a person's sex is determined by biology; gender is the culturally constructed and psychologically based perception of one's self as feminine, masculine, or **androgynous (having both feminine and masculine traits).** One's gender is learned and is socially reinforced by others, as well as by one's life experience and genetics. Some scholars prefer to study gender as a subset of culture (a co-culture), as a form of cultural diversity on the level of such other aspects as race, ethnicity, and religion. We view gender as one of many basic elements of culture; but because it so pervades our everyday existence, we choose to treat gender more fully in this chapter as we continue our focus on adapting to others.

At one time or another, you have probably thought, "Why doesn't she (or he) act like persons of *my* sex?" Have you ever heard yourself or someone else say, "You men are all alike," or "If women would just be more reasonable, like men are, life would be simpler"? You may also have heard (or said) "Vive la difference"—a French expression that celebrates the fact that men and women are different. Why celebrate? Because that difference makes us fascinating and mysterious, and it keeps the world from being awfully dull. Whatever your view of the relationship between the sexes, your day-to-day interaction with members of both sexes is a fact of life (unless you're a hermit). Women and men work, live, and play together, so it's important to explore the effects of gender on communication in order to improve our ability to relate to one another.

In fact, the likelihood that all of us will come into more frequent contact with members of both sexes is increasing, because Americans are working longer hours. Recent statistics reveal that we spent 10% more time on the job at the turn of the twenty-first century than in the 1960s.[39] Projections suggest that women will soon account for 63% of all employees.[40]

The Importance of Gender in Culture

In the predominant culture of the United States, someone's gender is an important thing to know. Think about it: What's the first question a new parent is asked? "Ten fingers and ten toes?" "Hairy or bald-headed?" "Blue eyes or brown?" No—usually the first question asked is, "Is it a boy or girl?" We place a great deal of importance on a person's sex in this culture, as do all cultures around the world. Some critics contend that we're too concerned with gender, with emphasizing differences between women and men and conditioning young boys to be masculine and girls to be feminine. Some men and women in our culture are chastised or ostracized because they don't conform to society's expectations for their sex.

Fascinating research reveals that sex-based expectations and conditioning start practically from birth. Adults, beginning with parents, talk to and respond to girls and boys differently.[41] Female babies are held more gingerly; as they become toddlers, they receive more attention from parents when they fall and are kept in closer proximity than male children. Boys are encouraged to rough and tumble, to "shake it off" when they fall, and to explore greater distances than girls. Girls are often allowed to reveal their emotions more readily than boys, while many boys may be taught to control or hide their emotions. When carried into adulthood, these early gender-based lessons may cause seri-

ous harm to our bodies, professional advancement, and relationships. For example, women who want to succeed in their careers often learn the hard way that revealing their emotions isn't considered professional. Many men find that years of suppressing emotion can lead to health problems and estrangement from family members.

An important question to consider is this: Just how different are you and members of your sex from members of the opposite sex? Do you think that women are from one planet and men another? Do you think that men constitute one cultural group and women another? Or do you think the media and other moneymaking enterprises oversell sex differences in an effort to create conflict and drama to generate high ratings and profits?

John Gray, author of the book *Men Are from Mars, Women Are from Venus*, would have us believe that the sexes are so different that we actually approach life from two distinct "planets" or spheres of perspective.[42] Although several of Gray's conclusions have been challenged by communication scholars because they are not supported by research, there are some research-documented differences in the ways men and women communicate.[43] Deborah Tannen, author of several books on the behavior of the sexes, views men and women as distinctly different cultural groups.[44] She suggests that female–male communication is cross-cultural communication, with all the challenges inherent in exchanging messages with persons of very different backgrounds and value systems. Perhaps these viewpoints are a bit extreme, and the sexes are actually more alike than different.

There are, however, some interesting differences based on research—not popular opinion or media hype—that are worthy of mention. We will discuss some of these in the next section. After reading that discussion, here's what we suggest you do:

- First, work to understand the differences we discuss.
- Second, make an insightful examination of your own behavior in light of the differences discussed and then determine how you conform to and differ from the description of members of your sex.

- Third, be a gender researcher yourself. Make a note of differences as well as similarities between you and members of the opposite sex. Be careful not to ascribe differences in communication only to gender, but also consider a host of other reasons such as age, personality, or culture.
- Finally, make a conscious effort to adapt your behavior appropriately. We don't mean that you have to always communicate as you think members of your sex would or should communicate, but be mindful of how you interact with others to enhance the quality of your relationships with them.

Why Women and Men Communicate Versus *How*

In an earlier section of this chapter, we explored ways in which whole cultures are typified by their emphasis on masculine or feminine values. Some of the values associated with masculinity include being assertive and getting things done. Classic sociological research has termed such qualities **an instrumental orientation, a term that implies assertiveness and action and a "me against the world" view of self.**[45] **Feminine cultural values emphasize**

connecting with others and fostering harmonious relationships, what has been termed an expressive orientation.

Translating these orientations into actual communication behavior is revealing. Research using multiple methods and originating in various disciplines consistently shows that differences in men's and women's communication have more to do with *why* we communicate than *how*. Men tend to talk to accomplish something or complete a task. Women often use conversation to establish and maintain relationships.

In Chapter 1.1, we discussed some basic characteristics of communication, the first being that communication is inescapable. We expanded on that characteristic by describing how every message has a content dimension and a relational dimension. **The content dimension is what is said, or the verbal message. The relational dimension involves how the verbal message is said, including tone of voice, facial expressions, and other nonverbal behaviors.** The content dimension is the *what*, the relational dimension is the *how*; the latter aspect tells you how to interpret the former. You also receive clues from the relational dimension about the state of the relationship between the two communicators. How are these characteristics of communication affected by gender?

Research reveals that men tend to approach communication from a content orientation, meaning that they view the purpose of communication as primarily information exchange. You talk when you have something to say. This is also consistent with the tendency for men to base their relationships, especially their male friendships, on sharing activities rather than talking. Women, research suggests, tend to use communication for the purpose of relating or connecting to others, of extending themselves to other persons to know them and be known by them. What you talk about is less important than the fact that you're talking, because talking implies relationship. There is a short way of summarizing this difference: *Men often communicate to report; women often communicate to establish rapport.*[46] So the point of difference isn't in the way the sexes actually communicate but in the motivations or reasons for communicating. The *how* may not be that different; the *why* may be very different.[47] Our instrumental and expressive orientations to the world translate into our communication behavior.

So here's one reason why adaptation is a premium skill. Can you see that by understanding both approaches to communication—content and relational (or instrumental and expressive)—and by developing the ability to accomplish both, you broaden what you can do? Just because you're female doesn't mean that you have to take an expressive approach to every interaction; just because you're male doesn't mean that conversations are always about information exchange. In a conversation with a member of the opposite sex, try to assess the person's communication motivation. Analyze what the other person must view as the purpose for the conversation, and adjust your response accordingly. Sometimes it's wise simply to ask the person what he or she wants.

RECAP

Gender-Based Approaches to Communication

Masculine Approach	Feminine Approach
More instrumental, often characterized by assertiveness and getting things done	More expressive, often characterized by an emphasis on connecting with others and fostering harmonious relationships
Usually more emphasis on the content of messages	Usually more emphasis on the relational elements of messages
Focuses more on the information being exchanged (the *what*) rather than on relational elements (the *how*) in the message	Focuses more on the quality of the relationship between communicators than on information exchanged
Attends more to verbal than nonverbal messages	Attends more to nonverbal elements, *how* something is said rather than *what* is said

QUICK
REVIEW

Barriers to Bridging Differences and Adapting to Others

Now that we've paid attention to how people are different from one another, let's identify barriers that increase the differences that exist between people. Differences, whether culture or gender based, often breed misunderstanding. And misunderstanding can lead to feelings of distrust, suspicion, and even hostility. The phrase "battle of the sexes" suggests that men and women perceive and respond to the world differently, which may result in disagreement and evolve into literal battles. Among the most common reasons for a woman to end up in an emergency room in the United States today is bodily harm inflicted by a male whom she knows.[48]

The front pages of newspapers continue to chronicle the prevalence of terrorism, war, and conflict around the globe, which are due, in part, to different cultural perspectives. Our hopes for harmony in our own country erode when we learn of hate crimes committed against members of co-cultural groups within the larger U.S. culture. Our hopes for peace and prosperity among all of the world's peoples are often dashed when we read of violent clashes between people of different religions, races, sexual orientations, and ethnicities.

Is it possible to develop effective relationships with people who are different from ourselves? The answer is "Of course." Although almost every relationship experiences some degree of conflict, most of the world's people do not witness annihilating destruction each day. Bridging culture and gender differences is possible.

The first step to bridging differences between people is to identify what hinders effective communication. Sometimes communication falters because of different meanings created by different languages or interpretations of nonverbal messages. And sometimes communication is not effective because of our inability to stop focusing exclusively on our own goals; we fail to consider the needs of our communication partners. To develop effective strategies to adapt to others who are different from ourselves, we'll examine some of the barriers that often separate us from one another.

Assuming Superiority

We shook our heads in absolute horror and disbelief as we watched TV images of the twin towers of the World Trade Center crumbling in a shroud of smoke and ash and the Pentagon erupting in flames. These indelible images of September 11, 2001, are seared in our consciousness. Collectively we asked "Why?" There are no easy answers. Part of the answer, however, may lie in the belief of self-righteous superiority held by those who seek to destroy cultural and religious traditions that are different from their own. Of course, terrorism and violence are not new; historical records document that differences, especially religious differences, have for centuries created conditions that have resulted in unspeakable human atrocities. One of the most powerful barriers to adapting to others is the belief that one's own culture or gender is better than that of others.

Ethnocentrism is the attitude that our own cultural approaches are superior to those of other cultures.[49] Extreme ethnocentrism is the opposite of being other-oriented. When fans from two rival high schools at a Friday-night football game scream, "We're number one!" they are hardly establishing quality communication. Competition is, of course, expected in sports; but when the mindset of unquestioned superiority is created through cultural or religious identification, the resulting mistrust and suspicion are breeding grounds for conflict. Ethnocentrism and cultural snobbery create a barrier that inhibits rather than enhances communication.

It would probably be impossible to avoid feeling most comfortable with our own culture and people who are like us. In fact, some degree of ethnocentrism can play a useful role in perpetuating our own cultural traditions; we form communities and groups based on common traditions, beliefs, and values. A problem occurs, however, if we become so extremely biased in favor of our own cultural traditions that we fail to recognize that people from other cultural traditions are just as comfortable with their approach to life as we are to ours. And when we mindlessly attack someone else's cultural traditions (which may be a prelude to physical aggression), we begin to erect communication barriers.

"My dad is smarter than your dad." "Boys are smarter than girls." "U.S. workers are more industrious than workers in other countries." What may start out as a child's chant may evolve into a cultural consciousness that leads

Because the communication process may be difficult between members of different cultures, both parties need to work to understand each other.

to perceptions of cultural and gender superiority. Cultural anthropologists caution against assuming that one culture is superior to another; as we just noted, this creates a barrier. If you have ever talked with someone with an overinflated ego, you know what a hindrance such a self-promoting attitude can be to communication. If a group or nation harbors that sense of unchallenged superiority and feeling of ordained righteousness, it will be difficult to establish quality communication relationships with that group.

A person who assumes superiority may also assume greater power and control over others. Conflicts are often about power—who has it and who wants more of it. Differences in power, therefore, are breeding grounds for mistrust and conflict. The nineteenth-century British scholar Lord Acton said that absolute power corrupts absolutely; although this may not always be the case, an ethnocentric mindset that assumes superiority may add to the perception of assumed power over others. Although it's true that there are cultural differences in attitudes toward power (whether power is centralized or decentralized), world history documents that those who are consistently pushed and pulled and pummeled eventually revolt and seek greater equity of power.

Assuming Similarity

Just as it is inaccurate to assume that all members of the opposite sex or all people who belong to other social groups or classes are worlds apart from you, it is also wrong to assume that others will act and think just like you. Even if they appear to be like you, all people do not behave the same way.[50] Anthropologists Clyde Kluckhohn and Henry Murray suggested that every person is, in some respects, (1) like all other people, (2) like some other people, and (3) like no other people.[51] Our challenge when meeting others is to sort out how we are alike and how we are unique. Focusing on superficial factors such as appearance, clothing, and even a person's occupation can lead to false impressions. Instead, we must take time to explore the person's background and cultural values before we can determine what we really have in common.

On meeting a new acquaintance, we usually explore what we may have in common. "Do you know so and so?" "Oh, you're from Missouri. Do you know Mamie Smith from Buckner?" The search for similarities helps us develop a common framework for communication. But even when we find a few similarities, it's a mistake to make too many assumptions about our new friend's attitudes and perceptions. Because of our human tendency to develop categories and use words to label our experiences, we may lump people into a common category and assume similarity where no similarity exists. Each of us perceives the world through our own frame of reference. As one ancient Greek sage put it, "Every tale can be told in a different way." We not only see the world differently, we express those differences in the way we talk, think, and interact with others. If we fail to be mindful that each of us is unique, we may take communication shortcuts, use unfamiliar words, and assume our communication will be more effective than it is.

Assuming Differences

Although it may seem contradictory to say so, given what we just noted about assuming similarities, another barrier that may keep you from bridging differences between yourself and someone else is to automatically assume that the other person will be different from you. It can be just as detrimental to communication to assume someone is essentially different from you as it is to assume someone is just like you. The fact is, human beings *do* share common experiences and characteristics despite their differences. So we suggest that while you don't want to assume everyone is just like you, it's also detrimental to communication to assume you have nothing in common with others.

Cultural anthropologists have spent considerable effort to identify cultural differences among people. The gist of this entire chapter is that people are different—in culture, gender, and a host of other factors such as personality, age, sexual orientation, and innate talents. Yet if we don't seek to connect with those factors that make us all members of the human family, we may miss opportunities for bridging the real differences that exist.

The point of noting that humans have similarities as well as differences is not to diminish the role of culture as a key element that influences communication, but to recognize that despite cultural differences we are all members of the human family. The words *communication* and *common* resemble one another. We communicate effectively and appropriately when we can connect to others based on discovering what we hold in common. Identifying common cultural issues and similarities can also help you establish common ground with your audience.

How are we all alike? Cultural anthropologist Donald Brown has compiled a list of hundreds of "surface" universals of behavior.[52] According to Brown, people in all cultures

- have beliefs about death
- have a childhood fear of strangers
- have a division of labor by sex
- experience certain emotions and feelings, such as envy, pain, jealousy, shame, and pride
- use facial expressions to express emotions
- have rules for etiquette
- experience empathy
- value some degree of collaboration or cooperation
- experience conflict and seek to manage or mediate conflict

Of course, not all cultures have the same beliefs about death or the same way of dividing labor according to sex, but all cultures address these issues. Communication researcher David Kale believes that another universal value is the dignity and worth of other people. Thus, he suggests that all people can identify with the struggle to enhance their own dignity and worth, although different cultures express that in different ways.[53] Another common value that Kale notes is world peace. Intercultural communication scholars Larry Samovar and Richard Porter assert that there are other common elements that cultures share.[54] They note that people from all cultures seek physical pleasure as well as emotional and psychological pleasure and seek to avoid personal harm. It's true that each culture and each person decides what is pleasurable or painful; nonetheless, argue Samovar and Porter, all people operate within this pleasure-pain continuum.

Another advocate for common human values was the Oxford and Cambridge professor and widely read author C. S. Lewis. In his book *The Abolition of Man*, Lewis argued for the existence of universal, natural laws, which he called the Tao, that serve as benchmarks for all human values.[55] Lewis identified such common values as do not murder; be honest; hold parents, elders, and ancestors with special honor; be compassionate to those who are less fortunate; keep your promises; honor the basic human rights of others.

Educators have long debated whether there are common human values and whether they can be taught. There are over 50 consulting organizations in the United States that develop "character education" programs for primary and secondary schools.[56] One district adopted a curriculum to teach "touch-stone character skills" that include caring, courage, fairness, honesty, integrity, perseverance, respect, responsibility, self-discipline, and trustworthiness.[57]

What are the practical implications of trying to identify common human values or characteristics? If you find yourself disagreeing with another person about a particular issue, identifying a larger common value such as the value of peace and prosperity or the importance of family can help you find common ground so that the other person will at least listen to your ideas. It's useful, we believe, not just to categorize our differences but also to explore how human beings are similar to one another. Discovering how we are alike can provide a starting point for human understanding. Yes, we are all different; but we share things in common as well. Communication effectiveness is diminished when we assume we're all different from one another in every aspect, just as communication is hindered if we assume we're all alike. We're more complicated than that.

Stereotyping and Prejudice

Closely related to ethnocentrism and feelings of cultural and gender superiority is the barrier of making a rigid judgment against a class or type of people.

All Russians like vodka.
All men like to watch wrestling.

Ethics and *Communication*

Stereotyping Others

*W*e've pointed out that being prejudiced toward others, as well as stereotyping people into predetermined, rigid categories (especially because of racial, ethnic, or cultural backgrounds), can hinder effective communication. Reaching conclusions about someone before you get to know him or her can result in a dishonest relationship. Most people are taught not to be prejudiced toward others. Yet might stereotypes sometimes serve a useful purpose, especially when a quick decision is needed and you have only partial information?

Imagine, for example, that you are driving your car late at night and have a flat tire in a neighborhood that's known to have a high crime rate. While wondering what to do, you see two people who have observed your plight and are moving toward you. Do you hop out of your car and seek their help? Or do you lock your doors and be thankful that you have your cell phone to call for assistance? Are there times when prejudging a situation and reaching stereotypical conclusions about others may make common sense? Could a case be made that the ability to create and respond stereotypically may be useful in times of stress when quick thinking is needed? We never know all of the facts about a situation, and we sometimes (maybe even often) have to respond with only the partial information we have at hand. Some might argue that we sometimes need to make stereotypical, snap judgments. Malcolm Gladwell, author of *Blink: The Power of Thinking Without Thinking,* describes how people often make quick, snap decisions and argues that sometimes these "thin-sliced," momentary decisions can be quite accurate.[58] Of course, sometimes snap judgments can be way off base. What do you think? Is it ever appropriate to hold stereotypical views of others and to make judgments about them without knowing all of the facts? When do stereotypical evaluations hinder communication? When is it preferable not to make stereotypical decisions?

All Asians are good at math.
All women like to go shopping.

These statements are stereotypes. They are all inaccurate. **To stereotype someone is to place him or her in an inflexible, all-encompassing category.** The term *stereotype* started out as a printing term to describe a process in which the typesetter uses the same type to print text again and again. When we stereotype, we "print" the same judgment over and over again, failing to consider the uniqueness of individuals, groups, or events. Such a "hardening of the categories" becomes a barrier to effective communication and inhibits our ability to adapt to others.

A related barrier, **prejudice, is a judgment based on the assumption that we already know all of the information we need to know about a person.** To prejudge someone as inept, inferior, or incompetent based on that person's ethnicity, race, sexual orientation, gender, or some other factor is a corrosive practice that can raise significant barriers to effective communication. Some prejudices are widespread. Although there are more females than males in the world, one study found that even when a male and a female held the same type of job, the male's job was considered more prestigious than the female's.[59] Even though it is illegal in the United States to discriminate because of a person's gender, race, or age in offering employment or promotions, women and members of minority groups may still be discriminated against. In the workplace, stereotyping and prejudice are still formidable barriers to communicating effectively with others.

Mark Twain once said, "It is discouraging to try and penetrate a mind such as yours. You ought to get out and dance on it. That would take some of the rigidity out of it." Learning how to break rigid stereotypes and overcome prejudice is an important part of the process of learning how to adapt to others.

Different Communication Codes

When Janice and Ron were on their vacation in Miami, Florida, they visited a market on Calle Ocho, in the heart of Little Havana—a district populated by many Cuban immigrants. When they tried to purchase some fruit, it was a frustrating experience for Janice and Ron as well as the market salesclerk; Janice and Ron spoke no Spanish, and the clerk knew no English. It is not uncommon today, when you travel within the United States, to encounter people who do not speak your language. Obviously, this kind of difference poses a formidable communication challenge. Even when you do speak the same language as another, he or she may come from a place where the words and gestures have different meanings. Your ability to communicate will depend on whether you can understand each other's verbal and nonverbal cues.

RECAP

Barriers to Bridging Differences and Adapting to Others

Assuming Superiority	Becoming ethnocentric—assuming that one's own culture and cultural traditions are superior to those of others
Assuming Similarity	Assuming that other people respond to situations as we respond; failing to acknowledge and consider differences in culture and background
Assuming Differences	Assuming that other people are always different from ourselves; failing to explore common values and experiences that can serve as bridges to better understanding
Stereotyping and Prejudice	Rigidly categorizing and prejudging others based on limited information
Different Communication Codes	Differences in language and the interpretation of nonverbal cues that lead to misunderstanding

QUICK REVIEW

Adapting to Others Who Are Different from You

It is not enough simply to identify some of the common barriers that highlight our differences. Although becoming "consciously competent" about what may keep us from adapting and connecting with others is important, there are also some strategies that can help in our quest to adapt to others. Eleanor Roosevelt once said, "We have to face the fact that either we, all of us, are going to die together or we are going to live together, and if we are to live together we have to talk."[60] In essence, she was saying that we need effective communication skills to overcome our differences. It is not enough just to point to the barriers we have identified and say, "Don't do that." Identifying the causes of misunderstanding is a good first step, but most people need more concrete advice with specific strategies to help them overcome these barriers.

To become competent at any task you need three things: knowledge, motivation, and skill. To help you become competent in appropriately adapting to others, we suggest that you use two strategies to help you increase your knowledge about others: seek information about a culture and ask questions and listen to the responses. To maintain your motivation to adapt when communicating with others who are different from you, we encourage you to be patient and to strive to tolerate ambiguity and uncertainty; in addition, being mindfully aware of the differences between you and others can help you adapt. Finally, the key skills for communicating with people who are different from you include becoming other-oriented and then appropriately adapting your communication to others.

Seek Information

Philosopher André Gide said, "Understanding is the beginning of approving." Prejudice often is the result of ignorance. Learning about another person's values, beliefs, and culture can help you understand his or her messages and their meaning. As you speak to a person from another culture, think of yourself as a detective, watching for implied, often unspoken messages that provide information about the values, norms, roles, and rules of that person's culture.

You can also prepare yourself by studying other cultures. If you are going to another country, start by reading a travel guide or another general overview of the culture. You may then want to learn more detailed information by studying the history, art, or geography of the culture. The Internet offers a wealth of information about the cultures and traditions of others. In addition to reading books and magazines and using cyber sources, talk to people from other cultures. If you are trying to communicate with someone closer to home who is from a different background, you can learn about the music, food, and other aspects of the culture. Given the inextricable link between language and culture, the more skilled you become at speaking another language, the better you will understand the traditions and customs of the culture where it is spoken.

As we discussed at the beginning of the chapter, the broad concept of culture also includes the notion of a co-culture, a cultural group within a larger culture. Learning how men and women, members of separate co-cultures, communicate differently can help improve your communication with members of the opposite sex.

As you read about other cultures or co-cultures, it is important not to develop rigid categories or stereotypes for the way others may talk or behave. Proclaiming "Oh, you're just saying that because you're a woman" or "You men are always saying things like that" can increase rather than decrease communication barriers. In this chapter, we will identify research-based gender differences in the way men and women communicate to improve your understanding of and communication with members of the opposite sex. But, as noted earlier, we don't recommend that you treat men and women as completely separate species from different planets and automatically assume you will be misunderstood. Such a stereotypical judgment does not enhance communication—it hinders it.

Ask Questions and Listen

When you talk with people who are different from you, you may feel some discomfort and uncertainty. This is normal. We are more comfortable talking with people we know and who are like us. Communication, through the give-and-take process of listening, talking, and asking questions, helps to reduce the uncertainty present in any relationship. When you meet people for the first time, you are typically not certain about their likes and dislikes, including whether they like or dislike you. When you communicate with a person from another culture or co-culture, the uncertainty level escalates. As you begin to talk, you exchange information that helps you develop greater understanding. If you continue to ask questions, eventually you will feel less anxiety and uncertainty. You will be more able to predict how the person will behave. When you meet a person who is different from you, ask thoughtful questions, then pause to listen. This is a simple technique for gathering information and also for confirming the accuracy of your expectations and assumptions.

Just asking questions and sharing information about yourself is not sufficient to remove communication barriers and bridge differences in culture and background, but it is a good beginning. The skills of stopping (focusing on the message of the other person), looking (observing nonverbal cues), and listening (noting both details and major ideas) that we presented in the last chapter will serve you well in enhancing communication with people from cultural traditions different from your own.

Tolerate Ambiguity

Many people become uncomfortable with uncertainty and ambiguity—especially if they are from a low-context culture such as those in North America. As we discussed earlier in the chapter, people from low-context cultures prefer a more direct approach to getting information. North Americans, for example, often say things like "Tell it to me straight," "Don't beat around the bush," or "Just tell me what you want."

Communicating with someone from a culture that does not value such directness produces uncertainty. It may take time and several exchanges to clarify a message. If you are from a cultural tradition that values certainty, and you are uncomfortable with uncertainty, you may have to acknowledge the cultural difference. Be patient and work at tolerating more ambiguity. Don't be in a hurry to have all of the details nailed down. Remind yourself that the other person does not have the same attitudes about knowing the future or appreciating details.

Develop Mindfulness

To be mindful is to be aware of how you communicate with others. A mindful communicator puts into practice the first communication principle we presented in this book: *Be aware of your communication with yourself and others.* To be a mindful communicator, you should constantly remind yourself that other people are not like you. Also, you should be aware that other people do not use different communication strategies to offend or to be rude, they just have different culturally based strategies of interacting with others. Intercultural communication scholar William Gudykunst suggests that being mindful is one of the best ways to approach any new cultural encounter.[61] Mindfulness is a conscious state of mind, a realization of what is happening to you at a given moment. If you are not mindful, you are oblivious to the world around you. You are on mental cruise control.

How can you cultivate the skill of being mindful? You can become more mindful through **self-talk (inner speech; communication with the self; the process of mentally verbalizing messages that help a person become more aware or mindful of how he or she is processing information and reacting to life situations)**, something we discussed earlier in the book. Self-talk consists of messages you tell yourself to help you manage your discomfort, emotions, or negative thoughts about situations. When Ron and Janice tried to purchase the fruit in the Cuban market in Miami, they could have become offended and muttered, "Doesn't anyone speak English around here?" Instead, Janice reminded Ron "You know, it's not surprising that only Spanish is spoken here. Yes, it would be more comfortable for us if the clerk spoke our language. But we have to realize that there is no intent to offend us." Janice was being mindful of the cultural differences; by acknowledging the differences rather than emotionally and mindlessly becoming offended, she was able to maintain her composure and communicate in a manner appropriate to the circumstances.

Become Other-Oriented

Scholars of evolution might argue that it is our tendency to look out for number one that ensures the continuation of the human race. But if we focus exclusively on ourselves, it is very unlikely that we will be effective communicators. As we noted earlier, assuming superiority is a major barrier to communicating with others. Most of us are **egocentric—focused on ourselves and our importance.**[62] Our first inclination is to focus on meeting our own needs before addressing the needs of others.[63]

In this chapter we have emphasized the principle of adapting to others. If we fail to adapt our message to listeners, especially listeners who are different from us (and isn't everyone different from you?), it is less likely that we will achieve our communication goal. As we noted earlier, adapting messages to others doesn't mean that we tell others only what they want to hear. That would be unethical, manipulative, and ineffective. Nor does being considerate of others mean we abandon all concern for our own interests. **Other-oriented communication takes into account the needs, motives, desires, and goals of our communication partners while still maintaining our own integrity.** The choices we make in forming messages and selecting the time and place to deliver them should consider the thoughts and feelings of others.

Becoming other-oriented is not a single skill but a family of skills anchored in a willingness to try to understand others' thoughts and feelings. Research in emotional intelligence documents that focusing on the needs and interests of others is essential to adapting communication messages to others.[64]

How do you become other-oriented? We suggest a two-stage process, using skills discussed previously. The first stage, which we previewed in Chapter 1.5, is called social decentering—consciously *thinking* about another's thoughts and feelings. The second stage is developing empathy, a set of skills we also discussed in the last chapter. To empathize is to respond *emotionally* to another's feelings and actions. We'll discuss each of these two stages in more detail.

Social Decentering   **Social decentering is a cognitive process through which we take into consideration another person's thoughts, values, background, and perspectives.** It is seeing the world from the other person's point of view. To socially decenter is not to be a mind reader but to use past experiences and our ability to interpret the cues of others to understand what others may be thinking or how they may be perceiving issues or situations. According to Mark Redmond, a scholar who has extensively studied the process of social decentering, there are three ways to socially decenter.[65]

First, develop an understanding of the other person, based on how you have responded when something similar has happened to you in the past.[66] You know what it's like when you've been late for a meeting or an important appointment. When someone you know says he or she feels frazzled because he or she was late for a major meeting, you can think about what would be going through your mind if the same thing happened to you.

A second way to socially decenter is to base your understanding of what another person might be thinking on your knowledge of how that person has responded in the past. In communicating with someone who is different from you, the more direct experience you have interacting with that person, the better able you usually are to make predictions about how that person will react and respond. Suppose, for example, you have never seen one particular friend of yours be late for a meeting; you know how generally punctual your friend is. You therefore can guess that your friend would be quite frustrated by being late for a meeting.

A third way we socially decenter is to use our understanding of how most people, in general, respond to situations. If your roommate is from France, you probably have some general sense of the cultural differences between you and your French friend. You may harbor some general theories or assumptions about other French people. The trick, however, is to avoid rigid stereotypes or prejudices that confine or limit your perceptions. The more you can learn about others' cultural or gender perspectives, the more accurate you can become in socially decentering. It is important, however, not to develop inaccurate, inflexible stereotypes and labels for others or to base your perceptions of others only on generalizations.

Developing Empathy   Socially decentering involves attempting to understand what another person may be thinking. **Developing empathy,** a second strategy for becoming other oriented, **is feeling the emotional reaction that the other person may be experiencing.** When we feel empathy, we feel what another person feels.

As we discussed in the last chapter, you develop the ability to empathize by being sensitive to your own feelings and assessing how you feel during certain situations and then projecting those feelings onto others.[67] To develop empathy, we suggested that you first *stop* focusing on only your own messages and thoughts and focus instead on the messages of others. We also recommended that you *look* for information about the emotional meaning of messages by focusing on nonverbal cues. Then *listen* by concentrating on what someone is telling you. In addition, *imagine* how you would feel if you were in your partner's position. Then *ask* appropriate questions, if you need to, to gain additional information. Finally, *paraphrase* your communication partner's message content and feelings and monitor his or her reactions to what you communicate.

Some emotional reactions are almost universal and cut across cultural boundaries. The ravages of war, famine, and natural disasters such as floods or

The first step in developing the ability to empathize is to stop focusing on your own messages and begin focusing on the messages of others.

earthquakes evoke universal emotions. As you see pictures on the news of people who have experienced tragedies, you empathize with them. If you've seen the now classic movie *E. T. the Extra Terrestrial,* you may remember that Elliott, the young boy who discovers E. T., experiences an emotional bond with the alien. Elliott feels what E. T. feels. Such extreme empathic bonding may only happen in the movies. It would be unusual, if not impossible, for us to develop such empathy in our everyday relationships with others. Yet it is possible to develop emotional connections to others, and some people are more skilled and sensitive than others in developing emotional, empathic bonds.

Empathy is different from sympathy. **When you offer sympathy, you tell others that you are sorry that they feel what they are feeling.** When you sympathize, you acknowledge someone's feelings. When you empathize, however, you experience an emotional reaction that is similar to the other person's; as much as possible, you strive to feel what he or she feels.

The late author and theologian Henri J. M. Nouwen suggested that empathy lies at the heart of enhancing the quality of our relationships with others. As Nouwen phrased it, in order to bridge our differences we need to "cross the road for one another":

> We become neighbors when we are willing to cross the road for one another. There is so much separation and segregation: between black people and white people, between gay people and straight people, between young people and old people, between sick people and healthy people, between prisoners and free people, between Jews and Gentiles, Muslims and Christians, Protestants and Catholics, Greek Catholics and Latin Catholics.
>
> There is a lot of road crossing to do. We are all very busy in our own circles. We have our own people to go to and our own affairs to take care of. But if we could cross the road once in a while and pay attention to what is happening on the other side, we might indeed become neighbors.[68]

Adapt to Others

Adapting to others gets to the bottom line of this chapter. After you have thought about how you may be different from others, considered culture and gender differences, and even identified potential barriers to communication, you reach this question: So now what do you *do?* What you do is appropriately adapt. **To adapt is to adjust your behavior in response to the other person or persons you are communicating with.** You don't just keep communicating in the same way you always did. You make an effort to change how you communicate, to enhance the quality of communication.

We adapt messages to others to enhance their understanding of the message, to help us achieve the goal or intended effect of our communication, to ensure that we are ethical in our communication with others, and to establish

RECAP

How to Become Other-Oriented

Socially Decenter

View the world from another person's point of view.

- Develop an understanding of someone, based on your own past experiences.
- Consider what someone may be thinking, based on your previous association with the person.
- Consider how most people respond to the situation at hand.

Develop Empathy

Consider what another person may be feeling.

- *Stop.* Avoid focusing only on your own ideas or emotions.
- *Look.* Determine the emotional meaning of messages by observing nonverbal messages.
- *Listen.* Focus on what the other person says.
- *Imagine.* Consider how you would feel in a similar situation.
- *Paraphrase.* Summarize your understanding of the other person's thoughts and feelings.

and develop satisfying relationships. To enhance understanding, you may need to slow your rate of speech or talk faster than you normally do. You may need to use more examples or speak in a very structured, organized way. To ensure that you achieve your communication objectives, you may need to draw on statistics and other forms of evidence to prove your point. Or your communication partner may not be impressed with statistics but might be quite moved by a story that poignantly illustrates your point. We also adapt messages to be ethical. Ethical communication gives your communication partner choices, rather than forcing or coercing him or her to do what you demand. Telling the truth, not withholding information, and identifying options are ways to adapt your message to be an ethical communicator. Finally, we adapt our communication to generate more positive feelings or regard for others, so as to enhance our relationships and improve our quality of life.

Can the skills and principles we have suggested here make a difference in your ability to communicate with others? The answer is a resounding "yes." Communication researcher Lori Carell found that students who had been exposed to lessons in empathy as part of their study of interpersonal and intercultural communication improved their ability to empathize with others.[69] There is evidence that if you master these principles and skills, you will be rewarded with greater ability to communicate with others who are different from you—which means everyone.

It is not possible to prescribe how to adapt to others in all situations. We can suggest that you draw on the other four communication principles for a lifetime that we have presented in this book. You will be more effective in adapting to others if you are aware of your own cultural traditions and gender-related behavior and how they are different from those of other people. Being able to use and interpret verbal and nonverbal symbols appropriately and effectively will also increase your ability to adapt and respond to others. The essential skills of listening and responding to others are key competencies in being able to adapt to others—to be other-oriented. To interpret spoken information accurately (as well as "listening" with your eyes to unspoken messages) is a linchpin of competence in adapting to others.

Adapting your messages to others does not mean you have to abandon your own ethical principles or personal positions. It would be unethical to change your opinions and point of view just to avoid conflict and keep the peace—like a politician who only tells his or her audience what they want to hear. It was President Harry Truman who said, "I wonder how far Moses would have gone if he'd taken a poll in Egypt?"[70] A spineless, wishy-washy approach to communication does not enhance the quality of your relationships with others. But you can be sensitive and mindful of how your comments may be received by others.

RECAP

Adapting to Others

Develop Knowledge

Seek Information	Learn about a culture's worldview.
Ask Questions and Listen	Reduce uncertainty by asking for clarification and listening to the answer.

Develop Motivation

Tolerate Ambiguity	Take your time and expect some uncertainty.
Develop Mindfulness	Be consciously aware of cultural differences, rather than ignoring the differences.

Develop Skill

Become Other-Oriented	Put yourself in the other person's mental and emotional frame of mind; socially decenter and develop empathy.
Adapt to Others	Listen and respond appropriately.

QUICK REVIEW

PRINCIPLES FOR A LIFETIME: Enhancing Your Skills

Adapt

Principle Five: Appropriately adapt messages to others.

- It's important to learn to ethically adapt messages to others to enhance understanding, because we're all different for a variety of reasons (culture, age, background, experience, sexual preference, attitudes, beliefs, values).
- Appropriately adapt messages to others based on whether an individual is from a high-context culture (in which an emphasis is placed on nonverbal messages and the surroundings) or a low-context culture (in which an emphasis is placed on words and explicitly communicated messages).
- Appropriately adapt messages to others based on the cultural value of individualism versus collectivism, preference for certainty versus tolerance of uncertainty, tendency to emphasize masculine versus feminine values, preference for centralized or decentralized power, and long-term versus short-term time orientation.
- Appropriately adapt messages based on gender differences in communication by doing the following four things: (1) seek to understand differences between genders; (2) consider your own preferences, needs, and communication goals; (3) avoid assuming that differences between people are solely the result of gender; and (4) consider both your needs and goals and those of the other person.
- Avoid being ethnocentric—always assuming that your cultural traditions and approaches are superior to other cultural traditions.
- Don't assume everyone does things the same way you do or holds the same attitudes, beliefs, or values that you hold.
- Don't assume that because someone is from another culture or geographic area, you don't have anything in common with the person; seek to establish common ground.
- Avoid making rigid, inflexible stereotypes and prejudgments of others based on limited information.
- Seek to bridge differences between yourself and others who speak a different language or have different interpretations for nonverbal expressions; learn the language of others.
- Bridge cultural differences by learning as much as you can about another culture.
- Listen and ask questions to enhance your understanding of others.
- Be patient and tolerate some ambiguity and uncertainty when you communicate with people who are different from you.
- Being mindful, or aware that differences will exist, can help you better tolerate differences.
- Develop your skills at being other-oriented: Focus on the needs and concerns of others while maintaining your personal integrity.
- Socially decenter: Think about how your communication partner would respond to information and situations; take into account people's thoughts, values, background, and perspectives.
- Empathize: Try to imagine how you would feel if you were in the other person's position.

SUMMARY

Human differences result in the potential for misunderstanding and miscommunication. Differences in culture and gender contribute to the challenge of communicating with others. The relevant communication principle is, *Effective communicators appropriately adapt their messages to others.* One concept that makes a difference when we communicate with others is taking into consideration cultural perspective or worldview. Culture is a system of knowledge that is shared by a group of people. Our worldview is the overarching set of expectations that helps us explain why events occur as they do and gives us a perspective for explaining what happens to us and others. Intercultural communication occurs when individuals or groups from different cultures communicate.

Culture and communication are clearly linked because of the powerful role culture plays in influencing our values. Cultural values reflect how individuals regard masculine perspectives (such as achieving results and being productive) and feminine perspectives (such as consideration for relationships), their tolerance of uncertainty or preference for certainty, their preference for centralized or decentralized power structures, the value they place on individual or collective accomplishment, and their long-term or short-term time orientation.

Two gender-related cultural values are the instrumental, or masculine, orientation, which involves assertiveness and action; and the expressive, or feminine, orientation, which emphasizes connection and the development of harmonious relationships and community. These orientations translate into communication behavior that differs depending on one's sex. Women tend to attend to the relational dimension of communication; that is, they focus on *how* something is said more than on *what*. Their purpose in communication typically is to establish and develop relationships and connections with others. In contrast, men tend to approach communication from a content perspective, meaning that they view communication as functioning primarily for information exchange. The principle of adaptation is quite useful in bridging gender differences in communication style. People can and should break out of sex-specific behavior to choose the best approach to communicating in a given situation.

Several barriers inhibit effective communication. When one culture or gender assumes superiority, communication problems often occur. Ethnocentrism is the belief that one's own cultural traditions and assumptions are superior to those of others. Sexism is the attitude that one sex is superior to the other. It is not productive when individuals or groups from different backgrounds or cultures assume that others behave with similar responses. But it is also important not to automatically assume that other people are different from you. We stereotype by placing a group or person into an inflexible, all-encompassing category. A related barrier is prejudice. When we prejudge someone before we know all the facts about him or her, we also create a potential communication problem. Stereotyping and prejudice can keep us from acknowledging others as unique individuals and therefore can hamper effective, open, honest communication. Differences in language codes and the way we interpret nonverbal messages interfere with effective communication.

Strategies for adapting to others include developing knowledge, motivation, and skill to bridge differences of culture and gender. To enhance understanding, actively seek information about others who are different from you, ask questions, and listen to the responses. Motivational strategies include being tolerant of ambiguity and uncertainty and being more conscious or mindful when interacting with others who are different from you. Finally, to develop skills in adapting to others, become other-oriented by socially decentering and emotionally empathizing with others. Then appropriately respond by adapting your messages to others; consider their thoughts and feelings.

DISCUSSION AND REVIEW

1. What is intercultural communication?
2. Describe the differences between high-context and low-context cultures.
3. What are the characteristics of masculine and feminine cultural values?
4. What are the differences between cultures that value certainty and those that have a greater tolerance for uncertainty?
5. How are decentralized and centralized cultural perspectives different?
6. What are the characteristics of and differences between individualistic and collectivistic cultures?
7. How important is a person's gender in U.S. culture?
8. What are the primary differences between the sexes in terms of listening behavior?
9. How can one adapt communication to bridge gender differences?
10. Identify and describe some barriers that hinder intercultural communication.
11. What communication strategies will help you bridge differences in communication and achieve the goal of adapting to others?

PUTTING PRINCIPLES INTO PRACTICE

1. Describe your perceptions of your cultural values, based on the discussion of cultural values beginning on page 185 in this chapter. Using a scale from 1 to 10, rate yourself in terms of the value of a masculine (1) versus a feminine (10) perspective; individual (1) versus group (10) achievement; tolerance of uncertainty (1) versus need for certainty (10); preference for decentralized (1) versus centralized (10) power, and long-term (1) versus short-term (10) time orientation. Provide an example of your reaction to an interpersonal communication encounter to illustrate each of these values. Share your answers with your classmates.

2. Role play with someone of the opposite sex a first conversation or a conflict or disagreement between dating partners. First, enact the roles from the perspective of your own sex— in other words, both you and your partner play the roles of people of your own sex. Then enact the conversation again, but with the roles reversed. Note any differences that emerge in how the conversation plays out. Do you detect any stereotypical behaviors that emerge when you swap roles? Do you

think an activity like this helps you better understand members of the opposite sex and their communication patterns?

3. This chapter presented five specific strategies or skills to help bridge differences in background and culture. Rank order these skills and strategies in terms of what you need to improve in your interactions with people from different backgrounds. Give a rank of 1 to the skill or strategy that you most need to develop, a rank of 2 to the next area you feel you need to work on, and so on. Rank yourself on all five strategies.

_____ Seek information about the culture

_____ Listen and ask questions of others

_____ Tolerate ambiguity

_____ Be mindful

_____ Be other-oriented

Write a journal entry about how you will develop skill in the areas in which you most need improvement. How will you put what you have learned in this chapter into practice?

4. With a group, go on an intercultural scavenger hunt. Your instructor will give you a time limit. Scavenge your campus or classroom area to identify influences of as many different cultures as you can find. For example, you could make note of ethnic foods offered in the dining hall; or you could identify clothing, music, or architecture that is influenced by certain cultures.

5. In a small group, identify examples from your own experiences of each barrier to effective intercultural communication discussed in the text. Use one of the examples as the basis for a skit to perform for the rest of the class. See if the class can identify which intercultural barrier your group is depicting. Also, suggest how the skills and principles discussed in the chapter might have improved the communication in the situation you role-played.

6. Try an exercise that will help clarify the different reasons men and women communicate. Ask the following questions of both men and women and then see if you note any major differences.

a. What is the general purpose or function of communication?

b. Which of the following statements best summarizes your preferred approach to communication?

1. It's better to get to the point when asking for information or making a request of someone.

2. It's better to take some time to talk about the background of a situation rather than quickly trying to get to "the bottom line" of what you're saying.

c. What bothers you the most when you talk to someone of the opposite sex?

d. What general impressions do you have about the way men and women listen to each other?

Compare the answers you collect with those collected by your classmates. Do you note any general trends or differences and similarities in light of the research conclusions we've summarized in this chapter?

Chapter 1.6 *Practice Test*

MULTIPLE CHOICE.   Choose the *best* answer to each of the following questions.

1. The cultural value of _____ means that people in the culture tend to value high achievement and more differentiation in sex roles.

   a. uncertainty avoidance

   b. power distribution

   c. individualism

   d. masculinity

2. _____ cultures tend to value group achievements.

   a. Individualistic

   b. Decentralized

   c. Collectivistic

   d. Centralized

3. The increased likelihood that you will interact with individuals from different cultural backgrounds because of increased interconnectedness is referred to as

   a. culture shock.

   b. intercultural communication.

   c. globalization.

   d. decentralized values.

4. Which type of culture below emphasizes connection with others and fostering harmonious relationships?

   a. feminine

   b. masculine

   c. individualist

   d. androgynous

5. While a particular culture is shared by a group of people, it is also true that cultures

   a. are not affected by the way people interact and are fairly consistent over time.

   b. are not affected by the way people interact and change over time.

   c. are affected by the way people interact and are fairly consistent over time.

   d. are affected by the way people interact and change over time.

6. Kai is discussing an assignment with his professor, and the professor's office is rather cold. Instead of saying something to the professor, Kai crosses his arms, exaggerates his shivering, and hunches forward slightly. Kai then continues the conversation and waits for the professor to notice. Kai's culture is likely

   a. high context.

   b. low context.

   c. ethnic.

   d. diverse.

7. According to your textbook, adapting your message to your audience means

   a. changing your message so that your audience will agree with it.

   b. going along with the ideas that are comfortable to the time, place, and situation.

   c. manipulating the way you express your ideas so that others interpret them correctly.

   d. doing what it takes to make sure that your goals are accomplished.

8. According to Thomas Friedman, globalization began in the

   a. 1490s.

   b. 1870s.

   c. 1940s.

   d. 1990s.

9. Cultures that tend to rely on explicit language to convey information are

   a. high power.

   b. low power.

   c. high context.

   d. low context.

10. People from countries with a preference for higher power distribution tend to

    a. be more accepting of those in power and prefer greater power differences among people.

    b. be less accepting of those in power and prefer greater power differences among people.

    c. be more accepting of those in power and prefer lesser power differences among people.

    d. be less accepting of those in power and prefer lesser power differences among people.

11. To feel what another person is feeling is called

    a. superiority.

    b. egocentrism.

    c. intellectualism.

    d. empathy.

12. Because the Japanese culture is collectivistic,

    a. Japanese workers work better by themselves.

    b. Japanese workers value personal honors and awards.

    c. Japanese workers work better in teams.

    d. Japanese workers tend to be more loosely knit socially.

13. The tendency to believe that one's own culture is superior to other cultures is called

    a. ethnocentrism.

    b. egocentrism.

    c. stereotyping.

    d. collectivism.

14. Emphasizing a connection to others is characteristic of

    a. a masculine and expressive approach.

    b. a feminine and expressive approach.

    c. a masculine and instrumental approach.

    d. a feminine and instrumental approach.

15. If you are uncomfortable with the uncertainty of intercultural interactions, you should do all of the following *except*

    a. have patience.

    b. get as many details as possible.

    c. learn to tolerate more ambiguity.

    d. be willing to engage in several exchanges to clarify a message.

16. When you try to understand someone from another culture by remembering how that person has responded in similar situations, you are

    a. practicing mindfulness.

    b. tolerating ambiguity.

    c. practicing social decentering.

    d. asking questions.

17. Most of the expectations we have about how men and women should act are formed

    a. practically from birth.

    b. during adolescence.

    c. during young adulthood.

    d. after the age of 25.

18. Kaitlan is highly ambitious and takes pride in making things happen. When she communicates, her communications reflect this attitude. Her orientation toward communication would be described as

    a. expressive.

    b. egocentric.

    c. instrumental.

    d. stereotypical.

19. On a recent Caribbean cruise, Cody commented to a friend, "I feel strange talking to the room stewards. They're all from interesting places and their English is excellent, but there's nothing we can talk about." Cody's dilemma can best be ascribed to

    a. different communication codes.

    b. assuming differences.

    c. prejudice.

    d. decentering.

20. While they are having coffee, Elijah's eighteen-year-old sister Trinity confides in him that she just found out she is pregnant. She has just started her first year of college and wants to get her degree. Even though she and her family are fundamentally opposed to abortion, she explains that she is considering getting one. As a competent and ethical communicator, Elijah should

a. explain to Trinity the seriousness of her situation.

b. discuss with Trinity the moral implications of her choice.

c. consider how Trinity is feeling and work to understand her point of view.

d. set aside his beliefs and tell Trinity what she needs to hear to make her feel okay.

TRUE/FALSE.   Indicate whether the following statements are *true* or *false.*

1. T or F   Many co-cultures may exist within a single society.

2. T or F   Becoming other-oriented is a wise strategy when communicating with people from a different culture.

3. T or F   Masculine communicators tend to interact in order to accomplish a task.

4. T or F   People from cultures with low scores on uncertainty avoidance tend to deal well with ambiguity about the future.

5. T or F   People from cultures with low scores on power distribution are more accepting of someone having authority over them.

6. T or F   All cultures experience empathy.

7. T or F   Competent communicators avoid assuming both similarities and differences.

8. T or F   Androgynous individuals are neither masculine nor feminine.

9. T or F   Empathy involves telling others that you are sorry they feel what they are feeling—simply acknowledging their feelings.

10. T or F   Being egocentric involves considering the needs, motives, desires, and goals of our communication partners while maintaining our own integrity.

FILL IN THE BLANK.   Complete the following statements.

1. _____ is the belief that your cultural perspective is better than others are.

2. Any culture that exists inside a larger culture is termed a _____.

3. A(n) _____ orientation is a more masculine approach to viewing self and reality.

4. Culture _____ is the stressful feeling you get when you encounter a culture different from your own.

5. _____ cultures rely heavily on words to make sense out of messages.

6. Collaboration, teamwork, and group achievement are key components of a _____ culture.

7. A learned system of knowledge, behaviors, attitudes, beliefs, values, and norms that is shared by a group of people is known as a _____.

8. _____ cultures rely heavily on nonverbal cues to make sense out of messages.

9. Individual achievement and personal accomplishment are key components of a(n) _____ culture.

10. A(n) _____ orientation is a more feminine approach to viewing self and reality.

Notes

CHAPTER 1.1

1. E. T. Klemmer and F. W. Snyder, "Measurement of Time Spent Communicating," *Journal of Communication 20* (June, 1972): 142.

2. F. E. X. Dance and C. Larson, *Speech Communication: Concepts and Behavior* (New York: Holt, Rinehart and Winston, 1972).

3. Dance and Larson, *Speech Communication.*

4. J. T. Masterson, S. A. Beebe, and N. H. Watson, *Invitation to Effective Speech Communication* (Glenview, IL: Scott, Foresman, 1989).

5. M. Gladwell, *Blink: The Power of Thinking without Thinking* (New York: Little Brown and Company, 2005).

6. This section is based on J. T. Masterson, S. A. Beebe, and N. H. Watson. We are especially indebted to J. T. Masterson for this discussion.

7. See R. P. Wolff, *About Philosophy* (Upper Saddle River, NJ: Prentice Hall, 2000), 308–335.

8. C. S. Lewis, *The Abolition of Man* (New York: Macmillan, 1947); also see A. M. Nicholi, Jr., *The Question of God: C. S. Lewis and Sigmund Freud Debate God, Love, Sex, and the Meaning of Life* (New York: The Free Press, 2002).

9. C. Christians and M. Traber, *Communication Ethics and Universal Values* (Beverly Hills, CA: Sage, 1997); also see S. Bok, *Common Values* (Columbia, MO: University of Missouri Press, 2002).

10. Christians and Traber, *Communication Ethics and Universal Values.*

11. For an excellent discussion of comparative religions and the common principle of being other oriented see W. Ham, *Man's Living Religions* (Independence, MO: Herald Publishing House, 1966), 39–40.

12. For additional discussion of the ethical values taught in the world's religions, see H. Smith, *The World's Religions* (San Francisco: HarperSanFrancisco, 1991).

13. National Communication Association, "NCA Credo for Communication Ethics," 1999 (June 27, 2001) <http://www.natcom.org/conferences/Ethics/ethicsconfcredo99.htm>.

14. We thank Tom Burkholder, University of Nevada, Las Vegas, for this idea.

15. D. Quinn, *My Ishmael* (New York: Bantam Books, 1996).

16. V. Marchant, "Listen Up!" *Time* (June 28, 1999): 72.

17. A. Vangelisti and J. Daly, "Correlates of Speaking Skills in the United States: A National Assessment," *Communication Education 38* (1989): 132–143.

18. M. Cronin, ed., "The Need for Required Oral Communication Education in the Undergraduate General Education Curriculum," unpublished paper, 1993, available from the National Communication Association, Washington, D.C.

19. J. Ayres and T. S. Hopf, "The Long-Term Effect of Visualization in the Classroom: A Brief Research Report," *Communication Education 39* (1990): 75–78.

20. See J. C. McCroskey and M. Beatty, "The Communibiological Perspective: Implications for Communication in Instruction," *Communication Education 49* (2000): 1. Also see J. C. McCroskey, J. A. Daly, M. M. Martin, and M. J. Beatty, eds., *Communication and Personality: Trait Perspectives* (Cresskill, NJ: Hampton Press, 1998).

21. J. H. McConnell, *Are You Communicating? You Can't Manage without It* (New York: McGraw-Hill, 1995).

22. J. L. Winsor, D. Curtis, and R. D. Stephens, "National Preferences in Business and Communication Education: A Survey Update," *Journal of the Association of Communication Administration 3* (1997): 170–179.

23. Winsor, Curtis, and Stephens, "National Preferences in Business and Communication Education."

24. K. E. Davis and M. Todd, "Assessing Friendship: Prototypes, Paradigm Cases, and Relationship Description." In *Understanding Personal Relationships*, edited by S. W. Duck and D. Perlman (London: Sage, 1985); B. Wellman, "From Social Support to Social Network." In *Social Support: Theory, Research and Applications*, edited by I. G. Sarason and B. R. Sarason (Dordrecht, Netherlands: Nijhoff, 1985); R. Hopper, M. L. Knapp, and L.

Scott, "Couples' Personal Idioms: Exploring Intimate Talk," *Journal of Communication* 31 (1981): 23–33.

25. M. Argyle and M. Hendershot, *The Anatomy of Relationships* (London: Penguin Books, 1985), 14.

26. D. Goleman, "Emotional Intelligence: Issues in Paradigms Building." In *The Emotionally Intelligent Workplace*, edited by C. Cherniss and D. Goleman (San Francisco: Jossey Bass, 2001), 13.

27. V. Satir, *Peoplemaking* (Palo Alto, CA: Science and Behavior Books, 1972).

28. M. Argyle, *The Psychology of Happiness* (London: Routledge, 2001).

29. J. J. Lynch, *The Broken Heart: The Medical Consequences of Loneliness* (New York: Basic Books, 1977).

30. D. P. Phillips, "Deathday and Birthday: An Unexpected Connection." In *Statistics: A Guide to the Unknown*, edited by J. M. Tanur (San Francisco: Holden Day, 1972). Also see F. Korbin and G. Hendershot, "Do Family Ties Reduce Mortality? Evidence from the United States 1968," *Journal of Marriage and the Family* 39 (1977): 737–746; K. Heller and K. S. Rook, "Distinguishing the Theoretical Functions of Social Ties: Implications of Support Interventions." In *Handbook of Personal Relationships* 2e, edited by S. W. Duck, K. Dindia, W. Ickes, R. Milardo, R. S. L. Mills, and B. R. Sarason (Chichester: Wiley, 1997); B. R. Sarason, I. G. Sarason, and R. A. R. Gurung, "Close Personal Relationships and Health Outcomes: A Key to the Role of Social Support." In *Handbook of Personal Relationships*, Duck et al., eds. Also see S. Duck, *Relating to Others* (Buckingham, England: Open University Press, 1999), 1.

31. H. Lasswell, "The Structure and Function of Communication in Society." In *The Communication of Ideas*, edited by L. Bryson (New York: Institute for Religious and Social Studies, 1948), 37.

32. See V. E. Cronen, W. B. Pearce, and L. M. Harris, "The Coordinated Management of Meaning: A Theory of Communication." In *Human Communication Theory: Comparative Essays*, edited by F. E. X. Dance (New York: Harper & Row, 1982), 61–89.

33. L. Barker, R. Edwards, C. Gaines, K. Gladney, and F. Holley, "An Investigation of Proportional Time Spent in Various Communication Activities of College Students," *Journal of Applied Communication Research 8* (1981): 101–109.

34. See D. Barnlund, *Interpersonal Communication: Survey and Studies* (Boston: Houghton Mifflin Company, 1968).

35. See C. R. Berger and J. J. Bradac, *Language and Social Knowledge: Uncertainty in Interpersonal Relations* (London: Arnold, 1982).

36. O. Wiio, *Wiio's Laws—and Some Others* (Espoo, Finland: Welin-Goos, 1978).

37. T. Watzlawick, J. B. Bavelas, and D. Jackson, *The Pragmatics of Human Communication* (New York: W. W. Norton, 1967).

38. S. B. Shimanoff, *Communication Rules: Theory and Research* (Beverly Hills: Sage, 1980).

39. We appreciate and acknowledge our friend and colleague M. V. Redmond for his contributions to our understanding of interpersonal communication. For more information, see S. A. Beebe, S. J. Beebe, and M. V. Redmond, *Interpersonal Communication: Relating to Others* 4e (Boston: Allyn & Bacon, 2005).

40. For an excellent discussion of the power of dialogue to enrich the quality of communication, see D. Yankelovich, *The Magic of Dialogue: Transforming Conflict into Cooperation* (New York: Simon & Schuster, 1999).

41. S. A. Beebe and J. T. Masterson, *Communicating in Small Groups: Principles and Practices* 8e (Boston: Allyn & Bacon, 2006).

42. For a discussion of group size, see Beebe and Masterson, *Communicating in Small Groups*.

CHAPTER 1.2

1. L. Garcia, "Dating Service Founder's Goal: Love That Lasts," *Dallas Morning News* (March 21, 2005): 1E, 4E; R. Konrad, "Dating Site Gets Patent: EHarmony Pushes Its Method for Love," *Corpus Christi Caller Times* (May 28, 2004): A2.

2. S. R. Covey, *The Seven Habits of Highly Effective People* (New York: Simon & Schuster, 1989), 67.

3. R. A. Baron, D. Byrne, and N. R. Branscombe, *Social Psychology* 11e (Boston: Allyn & Bacon, 2005).

4. K. Horney, *Neurosis and Human Growth* (New York: W. W. Norton & Co., 1950), 17.

5. B. Goss, *Processing Communication* (Belmont, CA: Wadsworth, 1982), 72.

6. J. T. Masterson, S. A. Beebe, and N. H. Watson, *Invitation to Effective Speech Communication* (Glenview, IL: Scott, Foresman and Company, 1989).

7. W. James, *Principles of Psychology* (New York: Henry Holt and Company, 1890).

8. M. Beck, "Makeover Madness," *O: The Oprah Winfrey Magazine* (April, 2005): 175–178; A. Botta, "Television Images and Adolescent Girls' Body Image Disturbance," *Journal of Communication* 49 (1999): 22–37; M. Wiederman and S. R. Hurst, "Body Size, Physical Attractiveness, and Body Image among Young Adult Women: Relationships to Sexual Experience and Sexual Esteem," *Journal of Sex Research* 35 (1998): 272–281; N. Wolf, *The Beauty Myth: How Images of Beauty Are Used against Women* (New York: William Morrow, 1991).

9. D. M. Garner, "The 1997 Body Image Survey Results," *Psychology Today* (January/February, 1997): 30–44, 74–75, 78, 80, 84.

10. T. Spiker, "How Men Really Feel About Their Bodies," *O: The Oprah Winfrey Magazine* (August, 2003): 150–151, 181–182; G. B. Forbes, L. E. Adams-Curtis, B. Rade, and P. Jaberg, "Body Dissatisfaction in Women and Men: The Role of Gender-Typing and Self-Esteem," *Sex Roles 44* (2001): 461–484.

11. A. N. Markham, *Life Online: Researching Real Experience in Virtual Space* (Walnut Creek, CA: AltaMira Press, 1998), 135; 202–203.

12. C. H. Cooley, *Human Nature and the Social Order* (New York: Scribner's, 1912).

13. G. H. Mead, *Mind, Self, and Society* (Chicago: University of Chicago Press, 1934).

14. J. Stewart, K. E. Zediker, and S. Witteborn, *Together: Communicating Interpersonally* 6e (Los Angeles: Roxbury, 2005).

15. D. K. Ivy and P. Backlund, *GenderSpeak: Personal Effectiveness in Gender Communication* 3e (New York: McGraw-Hill, 2004).

16. J. C. Pearson, L. Turner, and W. T. Mancillas, *Gender & Communication* 3e. (Dubuque, IA: William C. Brown, 1995).

17. J. E. Stake, "Gender Differences and Similarities in Self-Concept within Everyday Life Contexts," *Psychology of Women Quarterly 16* (1992): 349–363.

18. G. Steinem, *Revolution from Within: A Book of Self-Esteem* (Boston: Little, Brown and Company, 1993), 26.

19. Ivy and Backlund, *GenderSpeak*.

20. See C. Gilligan, *In a Different Voice: Psychological Theory and Women's Development* (Cambridge, MA: Harvard University Press, 1982); P. Orenstein, *Schoolgirls: Young Women, Self-Esteem, and the Confidence Gap* (New York: Doubleday, 1994); R. A. Josephs, H. R. Markus, and R. W. Tafarodi, "Gender and Self-Esteem," *Journal of Personality and Social Psychology 63* (1991): 391–402.

21. American Association of University Women, *Shortchanging Girls, Shortchanging America* (Washington, DC: AAUW Educational Foundation, 1991).

22. M. Sadker and D. Sadker, *Failing at Fairness: How America's Schools Cheat Girls* (New York: Charles Scribner's Sons, 1994), 77.

23. G. J. Carter, "The New Face: As Women's World Cup Soccer Kicks Off This Weekend, Girls around the Globe Finally Get the Role Model They Deserve: Mia Hamm," *USA Weekend* (June 18–20, 1999): 6–7.

24. "Shot of Brandi Lifts U.S.," *Corpus Christi Caller Times* (July 11, 1999): B1, B9.

25. L. Festinger, "A Theory of Social Comparison Processes," *Human Relations 2* (1954): 117–140.

26. J. S. Phinney, C. L. Cantu, and D. A. Kurtz, "Ethnic and American Identity as Predictors of Self-Esteem Among African American, Latino, and White Adolescents," *Journal of Youth and Adolescence 26* (1997): 165–185.

27. G. Flynn, "Self-Hate Crime: Misogynistic Makeover Show *The Swan* Is One Ugly Duckling," *Entertainment Weekly* (April 23, 2004): 69.

28. M. M. Martin and J. W. Gentry, "Stuck in the Model Trap." In *Taking Sides: Clashing Views on Controversial Issues in Mass Media and Society* 8e, edited by A. Alexander and J. Hanson (Dubuque, IA: McGraw-Hill/Dushkin, 2005), 52–61.

29. M. Cottle, "Turning Boys into Girls." In *Taking Sides*, Alexander and Hanson, eds.

30. J. Hattie, *Self-Concept* (Hillsdale, NJ: Lawrence Erlbaum, 1992).

31. A. Chatham-Carpenter and V. DeFrancisco, "Pulling Yourself Up Again: Women's Choices and Strategies for Recovering and Maintaining Self-Esteem," *Western Journal of Communication 61* (1997): 164–187.

32. Goss, *Processing Communication*.

33. L. C. Lederman, "The Impact of Gender on the Self and Self-Talk." In *Women and Men Communicating: Challenges and Changes* 2e, edited by L. P. Arliss and D. J. Borisoff (Prospect Heights, IL: Waveland, 2001), 78–89; J. R. Johnson, "The Role of Inner Speech in Human Communication," *Communication Education 33* (1984): 211–222; C. R. Streff, "The Concept of Inner Speech and Its Implications for an Integrated Language Arts Curriculum," *Communication Education 33* (1984): 223–230; J. L. McFarland, "The Role of Speech in Self-Development, Self-Concept, and Decentration," *Communication Education 33* (1984): 231–236; J. Ayres, "The Power of Positive Thinking," *Communication Education 37* (1988): 289–296.

34. C. J. Mruk, *Self-Esteem: Research, Theory, and Practice* (New York: Springer, 1995).

35. See J. Ayres and T. S. Hopf, "The Long-Term Effect of Visualization in the Classroom: A Brief Research Report," *Communication Education 39* (1990): 75–78; J. Ayres and T. S. Hopf, "Visualization: Is It More Than Extra-Attention?" *Communication Education 38* (1989): 1–5.

36. J. Ayres, T. S. Hopf, and D. M. Ayres, "An Examination of Whether Imaging Ability Enhances the Effectiveness of an Intervention Designed to Reduce Speech Anxiety," *Communication Education 43* (1994): 252–258.

37. Covey, *The Seven Habits of Highly Effective People*, 105.

38. P. R. Hinton, *The Psychology of Interpersonal Perception* (New York: Routledge, 1993).

39. U. Neisser, *Cognition and Reality: Principles and Implications of Cognitive Psychology* (San Francisco: W. H. Freeman and Company, 1976).

40. D. J. Schneider, A. H. Hastorf, and P. C. Ellsworth, *Person Perception* 2e (Reading, MA: Addison-Wesley, 1979).

41. D. T. Kenrick, S. L. Neuberg, and R. B. Cialdini, *Social Psychology: Unraveling the Mystery* 3e (Boston: Allyn & Bacon, 2004).

42. C. N. Macrae, G. V. Bodenhausen, A. B. Milne, and J. Jetten, "Out of Mind but Back in Sight: Stereotypes on the Rebound," *Journal of Personality and Social Psychology* 67 (1994): 808–817.

43. Macrae et al., "Out of Mind," 808.

44. This chapter benefited from the fine scholarship and work of M. V. Redmond, coauthor of *Interpersonal Communication: Relating to Others* 4e (Boston: Allyn & Bacon, 2005).

CHAPTER 1.3

1. S. Friess, "Yo, can u plz help me write English?: Parents Fear Online Chatting Ruins Kids' Language Skills," *USA Today* (April 1, 2003).

2. J. Scott, "I Feel," *Bitch: Feminist Response to Pop Culture* (Spring, 2003): 25.

3. "College Graduates Aren't Ready for the Real World," *The Chronicle of Higher Education* (February 18, 2005): B11.

4. B. Spitzberg and J. P. Dillard, "Social Skills and Communication." In *Interpersonal Communication Research: Advances Through Meta-Analysis*, edited by M. Allen, R. W. Preiss, B. M. Gayle, and N. Burrell (Mahwah, NJ: Lawrence Erlbaum, 2002), 89–107.

5. D. Spender, *Man Made Language* 2e (London: Routledge & Kegan Paul, 1985).

6. B. L. Whorf, "Science and Linguistics." In *Language, Thought, and Reality*, edited by J. B. Carroll (Cambridge: Massachusetts Institute of Technology Press, 1956).

7. W. Johnson, *People in Quandaries: The Semantics of Personal Adjustment* (New York: Harper & Row, 1946).

8. *Oxford Desk Dictionary and Thesaurus, American Edition* (New York: Oxford University Press, 1997).

9. A. G. Smith, ed., *Communication and Culture* (New York: Holt, Rinehart, & Winston, 1966).

10. D. K. Ivy and P. Backlund, *GenderSpeak: Personal Effectiveness in Gender Communication* 3e (New York: McGraw-Hill, 2004).

11. A. Ellis, *A New Guide to Rational Living* (North Hollywood, CA: Wilshire Books, 1977).

12. C. Peterson, M. E. P. Seligman, and G. E. Vaillant, "Pessimistic Explanatory Style Is a Risk Factor for Physical Illness: A 35-Year Longitudinal Study," *Journal of Personality and Social Psychology* 55 (1988): 23–27.

13. J. Barlow, "E-Mail Etiquette Has Its Own Rules," *Houston Chronicle* (March 11, 1999): C1.

14. D. A. Lieberman, *Public Speaking in the Multicultural Environment* 2e (Boston: Allyn & Bacon, 1997), 34–35.

15. *Newsweek* (November 20, 1995): 81.

16. "Y? The National Forum on People's Differences," *Entertainment Weekly* (July 12, 1999): 30.

17. L. Pitts, "African-American? Hispanic? Indian? Does It Really Matter What We Call Ourselves?" *Corpus Christi Caller Times* (May 25, 2003): A15.

18. See J. K. Swim, R. Mallett, and C. Stangor, "Understanding Subtle Sexism: Detection and Use of Sexist Language," *Sex Roles* 51 (2004): 117–128; J. Briere and C. Lanktree, "Sex-Role Related Effects of Sex Bias in Language," *Sex Roles* 9 (1983): 625–632; L. Brooks, "Sexist Language in Occupational Information: Does It Make a Difference?" *Journal of Vocational Behavior* 23 (1983): 227–232; A. Stericker, "Does This 'He or She' Business Really Make a Difference? The Effect of Masculine Pronouns as Generics on Job Attitudes," *Sex Roles* 7 (1981): 637–641.

19. H. S. O'Donnell, "Sexism in Language," *Elementary English* 50 (1973): 1067–1072, as cited by J. C. Pearson, L. Turner, and W. Todd Mancillas, *Gender & Communication* 3e (Dubuque, IA: William C. Brown, 1995).

20. See J. L. Stinger and R. Hopper, "Generic *He* in Conversation?" *Quarterly Journal of Speech* 84 (1998): 209–221; J. Gastil, "Generic Pronouns and Sexist Language: The Oxymoronic Character of Masculine Generics," *Sex Roles* 23 (1990): 629–641; D. K. Ivy, L. Bullis-Moore, K. Norvell, P. Backlund, and M. Javidi, "The Lawyer, the Babysitter, and the Student: Inclusive Language Usage and Instruction," *Women & Language* 18 (1994): 13–21; W. Martyna, "What Does 'He' Mean? Use of the Generic Masculine," *Journal of Communication* 28 (1978): 131–138.

21. L. Madson and R. M. Hessling, "Does Alternating between Masculine and Feminine Pronouns Eliminate Perceived Gender Bias in a Text?" *Sex Roles* 41 (1999): 559–576; D. Kennedy, "Review Essay: She or He in Textbooks," *Women and Language* 15 (1992): 46–49.

22. See R. Maggio, *The Nonsexist Word Finder: A Dictionary of Gender-Free Usage* (Boston: Beacon, 1988); C. Miller, K. Swift, and R. Maggio, "Liberating Language," *Ms.* (September/October, 1997): 50–54.

23. *Fox News* Broadcast, May 6, 2003.

24. C. H. Palczewski, " 'Tak[e] the Helm,' Man the Ship . . . and I Forgot My Bikini! Unraveling Why Woman Is Not Considered a Verb," *Women & Language* 21 (1998): 1–8; Maggio, *The Nonsexist Word Finder*.

25. A. Walker, as cited in A. Bilger, "The Common *Guy*: One Seemingly Benign Phrase Makes a Man Out of All of Us," *Bitch: Feminist Response to Pop Culture* (Fall, 2002): 87.

26. Ivy and Backlund, *GenderSpeak*.

27. J. S. Seiter, J. Larsen, and J. Skinner, "'Handicapped' or 'Handicapable'? The Effects of Language about Persons with Disabilities on Perceptions of Source Credibility and Persuasiveness," *Communication Reports 11* (1998): 21–31.

28. D. O. Braithwaite and C. A. Braithwaite, "Understanding Communication of Persons with Disabilities as Cultural Communication." In *Intercultural Communication: A Reader* 10e, edited by L. A. Samovar and R. E. Porter (Belmont, CA: Wadsworth, 2002), 136–145.

29. J. R. Gibb, "Defensive Communication," *Journal of Communication 11* (1961): 141–148. Also see R. Bolton, *People Skills* (New York: Simon & Schuster, 1979), 14–26; O. Hargie, C. Sanders, and D. Dickson, *Social Skills in Interpersonal Communication* (London: Routledge, 1994); O. Hargie, ed., *The Handbook of Communication Skills* (London: Routledge, 1997).

30. M. V. Redmond, "The Functions of Empathy (Decentering) in Human Relations," *Human Relations 42* (1993): 593–606.

CHAPTER 1.4

1. A. Mehrabian, *Nonverbal Communication* (Chicago: Aldine-Atherton, 1972).

2. L. E. Boone and D. L. Kurtz, *Contemporary Business* (New York: Dryden Press, 1997); V. Quercia, *Internet in a Nutshell* (Cambridge, MA: O'Reilly, 1997).

3. R. L. Birdwhistell, *Kinesics and Context* (Philadelphia: University of Pennsylvania Press, 1970).

4. J. H. Bert and K. Piner, "Social Relationships and the Lack of Social Relations." In *Personal Relationships and Social Support*, edited by S. W. Duck with R. C. Silver (London: Sage, 1989).

5. W. E. Chaplin, J. B. Phillips, J. D. Brown, N. R. Clanton, and J. L. Stein, "Handshaking, Gender, Personality, and First Impressions," *Journal of Personality and Social Psychology 79* (2000): 110–117.

6. J. K. Burgoon, L. A. Stern, and L. Dillman, *Interpersonal Adaptation: Dyadic Interaction Patterns* (Cambridge, England: Cambridge University Press, 1995).

7. P. Ekman, "Communication through Nonverbal Behavior: A Source of Information about an Interpersonal Relationship." In *Affect, Cognition, and Personality*, edited by S. S. Tomkins and C. E. Izard (New York: Springer, 1965).

8. M. Argyle, *Bodily Communication* (New York: Methuen & Company, 1988).

9. P. Ekman and W. V. Friesen, "Constants across Cultures in the Face and Emotion," *Journal of Personality and Social Psychology 17* (1971): 124–129; Argyle, *Bodily Communication*, 157; I. Eibl-Eibesfeldt, "Similarities and Differences between Cultures in Expressive Movements." In *Nonverbal Communication*, edited by R. A. Hinde (Cambridge, England: Royal Society and Cambridge University Press, 1972); P. Collett, "History and Study of Expressive Action." In *Historical Social Psychology*, edited by K. Gergen and M. Gergen (Hillsdale, NJ: Lawrence Erlbaum, 1984); E. T. Hall, *The Silent Language* (Garden City, NY: Doubleday, 1959); R. Shuter, "Proxemics and Tactility in Latin America," *Journal of Communication 26* (1976): 46–55; E. T. Hall, *The Hidden Dimension* (New York: Doubleday, 1966).

10. R. E. Porter and L. A. Samovar, "An Introduction to Intercultural Communication." In *Intercultural Communication: A Reader* 10e, edited by L. A. Samovar and R. E. Porter (Belmont, CA: Wadsworth, 2002).

11. J. Douglas, Jr., "Outside Texas, 'Hook 'em Horns' Gesture Has Different and Unflattering Meanings," *Fort Worth Star Telegram* (January 23, 2005): 2A.

12. "Watch Your Tongue; This Isn't Tibet," *Fort Worth Star Telegram* (October 10, 2004): 2A; E. Adams, "Manners Can Sink International Business Dealings," *Corpus Christi Caller Times* (November 2, 2003): K2.

13. See J. K. Burgoon and S. B. Jones, "Toward a Theory of Personal Space Expectations and Their Violations," *Human Communication Research 2* (1976): 131–146. For recent applications of expectancy violations theory, see S. Campo, K. A. Cameron, D. Brossard, and M. S. Frazer, "Social Norms and Expectancy Violation Theories: Assessing the Effectiveness of Health Communication Campaigns," *Communication Monographs 71* (2004): 448–470; L. A. Erbert and K. Floyd, "Affectionate Expression as Face-Threatening Acts: Receiver Assessments," *Communication Studies 55* (2004): 254–270; J. L. Bevan, "General Partner and Relational Uncertainty as Consequences of Another Person's Jealousy Expression," *Western Journal of Communication 68* (2004): 195–218; J. L. Bevan, "Expectancy Violation Theory and Sexual Resistance in Close, Cross-Sex Relationships." *Communication Monographs 70* (2003): 68–82; W. A. Afifi and J. K. Burgoon, "The Impact of Violations on Uncertainty and the Consequences for Attractiveness," *Human Communication Research 26* (2000): 203–233.

14. J. Fast, *Body Language* (New York: M. Evans, 1970).

15. P. Ekman and W. V. Friesen, "The Repertoire of Nonverbal Behavior: Categories, Origins, Usage, and Coding," *Semiotica 1* (1969): 49–98.

16. E. Tenner, "Political Timber: Glitter, Froth, and Measuring Tape," *The Chronicle of Higher Education* (October 1, 2004): B12–B13.

17. G. Montell, "Do Good Looks Equal Good Evaluations?" *The Chronicle of Higher Education: Career Network* (October 15, 2003) <http://chronicle.com>.

18. G. B. Forbes, L. E. Adams-Curtis, B. Rade, and P. Jaberg, "Body Dissatisfaction in Women and Men: The Role of Gender-Typing and Self-Esteem," *Sex Roles 44* (2001): 461–484; R. A. Botta, "Television Images and

Adolescent Girls' Body Image Disturbance," *Journal of Communication* 49 (1999): 22–37; M. Wiederman and S. Hurst, "Body Size, Physical Attractiveness, and Body Image among Young Adult Women: Relationships to Sexual Experience and Sexual Esteem," *Journal of Sex Research* 35 (1998): 272–281.

19. E. Hatfield and S. Sprecher, *Mirror, Mirror . . .: The Importance of Looks in Everyday Life* (Albany: SUNY Press, 1986); C. M. Marlowe, S. L. Schneider, and C. E. Nelson, "Gender and Attractiveness Biases in Hiring Decisions: Are More Experienced Managers Less Biased?" *Journal of Applied Psychology* 81 (1998): 11–21; W. R. Zakahi, R. L. Duran, and M. Adkins, "Social Anxiety, Only Skin Deep? The Relationships between Ratings of Physical Attractiveness and Social Anxiety," *Communication Research Reports* 11 (1994): 23–31; L. A. Zebrowitz, *Reading Faces: Window to the Soul?* (Boulder, CO: Westview, 1997).

20. J. Gorham, S. H. Cohen, and T. L. Morris, "Fashion in the Classroom III: Effects of Instructor Attire and Immediacy in Natural Classroom Interactions," *Communication Quarterly* 47 (1999): 281–299; K. D. Roach, "Effects of Graduate Teaching Assistant Attire on Student Learning, Misbehaviors, and Ratings of Instruction," *Communication Quarterly* 45 (1997): 125–141; S. E. White, "A Content Analytic Technique for Measuring the Sexiness of Women's Business Attire in Media Presentations," *Communication Research Reports* 12 (1995): 178–185; J. M. Townsend and G. D. Levy, "Effects of Potential Partners' Costume and Physical Attractiveness on Sexuality and Partner Selection," *Journal of Psychology* 124 (1990): 371–389; F. B. Furlow, "The Smell of Love." In *The Nonverbal Communication Reader: Classic and Contemporary Readings* 2e, edited by L. K. Guerrero, J. DeVito, and M. L. Hecht (Prospect Heights, IL: Waveland, 1999), 118–125; R. K. Aune, "The Effects of Perfume Use on Perceptions of Attractiveness and Competence." In Guerrero, *The Nonverbal Communication Reader*, 126–132.

21. J. T. Molloy, *New Dress for Success* (New York: Warner Books, 1988); J. T. Molloy, *New Woman's Dress for Success Book* (New York: Warner, 1996).

22. L. Averyt, "Casual-Attire Fridays Are Spreading to Rest of Week in Many Companies," *Corpus Christi Caller Times* (August 31, 1997): A1, A6; M. G. Frank and T. Gilovich, "The Dark Side of Self- and Social Perception: Black Uniforms and Aggression in Professional Sports," *Journal of Personality and Social Psychology* 54 (1988): 74–85; P. A. Andersen, *Nonverbal Communication: Forms and Functions* (Mountain View, CA: Mayfield, 1999); V. Santos-Garza, "School Code Is Dressed in Stress," *Corpus Christi Caller Times* (August 1, 2004): C1; O. Garcia Hunter,

"Goodbye Grunge," *Corpus Christi Caller Times* (July 18, 2004): A1, A8.

23. N. Armstrong and M. Wagner, *Field Guide to Gestures: How to Identify and Interpret Virtually Every Gesture Known to Man* (Philadelphia: Quirk Books, 2003).

24. Birdwhistell, *Kinesics and Context*; D. G. Leathers, *Successful Nonverbal Communication: Principles and Applications* 3e (Boston: Allyn & Bacon, 1997).

25. Ekman and Friesen, "The Repertoire of Nonverbal Behavior."

26. G. Beattie and H. Shovelton, "Mapping the Range of Information Contained in the Iconic Hand Gestures That Accompany Spontaneous Speech," *Journal of Language & Social Psychology* 18 (1999): 438–462; J. Streeck, "Gesture as Communication I: Its Coordination with Gaze and Speech," *Communication Monographs* 60 (1993): 275–299.

27. W. G. Woodall and J. P. Folger, "Nonverbal Cue Context and Episodic Memory: On the Availability and Endurance of Nonverbal Behaviors as Retrieval Cues," *Communication Monographs* 52 (1985): 320–333; A. A. Cohen and R. P. Harrison, "Intentionality in the Use of Hand Illustrators in Face-to-Face Communication Situations," *Journal of Personality and Social Psychology* 28 (1973): 276–279.

28. C. Darwin, *Expression of Emotions in Man and Animals* (London: Appleton; reprinted University of Chicago Press, 1965).

29. E. McClure and K. Pope, "Facial Expression Recognition in Adolescents with Mood and Anxiety Disorders," *Journal of Psychology* 160 (2003): 1172–1175; V. Lee and H. Wagner, "The Effect of Social Presence on the Facial and Verbal Expression of Emotion and the Interrelationships among Emotion Components," *Journal of Nonverbal Behavior* 26 (2002): 3–23; P. Gosselin, M. Perron, M. Legault, and P. Campanella, "Children's and Adults' Knowledge of the Distinction between Enjoyment and Nonenjoyment Smiles," *Journal of Nonverbal Behavior* 26 (2002): 83–107; L. Goos and I. Silverman, "Sex Related Factors in the Perception of Threatening Facial Expressions," *Journal of Nonverbal Behavior* 26 (2002): 27–41; M. Thunberg and D. Dimberg, "Gender Differences in Facial Reactions to Fear-Relevant Stimuli," *Journal of Nonverbal Behavior* 24 (2000): 44–50; D. LaPlante and N. Ambady, "Multiple Messages: Facial Recognition Advantage for Compound Expressions," *Journal of Nonverbal Behavior* 24 (2000): 211–221.

30. L. A. Renninger, T. J. Wade, and K. Grammer, "Getting That Female Glance: Patterns and Consequences of Male Nonverbal Behavior in Courtship Contexts," *Evolution and Human Behavior* 25 (2004): 416–431; D. Singh, "Mating Strategies of Young Women: Role of Physical Attractiveness," *Journal of Sex Research* 41 (2004): 43–54; K. Grammer, K. Kruck, A. Juette, and

B. Fink, "Nonverbal Behavior as Courtship Signals: The Role of Control and Choice in Selecting Partners," *Evolution and Human Behavior 21* (2000): 371–390; M. F. Abrahams, "Perceiving Flirtatious Communication: An Exploration of the Perceptual Dimensions Underlying Judgments of Flirtatiousness," *Journal of Sex Research 31* (1994): 283–292; K. Grammer, "Strangers Meet: Laughter and Nonverbal Signs of Interest in Opposite-Sex Encounters," *Journal of Nonverbal Behavior 14* (1990): 209–235.

31. M. M. Moore, "Nonverbal Courtship Patterns in Women: Context and Consequences," *Ethology and Sociobiology 6* (1985): 237–247; D. Knox and K. Wilson, "Dating Behaviors of University Students," *Family Relations 30* (1981): 255–258.

32. D. D. Henningsen, "Flirting with Meaning: An Examination of Miscommunication in Flirting Interactions," *Sex Roles 50* (2004): 481–489; M. M. Moore, "Courtship Communication and Perception," *Perceptual and Motor Skills 94* (2002): 97–105; E. Koukounas and N. M. Letch, "Psychological Correlates of Perception of Sexual Intent in Women," *Journal of Social Psychology 141* (2001): 443–456; A. Abbey, "Sex Differences in Attributions for Friendly Behavior: Do Males Misperceive Females' Friendliness?" *Journal of Personality and Social Psychology 42* (1982): 830–838; L. B. Koeppel, Y. Montagne, D. O'Hair, and M. J. Cody, "Friendly? Flirting? Wrong?" In Guerrero, *The Nonverbal Communication Reader*, 290–297.

33. A. Abbey, T. Zawacki, and P. O. Buck, "The Effects of Past Sexual Assault Perpetration and Alcohol Consumption on Reactions to Women's Mixed Signals," *Journal of Social and Clinical Psychology 24* (2005): 129–157; H. J. Delaney and B. A. Gluade, "Gender Differences in Perception of Attractiveness of Men and Women in Bars," *Journal of Personality and Social Psychology 16* (1990): 378–391.

34. A. E. Scheflen, "Quasi-Courtship Behavior in Psychotherapy," *Psychiatry 28* (1965): 245–257; K. Grammer, K. B. Knuck, and M. S. Magnusson, "The Courtship Dance: Patterns of Nonverbal Synchronization in Opposite Sex Encounters," *Journal of Nonverbal Behavior 22* (1998): 3–25.

35. J. A. Daly, E. Hogg, D. Sacks, M. Smith, and L. Zimring, "Sex and Relationship Affect Social Self-Grooming," *Journal of Nonverbal Behavior 7* (1983): 183–189.

36. M. L. Knapp and J. A. Hall, *Nonverbal Communication in Human Interaction* 5e (Fort Worth, TX: Harcourt Brace, 2002), 390–391.

37. S. A. Beebe, "Eye Contact: A Nonverbal Determinant of Speaker Credibility," *Speech Teacher 23* (1974): 21–25.

38. M. G. Frank and T. H. Feeley, "To Catch a Liar: Challenges for Research in Lie Detection Training," *Journal of Applied Communication Research 31* (2003): 58–75; D. Goleman, "Can You Tell When Someone Is Lying to You?" In Guerrero, *The Nonverbal Communication Reader*, 358–366; T. H. Feeley and M. A. deTurck, "The Behavioral Correlates of Sanctioned and Unsanctioned Deceptive Communication," *Journal of Nonverbal Behavior 22* (1998): 189–204; L. A. Zebrowitz, L. Voinescu, and M. A. Collins, "'Wide-Eyed' and 'Crooked-Faced': Determinants of Perceived and Real Honesty across the Life Span," *Personality and Social Psychology Bulletin 22* (1996): 1258–1269.

39. D. G. Leathers, L. Vaughn, G. Sanchez, and J. Bailey, "Who Is Lying in the Anita Hill–Clarence Thomas Hearing?: Nonverbal Communication Profiles." Paper presented at the meeting of the Speech Communication Association, October, 1992.

40. P. Ekman and W. Friesen, *Unmasking the Face* (Englewood Cliffs, NJ: Prentice-Hall, 1975).

41. Ekman and Friesen, *Unmasking the Face*.

42. Lee and Wagner, "The Effect of Social Presence on the Facial and Verbal Expression of Emotion and the Interrelationships among Emotion Components"; M. T. Motley, "Facial Affect and Verbal Context in Conversation," *Human Communication Research 20* (1993): 3–40; D. S. Berry, "Accuracy in Social Perception: Contributions of Facial and Vocal Information," *Journal of Personality and Social Psychology 61* (1991): 298–307.

43. Ekman and Friesen, *Unmasking the Face*.

44. P. M. Cole, "Children's Spontaneous Control of Facial Expression," *Child Development 57* (1986): 1309–1321.

45. S. Dang, "Abused Kids More Sensitive to Anger: Study Shows Victims Identify More Faces as 'Angry' Than Non-Abused," *Corpus Christi Caller Times* (June 23, 2002): A26.

46. S. E. Jones and A. E. Yarbrough, "A Naturalistic Study of the Meanings of Touch," *Communication Monographs 52* (1985): 19–56.

47. A. Montague, *Touching: The Human Significance of the Skin* (New York: Harper & Row, 1978).

48. M. S. Remland, T. S. Jones, and H. Brinkman, "Proxemic and Haptic Behavior in Three European Countries," *Journal of Nonverbal Behavior 15* (1991): 215–231; M. S. Remland, T. S. Jones, and H. Brinkman, "Interpersonal Distance, Body Orientation and Touch: Effect of Culture, Gender, and Age," *Journal of Social Psychology 135* (1995): 281–295; S. M. Jourard, "An Exploratory Study of Body-Accessibility," *British Journal of Social and Clinical Psychology 26* (1966): 235–242; D. C. Barnlund, "Communicative Styles in Two Cultures: Japan and the United States." In *Organization of Behavior in Face-to-Face Interaction*, edited by A. Kendon, R. M. Harris, and M. R. Key (The Hague: Mouton, 1975).

49. M. A. Beres, E. Herold, and S. B. Maitland, "Sexual Consent Behaviors in Same-Sex Relationships," *Archives of Sexual Behavior 33* (2004): 475–486; J. W. Lee and L. K. Guerrero, "Types of Touch in Cross-Sex Relationships between Coworkers: Perceptions of Relational and Emotional Messages, Inappropriateness, and Sexual Harassment," *Journal of Applied Communication Research 29* (2001): 197–220; M. S. Remland, *Nonverbal Communication in Everyday Life* (Boston: Houghton Mifflin, 2000); J. D. Murphy, D. M. Driscoll, and J. R. Kelly, "Differences in the Nonverbal Behavior of Men Who Vary in the Likelihood to Sexually Harass," *Journal of Social Behavior and Personality 14* (1999): 113–128; D. K. Ivy and S. Hamlet, "College Students and Sexual Dynamics: Two Studies of Peer Sexual Harassment," *Communication Education 45* (1996): 149–166.

50. L. M. Kneidinger, T. L. Maple, and S. A. Tross, "Touching Behavior in Sport: Functional Components, Analysis of Sex Differences, and Ethological Considerations," *Journal of Nonverbal Behavior 25* (2001): 43–62; L. K. Guerrero and P. A. Andersen, "Public Touch Behavior in Romantic Relationships between Men and Women." In Guerrero, *The Nonverbal Communication Reader*, 202–210; S. E. Jones, "Sex Differences in Touch Communication," *Western Journal of Speech Communication 50* (1986): 227–241; J. A. Hall and E. M. Veccia, "More 'Touching' Observations: New Insights on Men, Women, and Interpersonal Touch," *Journal of Personality and Social Psychology 59* (1990): 1155–1162; F. N. Willis, Jr., and L. F. Briggs, "Relationship and Touch in Public Settings," *Journal of Nonverbal Behavior 16* (1992): 55–63; B. Major, A. Schmidlin, and L. Williams, "Gender Patterns in Social Touch: The Impact of Setting and Age," *Journal of Personality and Social Psychology 58* (1990): 634–643.

51. L. L. Hinkle, "Perceptions of Supervisor Nonverbal Immediacy, Vocalics, and Subordinate Liking," *Communication Research Reports 18* (2001): 128–136.

52. T. DeGroot and S. J. Motowidlo, "Why Visual and Vocal Interview Cues Can Affect Interviewers' Judgments and Predict Job Performance," *Journal of Applied Psychology 84* (1999): 986–993; L. L. Carli, S. J. LaFleur, and C. C. Loeber, "Nonverbal Behavior, Gender, and Influence," *Journal of Personality and Social Psychology 68* (1995): 1030–1041; N. Christenfeld, "Does It Hurt to Say Um?" *Journal of Nonverbal Behavior 19* (1995): 171–186; J. K. Burgoon, T. Birk, and M. Pfau, "Nonverbal Behaviors, Persuasion, and Credibility," *Human Communication Research 17* (1990): 140–169; R. L. Street, Jr., R. M. Brady, and R. Lee, "Evaluative Responses to Communicators: The Effects of Speech Rate, Sex, and Interaction Context," *Western Journal of Speech Communication 48* (1984): 14–27.

53. K. Tracy, *Everyday Talk: Building and Reflecting Identities* (New York: Guilford Press, 2005).

54. C. A. Braithwaite, "Cultural Uses and Interpretations of Silence." In Guerrero, *The Nonverbal Communication Reader*, 163–172.

55. M. L. Knapp and A. L. Vangelisti, *Interpersonal Communication and Human Relationships* 5e (Boston: Allyn & Bacon, 2005); A. Jaworski, "The Power of Silence in Communication." In Guerrero, *The Nonverbal Communication Reader*, 156–162.

56. D. D. Henningsen, D. Dryden, M. G. Cruz, and M. C. Morr, "Pattern Violations and Perceptions of Deception," *Communication Reports 13* (2000): 1–10; M. A. deTurck, T. H. Feeley, and L. A. Roman, "Vocal and Visual Cue Training in Behavioral Lie Detection," *Communication Research Reports 14* (1997): 249–259; T. H. Feeley and M. A. deTurck, "Global Cue Usage in Behavioral Lie Detection," *Communication Quarterly 43* (1995): 420–430.

57. S. J. Baker, "The Theory of Silence," *Journal of General Psychology 53* (1955): 145–167.

58. J. Sandberg, "Want to Know Someone's Job Status? Look at Desk Location," *Corpus Christi Caller Times* (March 2, 2003): D4.

59. D. R. Peterson, "Interpersonal Relationships as a Link between Person and Environment." In *Person–Environment Psychology*, edited by W. B. Walsh, K. H. Craig, and R. H. Price (Hillsdale, NJ: Lawrence Erlbaum, 1991), 154.

60. A. Rapoport, *The Meaning of the Built Environment: A Nonverbal Communication Approach* (Beverly Hills: Sage, 1982).

61. A. H. Maslow and N. L. Mintz, "Effects of Esthetic Surroundings: I," *Journal of Psychology 41* (1956): 247–254.

62. M. H. Eaves and D. G. Leathers, "Context as Communication: McDonald's vs. Burger King," *Journal of Applied Communication Research 19* (1991): 263–289; E. J. Langan, "Environmental Features in Theme Restaurants." In Guerrero, *The Nonverbal Communication Reader*, 255–263.

63. Hall, *The Hidden Dimension*.

64. R. Sommer, "Studies in Personal Space," *Sociometry 22* (1959): 247–260; L. Smeltzer, J. Waltman, and D. Leonard, "Proxemics and Haptics in Managerial Communication." In Guerrero, *The Nonverbal Communication Reader*, 184–191.

65. J. A. Hall, *Nonverbal Sex Differences: Communication Accuracy and Expressive Style* (Baltimore: Johns Hopkins University Press, 1984); P. A. Bell, L. M. Kline, and W. A. Barnard, "Friendship and Freedom of Movement as Moderators of Sex Differences in Interpersonal Distancing," *Journal of Social Psychology 128* (1998): 305–310; M. Remland, T. S. Jones, and H. Brinkman, "Interpersonal Distance, Body Orientation

and Touch: Effect of Culture, Gender, and Age," *Journal of Social Psychology 135* (1995): 281–295.

66. S. M. Lyman and M. B. Scott, "Territoriality: A Neglected Sociological Dimension." In Guerrero, *The Nonverbal Communication Reader*, 175–183.

67. A. L. S. Buslig, "'Stop' Signs: Regulating Privacy with Environmental Features." In Guerrero, *The Nonverbal Communication Reader*, 241–249.

68. R. L. Paetzold and A. M. O'Leary-Kelly, "Organizational Communication and the Legal Dimensions of Hostile Work Environment Sexual Harassment." In *Sexual Harassment: Communication Implications*, edited by G. L. Kreps (Cresskill, NJ: Hampton Press, 1993), 63–77.

69. Mehrabian, *Nonverbal Communication*. For interesting applications of Mehrabian's immediacy principle to the instructional context, see S. D. Johnson and A. N. Miller, "A Cross-Cultural Study of Immediacy, Credibility, and Learning in the U.S. and Kenya," *Communication Education 51* (2002): 280–292; M. A. Jaasma and R. J. Koper, "Out-of-Class Communication between Female and Male Students and Faculty: The Relationship to Student Perceptions of Instructor Immediacy," *Women's Studies in Communication 25* (2002): 119–137; J. L. Chesebro and J. C. McCroskey, "The Relationship of Teacher Clarity and Immediacy with Student State Receiver Apprehension, Affect, and Cognitive Learning," *Communication Education 50* (2001): 59–68; P. L. Witt and L. R. Wheeless, "An Experimental Study of Teachers' Verbal and Nonverbal Immediacy and Students' Affective and Cognitive Learning," *Communication Education 50* (2001): 327–342; D. K. Baringer and J. C. McCroskey, "Immediacy in the Classroom: Student Immediacy," *Communication Education 49* (2000): 178–186; J. W. Neuliep, "A Comparison of Teacher Immediacy in African-American and Euro-American College Classrooms," *Communication Education 44* (1995): 267–277; J. F. Andersen, "Teacher Immediacy as a Predictor of Teaching Effectiveness." In *Communication Yearbook 3*, edited by D. Nimmo (New Brunswick, NJ: Transaction Books, 1979), 543–559.

70. Argyle, *Bodily Communication*.

71. Andersen, *Nonverbal Communication*.

72. K. McGinty, D. Knox, and M. E. Zusman, "Nonverbal and Verbal Communication in 'Involved' and 'Casual' Relationships among College Students," *College Student Journal 37* (2003): 68–71; C. C. Weisfeld and M. A. Stack, "When I Look into Your Eyes: An Ethological Analysis of Gender Differences in Married Couples' Nonverbal Behaviors," *Psychology, Evolution, and Gender 4* (2002): 125–147; B. Le Poire, A. Duggan, C. Shepard, and J. Burgoon, "Relational Messages Associated with Nonverbal Involvement, Pleasantness, and Expressiveness in Romantic Couples," *Communication Research Reports 19* (2002): 195–206.

73. M. S. Mast and J. A. Hall, "Who Is the Boss and Who Is Not? Accuracy of Judging Status," *Journal of Nonverbal Behavior 28* (2004): 145–165; M. Helweg-Larsen, S. J. Cunningham, A. Carrico, and A. M. Pergram, "To Nod or Not to Nod: An Observational Study of Nonverbal Communication and Status in Female and Male College Students," *Psychology of Women Quarterly 28* (2004): 358–361; L. Z. Tiedens and A. R. Fragale, "Power Moves: Complementarity in Dominant and Submissive Nonverbal Behavior," *Journal of Personality and Social Psychology 84* (2003): 558–568; H. Aguinis and C. A. Henle, "Effects of Nonverbal Behavior on Perceptions of a Female Employee's Power Bases," *Journal of Social Psychology 141* (2001): 537–549; J. A. Hall, L. S. LeBeau, J. G. Reinoso, and F. Thayer, "Status, Gender, and Nonverbal Behavior in Candid and Posed Photographs: A Study of Conversations between University Employees," *Sex Roles 44* (2001): 677–692; Mehrabian, *Nonverbal Communication*.

CHAPTER 1.5

1. L. Barker, et al., "An Investigation of Proportional Time Spent in Various Communication Activities of College Students," *Journal of Applied Communication Research 8* (1981): 101–109.

2. J. Brownell, "Perceptions of Effective Listeners: A Management Study," *The Journal of Business Communication* (Fall, 1990): 401–415; D. A. Romig, *Side by Side Leadership* (Austin, TX: Bard, 2001).

3. Adapted from the International Listening Association's definition of listening, which may be found on their Web site <http://www.listen.org>.

4. K. W. Watson, L. L. Barker, and J. B. Weaver, *The Listener Style Inventory* (New Orleans: SPECTRA, 1995).

5. M. D. Kirtley and J. M. Honeycutt, "Listening Styles and Their Correspondence with Second Guessing," *Communication Research Reports 13* (1996): 174–182.

6. S. L. Sargent and J. B. Weaver, "Correlates Between Communication Apprehension and Listening Style Preferences," *Communication Research Reports 14* (1997): 74–78.

7. Sargent and Weaver, "Correlates Between Communication Apprehension and Listening Style Preferences."

8. C. Y. Cheng, "Chinese Philosophy and Contemporary Communication Theory." In *Communication Theory: Eastern and Western Perspectives*, edited by D. L. Kincaid (New York, 1987).

9. T. S. Lebra, *Japanese Patterns of Behavior* (Honolulu: University Press of Hawaii, 1976).

10. A. Yugi, (trans. N. Chung), *Ilbon-in ye usik koo-jo (Japanese Thought Patterns)* (Seoul: Baik Yang Publishing Co. [in Korean], 1984).

11. J. O. Yum, "The Impact of Confucianism on Interpersonal Relationships and Communication Patterns in East Asia." In *Intercultural Communication: A Reader*, edited by L. A. Samovar and R. E. Porter (Belmont, CA: Wadsworth, 2000), 86.

12. W. Winter, A. J. Ferreira, and N. Bowers, "Decision-Making in Married and Unrelated Couples," *Family Process 12* (1973): 83–94.

13. R. Montgomery, *Listening Made Easy* (New York: AMACOM, 1981). Also see O. Hargie, C. Sanders, and D. Dickson, *Social Skills in Interpersonal Communication* (London: Routledge, 1994); O. Hargie, ed., *The Handbook of Communication Skills* (London: Routledge, 1997).

14. R. G. Owens, "Handling Strong Emotions." In *The Handbook of Communication Skills*, edited by O. Hargie (London: Croom Helm/New York University Press, 1986).

15. D. Goleman, *Emotional Intelligence: Why It Can Matter More Than IQ* (New York: Bantam Books, 1995). Also see D. Goleman, "Emotional Intelligence: Issues in Paradigms Building." In *The Emotionally Intelligent Workplace*, edited by C. Cherniss and D. Goleman (San Francisco: Jossey Bass, 2001), 13.

16. J. L. Gonzalez-Balado, ed., *Mother Teresa: In My Own Words* (New York: Gramercy Books, 1997).

17. R. G. Nichols, "Factors in Listening Comprehension," *Speech Monographs 15* (1948): 154–163; G. M. Goldhaber and C. H. Weaver, "Listener Comprehension of Compressed Speech When the Difficulty, Rate of Presentation, and Sex of the Listener Are Varied," *Speech Monographs 35* (1968): 20–25.

18. M. Fitch-Hauser, D. A. Barker, and A. Hughes, "Receiver Apprehension and Listening Comprehension: A Linear or Curvilinear Relationship?" *Southern Communication Journal* (1988): 62–71.

19. Fitch-Hauser et al., "Receiver Apprehension and Listening Comprehension."

20. K. Watson, L. Barker, and J. Weaver, "The Listening Styles Profile (LPP16): Development and Validation of an Instrument to Assess Four Listening Styles," *Journal of the International Listening Association* (1995). Research cited on *20/20*, ABC television network, September 1998.

21. A. Carruthers, "Listening, Hearing and Changing," *Business Communicator 5* (2004): 3.

22. I. W. Johnson, C. G. Pearce, T. L. Tuten, and L. Sinclair, "Self-Imposed Silence and Perceived Listening Effectiveness," *Business Communication Quarterly 66* (2003): 23–45.

23. M. V. Redmond, "The Functions of Empathy (Decentering) in Human Relations," *Human Relations 42* (1993): 593–606.

24. A. Mehrabian, *Nonverbal Communication* (Chicago: Aldine Atherton, 1970). A. Mehrabian, *Silent Messages* (Belmont, CA: Wadsworth, 1981). Also see D. Lapakko, "Three Cheers for Language: A Closer Examination of a Widely Cited Study of Nonverbal Communication," *Communication Education 46* (1997): 63–67.

25. M. Argyle and M. Cook, *Gaze and Mutual Gaze* (Cambridge, MA: Cambridge University Press, 1976).

26. Hargie et al., *Social Skills in Interpersonal Communication*; Hargie, *The Handbook of Communication Skills*.

27. For a review of the literature on gender, listening, and communication see D. K. Ivy and P. Backlund, *GenderSpeak: Personal Effectiveness in Gender Communication* 3e (New York: McGraw-Hill, 2004).

28. S. L. Sargent and J. B. Weaver, "Listening Styles: Sex Differences in Perceptions of Self and Others," *International Journal of Listening 17* (2003): 5–18.

29. C. G. Pearce, I. W. Johnson, and R. T. Barker, "Assessment of the Listening Styles Inventory," *Journal of Business & Technical Communication 17* (2003): 84–113.

30. M. K. Johnston, J. B. Weaver, K. W. Watson, and L. L. Barker, "Listening Styles: Biological or Psychological Differences?" *International Journal of Listening 14* (2000): 32–46; Sargent and Weaver, "Listening Styles."

31. J. Silverman, "Attentional Styles and the Study of Sex Differences." In *Attention: Contemporary Theory and Analysis*, edited by D. I. Mostofsky (New York: Appleton-Century-Crofts, 1970): 61–79.

32. See R. G. Nichols and L. A. Stevens, "Listening to People," *Harvard Business Review 35* (September–October, 1957): 85–92.

33. K. K. Halone and L. L. Pecchioni, "Relational Listening: A Grounded Theoretical Model," *Communication Reports 14* (2001): 59–71.

34. Pearce et al., "Assessment of the Listening Styles Inventory."

35. Pearce et al., "Assessment of the Listening Styles Inventory."

36. J. B. Weaver and M. B. Kirtley, "Listening Styles and Empathy," *The Southern States Communication Journal 60* (1995): 131–140.

37. Goleman, "Emotional Intelligence."

38. Goleman, "Emotional Intelligence."

39. H. J. M. Nouwen, "Listening as Spiritual Hospitality." In *Bread for the Journey* (New York: HarperCollins, 1997).

40. J. C. McCroskey and M. J. Beatty, "The Communibiological Perspective: Implications for Communication in Instruction," *Communication Education 49* (2000): 1–6; M. J. Beatty and J. C. McCroskey, "Theory, Scientific Evidence and the Communibiological Paradigm:

Reflections on Misguided Criticism," *Communication Education* 49 (2001): 36–44.

41. Goleman, "Emotional Intelligence."

42. "Personality Typing," *Wired* (July, 1999): 71.

43. "Personality Typing."

44. Hargie et al., *Social Skills in Interpersonal Communication*; R. Boulton, *People Skills* (New York: 1981). We also acknowledge others who have presented excellent applications of listening and responding skills in interpersonal and group contexts: D. A. Romig and L. J. Romig, *Structured Teamwork* (D Guide) (Austin, TX: Performance Resources, 1990); S. Deep and L. Sussman, *Smart Moves* (Reading, MA: Addison-Wesley, 1990); P. R. Scholtes, *The Team Handbook* (Madison, WI: Joiner Associates, 1988); Hargie et al., *Social Skills in Interpersonal Communication*; Hargie, *The Handbook of Communication Skills*.

45. L. B. Comer and T. Drollinger, "Active Empathic Listening and Selling Success: A Conceptual Framework," *Journal of Personal Selling & Sales Management* 19 (1999): 15–29; S. B. Castleberry, C. D. Shepherd, and R. Ridnour, "Effective Interpersonal Listening in the Personal Selling Environment: Conceptualization, Measurement, and Nomological Validity," *Journal of Marketing Theory and Practice* (Winter, 1999): 30–38.

46. F. C. B. Hansen, H. Resnick, and J. Galea, "Better Listening: Paraphrasing and Perception Checking—A Study of the Effectiveness of a Multimedia Skills Training Program," *Journal of Technology in Human Services* 20 (2002): 317–331.

47. Pearce et al., "Assessment of the Listening Styles Inventory."

CHAPTER 1.6

1. Research documents several culture-based differences in communication, including approaches to leadership, deception, and conflict management styles. See N. Ensari and S. E. Murphy, "Cross-Cultural Variations in Leadership Perceptions and Attribution of Charisma to the Leader," *Organizational Behavior and Human Decision Processes* 92 (2003): 52–66; M. K. Lapinski and T. R. Levine, "Culture and Information Manipulation Theory: The Effects of Self-Construal and Locus of Benefit on Information Manipulation," *Communication Studies* 5 (2000): 55–73; D. Cai and E. L. Fink, "Conflict Style Differences Between Individualists and Collectivists," *Communication Monographs* 69 (2002): 67–87.

2. S. Roberts, *Who We Are Now: The Changing Face of America in the Twenty-First Century* (New York: Henry Holt, 2004).

3. M. E. Ryan, "Another Way to Teach Migrant Students," *Los Angeles Times* (March 31, 1991): B20, as cited by M. W. Lustig and J. Koester, *Intercultural Competence: Interpersonal Communication across Cultures* (New York: HarperCollins, 1999), 11.

4. U.S. Census Bureau. <http:www.prb.org/Ameristat Template>. Accessed December 17, 2001.

5. G. Chen and W. J. Starosta, "A Review of the Concept of Intercultural Sensitivity," *Human Communication* 1 (1997): 7.

6. Lustig and Koester, *Intercultural Competence*.

7. *Newsweek* (July 12, 1999): 51.

8. U.S. Census Bureau, *Statistical Abstract of the United States: 1996*, 116e (Washington, DC, 1996), as cited by Lustig and Koester, *Intercultural Competence*, 8.

9. U.S. Census Bureau Report 1999, as reported in R. E. Schmid, *Austin-American Statesman* (September 17, 1999): A20.

10. "One Nation, One Language?" *U.S. News & World Report* (September 25, 1995): 40, as cited by Lustig and Koester, *Intercultural Competence*, 10.

11. Roberts, *Who We Are Now*, 122

12. Roberts, *Who We Are Now*, 122; A. Caldwell, "Census: More Than Half of Texans Are Minorities," *Austin-American Statesman* (August 11, 2005): 1B.

13. Roberts, *Who We Are Now*, 126.

14. Adapted from *Information Please Almanac* (Boston: Houghton Mifflin, 1990) and *World Almanac and Book of Facts* (New York: World Almanac, 1991), as cited by Lustig and Koester, *Intercultural Competence*, 11.

15. T. Friedman, *The World Is Flat: A Brief History of the Twenty-First Century* (New York: Farrar, Straus and Giroux, 2005).

16. Friedman, *The World Is Flat*, 10.

17. A. G. Smith, ed., *Communication and Culture* (New York: Holt, Rinehart & Winston, 1966).

18. E. T. Hall, *Beyond Culture* (Garden City, NY: Doubleday, 1976).

19. For example, see A. V. Matveeve and P. E. Nelson, "Cross Cultural Competence and Multicultural Team Performance: Perceptions of American and Russian Managers," *International Journal of Cross Cultural Management* 4 (2004): 253–270.

20. G. Hofstede, *Culture's Consequences: International Differences in Work-Related Values* (Beverly Hills: Sage, 1980); G. Hofstede and G. J. Hofstede, *Cultures and Organization: Software of the Mind* 2e (New York: McGraw-Hill, 2005).

21. See J. B. Walter, "Interpersonal Effects in Computer-Mediated Interaction: A Relational Perspective," *Communication Research* 19 (1992): 52–90; J. B. Walter, "Relational Aspects of Computer-Mediated Communication: Experimental and Longitudinal Observations," *Organizational Science* 6 (1995): 186–203; J. B. Walther, J. F. Anderson, and D. Park, "Interpersonal Effects in Computer-Mediated Interaction: A Meta-Analysis of Social and Anti-Social Com-

munication, *Communication Research* 21 (1994): 460–487.

22. C. Ward, S. Bochner, and A. Furnham, *The Psychology of Culture Shock* (Hove, England: Routledge, 2001).

23. For an excellent discussion of worldview and its implications for intercultural communication, see C. H. Dodd, *Dynamics of Intercultural Communication* (New York: McGraw-Hill, 1998).

24. Hall, *Beyond Culture.*

25. L. A. Samovar, R. E. Porter, and L. A. Stefani, *Communication between Cultures* (Belmont, CA: Wadsworth, 1998).

26. Hofstede, *Culture's Consequences*; Hofstede and Hofstede, *Cultures and Organization*. For an excellent summary of Geert Hofstede's cultural values, see Lustig and Koester, *Intercultural Competence*, 111–125.

27. H. C. Triandis, "The Many Dimensions of Culture," *Academy of Management Executive* 18 (2004): 88–93.

28. M. Voronov and J. A. Singer, "The Myth of Individualism-Collectivism: A Critical Review," *Journal of Social Psychology* 142 (2002): 461–480.

29. For an excellent review of Hofstede's work, see J. W. Bing, "Hofstede's Consequences: The Impact of His Work on Consulting and Business Practices," *Academy of Management Executive* 18 (2004): 80–87.

30. Hofstede, *Culture's Consequences*; Hofstede and Hofstede, *Cultures and Organization.*

31. W. B. Gudykunst, *Bridging Differences: Effective Intergroup Communication* (Newbury Park, CA: Sage, 1998).

32. Gudykunst, *Bridging Differences.*

33. Hofstede, *Culture's Consequences*; Hofstede and Hofstede, *Cultures and Organization.*

34. Hofstede, *Culture's Consequences*; Hofstede and Hofstede, *Cultures and Organization.*

35. Hofstede, *Culture's Consequences*; Hofstede and Hofstede, *Cultures and Organization.*

36. G. Hofstede, "Cultural Dimensions in Management and Planning," *Asia Pacific Journal of Management* (January, 1984): 81–98; Hofstede and Hofstede, *Cultures and Organization.*

37. For a discussion of long- and short-term oriented national cultures, see Hofstede and Hofstede, *Cultures and Organization*, 210–238.

38. Hofstede and Hofstede, *Cultures and Organization.*

39. J. Cloud, "Sex and the Law," *Time* (March 23, 1998): 48–54.

40. W. W. Neher, *Organizational Communication: Challenges of Change, Diversity, and Continuity* (Boston: Allyn & Bacon, 1997).

41. E. E. Maccoby, "Gender and Relationships: A Developmental Account," *American Psychologist* 45 (1990): 513–520.

42. J. Gray, *Men Are from Mars, Women Are from Venus* (New York: Harper Collins, 1992).

43. D. K. Ivy and P. Backlund, *GenderSpeak: Personal Effectiveness in Gender Communication* 3e (New York: McGraw-Hill, 2004); D. J. Canary and T. R. Emmers-Sommer, *Sex and Gender Differences in Personal Relationships* (New York: Guilford, 1997).

44. D. Tannen, *You Just Don't Understand* (New York: William Morrow, 1990).

45. T. Parsons and R. F. Bales, *Family, Socialization, and Interaction Processes* (New York: Free Press of Glencoe, 1955). Also see D. Bakan, *The Duality of Human Existence* (Chicago: McNally, 1966).

46. A. C. Selbe, *Are You from Another Planet or What?* Workshop presented at the Joint Service Family Readiness Matters Conference, Phoenix, AZ, July, 1999.

47. R. B. Rubin, E. M. Perse, and C. A. Barbato, "Conceptualization and Measurement of Interpersonal Communication Motives," *Human Communication Research* 14 (1988): 602–628; D. Tannen, *That's Not What I Meant!* (London: Dent, 1986).

48. See L. Davis, "Domestic Violence," in *Encyclopedia of Social Work*, vol. 1 (Washington, DC: National Association of Social Work), 780–789; Federal Bureau of Investigation, *Violence against Women: Estimates from the Redesigned Survey*, August, 1995 <http://www.ojp.usdoj.gov>; L. K. Hamberger, D. G. Saunders, and M. Hovey, "The Prevalence of Domestic Violence in Community Practice and Rate of Physician Inquiry," *Family Medicine* 24 (1992): 283–287; Women's Action Coalition, *WAC Stats: The Facts about Women* (New York: The New Press, 1993).

49. J. W. Neuliep, "Assessing the Reliability and Validity of the Generalized Ethnocentrism Scale," *Journal of Intercultural Communication Research* 31 (2002): 201–215. For additional research on the role of ethnocentrism in communication, see Y. Lin, A. Rancer, and A. Sunhee Lim, "Ethnocentrism and Intercultural Willingness to Communicate: A Cross-Cultural Comparison between Korean and American College Students," *Journal of Intercultural Communication Research* 32 (2003).

50. See Ensari and Murphy, "Cross-Cultural Variations in Leadership Perceptions and Attribution of Charisma to the Leader"; Lapinski and Levine, "Culture and Information Manipulation Theory"; Cai and Fink, "Conflict Style Differences Between Individualists and Collectivists."

51. C. Kluckhohn and S. Murray, 1953, as quoted by J. S. Caputo, H. C. Hazel, and C. McMahon, *Interpersonal Communication* (Boston: Allyn & Bacon, 1994), 304.

52. D. E. Brown, "Human Universals and Their Implications." In *Being Humans: Anthropological Universality and Particularity in Transdisciplinary Perspectives*, edited by N. Roughley (New York: Walter de Gruyter, 2000). For an applied discussion of these universals, see S.

Pinker, *The Blank Slate: The Modern Denial of Human Nature* (London: Penguin Books, 2002).

53. D. W. Kale, "Ethics in Intercultural Communication." In *Intercultural Communication: A Reader* 6e, edited by L. A. Samovar and R. E. Porter (Belmont, CA: Wadsworth, 1991).

54. L. A. Samovar and R. E. Porter, *Communication between Cultures* (Stamford, CT: Wadsworth and Thomson Learning, 2001), 29.

55. C. S. Lewis, *The Abolition of Man* (New York: Macmillan Publishing Company, 1944).

56. As reported by M. Obernauer, "Lessons on Values to Go Beyond Schools," *Austin-American Statesman* (March 30, 2005): B1, B5.

57. Obernauer, "Lessons on Values to Go Beyond Schools."

58. M. Gladwell, *Blink: The Power of Thinking without Thinking* (New York: Little Brown, 2005).

59. S. Kamekar, M. B. Kolsawalla, and T. Mazareth, "Occupational Prestige as a Function of Occupant's Gender," *Journal of Applied Social Psychology* 19 (1988): 681–688.

60. Eleanor Roosevelt, as cited by Lustig and Koester, *Intercultural Competence.*

61. W. B. Gudykunst and Y. Kim, *Communicating with Strangers* (New York: Random House, 1984); Gudykunst, *Bridging Differences.*

62. For a classic discussion of egocentrism and ethnocentrism, see T. W. Adorno, E. Frenkel-Brunswik, D. J. Levinson, and R. N. Sanford, *The Authoritarian Personality* (New York: Harper & Brothers, 1950).

63. Neuliep, "Assessing the Reliability and Validity of the Generalized Ethnocentrism Scale"; Lin, "Ethnocentrism and Intercultural Willingness to Communicate."

64. S. DeTurk, "Intercultural Empathy: Myth, Competency, or Possibility for Alliance Building?" *Communication Education* 50 (2001): 374–384.

65. M. V. Redmond, "The Functions of Empathy (Decentering) in Human Relations," *Human Relations* 42 (1993): 593–606. Also see M. V. Redmond, "A Multidimensional Theory and Measure of Social Decentering," *Journal of Research in Personality* (1995); for an excellent discussion of the role of emotions in establishing empathy, see D. Goleman, *Emotional Intelligence* (New York: Bantam, 1995).

66. See B. J. Broome, "Building Shared Meaning: Implications of a Relational Approach to Empathy for Teaching Intercultural Communication," *Communication Education* 40 (1991): 235–249. Much of this discussion is based on the treatment of social decentering and empathy in S. A. Beebe, S. J. Beebe, and M. V. Redmond, *Interpersonal Communication: Relating to Others* 4e (Boston: Allyn & Bacon, 2005).

67. For an excellent discussion of empathy as it relates to intercultural communication, see D. W. Augsburger, *Pastoral Counseling Across Cultures* (Philadelphia: The Westminister Press, 1986), 28–30.

68. H. J. M. Nouwen, *Bread for the Journey* (New York: HarperCollins, 1997).

69. L. J. Carrell, "Diversity in the Communication Curriculum: Impact on Student Empathy," *Communication Education* 46 (1997): 234–244.

70. R. H. Farrell, ed., *Off the Record: The Private Papers of Harry S. Truman* (New York: Harper & Row, 1980), 310.

Photo Credits

Answers to Practice Tests

CHAPTER 1.1

Multiple Choice

1. c	11. d
2. b	12. c
3. b	13. b
4. d	14. b
5. d	15. b
6. d	16. c
7. d	17. c
8. a	18. b
9. c	19. c
10. b	20. b

True/False

1. T
2. F
3. T
4. T
5. F
6. F
7. F
8. F
9. T
10. T

Fill in the Blank

1. two
2. decoding
3. rule
4. intrapersonal
5. rhetoric
6. nonverbal
7. interpersonal
8. source
9. message
10. objects

CHAPTER 1.2

Multiple Choice

1. a	11. a
2. b	12. b
3. d	13. d
4. c	14. b
5. b	15. d
6. a	16. d
7. a	17. b
8. d	18. c
9. b	19. c
10. c	20. b

True/False

1. T
2. T
3. F
4. F
5. T
6. F
7. T
8. F
9. F
10. F

Fill in the Blank

1. self-concept
2. attitude
3. avowed
4. reframing
5. stereotypes
6. values
7. beliefs
8. self-worth
9. symbolic
10. closure

CHAPTER 1.3

Multiple Choice

1. b	11. c
2. c	12. d
3. b	13. b
4. b	14. d
5. b	15. a
6. a	16. d
7. b	17. b
8. b	18. c
9. d	19. d
10. a	20. c

True/False

1. T
2. T
3. F
4. T
5. T
6. F
7. F
8. F
9. F
10. T

Fill in the Blank

1. meaning
2. denotative
3. empathy
4. defensive
5. symbol
6. connotative
7. abstract
8. language
9. supportive
10. concrete

CHAPTER 1.4

Multiple Choice

1. b	11. c
2. a	12. d
3. d	13. b
4. d	14. d
5. b	15. b
6. c	16. c
7. d	17. d
8. c	18. a
9. a	19. b
10. a	20. d

True/False

1. T
2. T
3. F
4. T
5. F
6. F
7. F
8. F
9. F
10. T

Fill in the Blank

1. nonverbal
2. paralanguage
3. perception checking
4. artifact
5. proxemics
6. quasi-courtship
7. haptics
8. ethic
9. response latency
10. kinesics

CHAPTER 1.5

Multiple Choice

1. b	11. a
2. b	12. a
3. b	13. d
4. a	14. b
5. c	15. d
6. c	16. c
7. b	17. d
8. c	18. c
9. d	19. b
10. d	20. d

True/False

1. T
2. T
3. T
4. F
5. F
6. T
7. T
8. T
9. F
10. T

Fill in the Blank

1. selecting
2. responding
3. hearing
4. attending
5. decentering
6. understanding
7. listening style
8. receiver apprehension
9. active
10. stop, look, listen

CHAPTER 1.6

Multiple Choice

1. d	11. d
2. c	12. c
3. c	13. a
4. a	14. b
5. d	15. b
6. a	16. c
7. c	17. a
8. a	18. c
9. d	19. b
10. a	20. c

True/False

1. T
2. T
3. T
4. T
5. F
6. T
7. T
8. F
9. F
10. F

Fill in the Blank

1. ethnocentrism
2. co-culture
3. instrumental
4. shock
5. low-context
6. collectivistic
7. culture
8. high-context
9. individualistic
10. expressive

Key to the MyCommunicationLab Media Assets

The MyCommunicationLab assets are listed by type and title in the order in which they appear throughout each chapter.

CHAPTER 1.1

Explore	Principles of Communication
Quick Review	Communication Defined
Explore	Ethical Speaking
Homework	Credo for Ethical Communication
Homework	Ethical Dilemma
Quick Review	Communication Competence
Watch	Juggling Act
Watch	The Switch
Quick Review	Why Study Communication?
Watch	The Saga of Susan and Juan
Watch	In the Classroom
Quick Review	Communication Models
Visual Literacy	Types of Intentional and Unintentional Communication
Homework	What You Say
Watch	Jack and Jim Joust
Quick Review	Communication Characteristics
Profile	Willingness to Communicate Scale
Explore	Teams: Leadership Styles
Watch	Virtual Miscommunication
Watch	Oral Report (Professional Version)

Watch	Adapting to Serve a Client
Quick Review	Communicating with Others

CHAPTER 1.2

Profile	Assertiveness Responsiveness Measure
Homework	I Am
Explore	Self-Awareness and Communication
Quick Review	Self-Awareness
Visual Literacy	Self/Self-Concept
Visual Literacy	The Self-Concept
Watch	Do You Come Here Often?
Visual Literacy	Young/Old Women
Watch	Name Game
Profile	Self-Perceived Communication Competence Questionnaire
Watch	The Saga of Susan and Juan
Watch	Sarah's Blog
Quick Review	Self-Concept
Quick Review	Self-Esteem
Watch	Aisha's Paper
Profile	Introversion Scale
Quick Review	Communication and Self-Esteem
Explore	Perception
Homework	Understanding Perception
Quick Review	The Perception Process
Explore	Go There

Watch	Art Appreciation
Quick Review	Communication and Perceptual Accuracy

CHAPTER 1.3

Homework	Slang
Profile	Talkaholic Scale
Quick Review	Bias in Language
Quick Review	Why Focus on Language?
Explore	The Power of Words
Homework	What Do You Mean?
Homework	What's in a Name?
Explore	Verbal Communication
Watch	Chair's Office
Watch	The Saga of Susan and Juan
Quick Review	The Nature of Language
Explore	Language
Quick Review	The Power of Words
Explore	Biased Language Survey
Explore	Sexist Language
Quick Review	Confronting Bias in Language
Watch	Job Promotion
Watch	Virtual Miscommunication
Watch	Helping Annie
Explore	Empathy
Quick Review	Using Words to Establish Supportive Relationships

CHAPTER 1.4

Watch	Sam's Surprise
Profile	Shyness Scale
Quick Review	Why Focus on Nonverbal Communication?
Profile	Cheek and Buss Shyness Scale
Quick Review	The Nature of Nonverbal Communication
Explore	Appearance
Explore	Professional Appearance
Watch	Jack and Jim Joust

Explore	Nonverbal Communication
Visual Literacy	The Five Body Movements
Explore	The Human Face
Explore	Recognizing Facial Expressions of Emotions
Explore	The Human Voice
Watch	Going Up
Explore	Space Speaks
Explore	Spatial Communication
Watch	The Interns
Quick Review	Codes of Nonverbal Communication
Watch	What Was That?
Quick Review	How to Interpret Nonverbal Cues More Accurately

CHAPTER 1.5

Visual Literacy	We Spend Most of Our Time as Listeners
Watch	The Politics of Sociology
Explore	Listening
Explore	How Good Is Your Memory for Stories?
Quick Review	How We Listen
Profile	Januski/Wolvin Student Listening Inventory
Quick Review	Listening Styles
Explore	Steps in Listening
Watch	What Was That?
Quick Review	Adapting to Your Listening Style
Explore	Effective Listening
Watch	Sam's Surprise
Watch	Art Appreciation
Watch	Fast Food
Watch	Talk, Talk, Talk
Profile	Listening Problems Inventory
Profile	Communication Apprehension in Generalized Contexts
Profile	SCAM

Visual Literacy	Filter Out Sounds	*Explore*	Culture
Quick Review	Listening Barriers	*Explore*	How to Say No
Profile	Listening Skills Inventory	*Visual Literacy*	A Model of Intercultural Communication
Explore	Listening with Empathy		
Watch	Aisha's Paper	*Quick Review*	Culture and Communication
Explore	Active Listening	*Watch*	What Was That?
Quick Review	Improving Your Listening Skills	*Explore*	Take Me to the Other Side
		Quick Review	Gender and Communication
Homework	Listening Perception Check	*Visual Literacy*	Ethnocentrism Scale
Quick Review	Responding Skills	*Watch*	Talk, Talk, Talk
Explore	Empathy	*Quick Review*	Barriers to Bridging Differences and Adapting to Others
Watch	Trust Troubles		
Quick Review	Responding with Empathy		
		Watch	Tonya in the Classroom

CHAPTER 1.6

		Quick Review	Adapting to Others Who Are Different from You
Watch	Words That Wound	*Watch*	Effective Communication
Quick Review	Ethically Adapt Your Communication to Others		

Index